Magic Moments

collaboration between artists and young people

edited by Anna Harding

Black Dog Publishing

contents

introduction

Magic Moments Collaboration Between
Artists and Young People

4

one

Artists' Perspectives on working
with young people

22

The Jar of Sawdust and the Lawned Sheep
Richard Wentworth and Ruth Maclennan
25

Creativity with Purpose
Faisal Abdu' Allah
36

Bare Dust
Shona Illingworth
42

Bob, Roberta and Etta: the Art of Collaboration
50

Sound Mirrors a Proposed Artwork Involving
secondary school pupils in kent, England and in
Dunkirk, France
Lise Autogena
56

two

Artists and schools: Interventions
in Education systems

66

From a Certain Perspective a Child's Perpective can
Be Somewhat Complex
Ben Sadler
68

Macht und Gehorsam – schule Unterrichtet
Power and Obedience – school Instructs
Martin Krenn
74

Room 13: One Artist, 11 Years, One School
84

Finally Not Fully Under Control... Notes on
subjectivity and social Politics in the Collaborative
Art Praxis of Dias & Riedweg
Dias & Riedweg
92

Adaptation for Change: The Southwark Educational
Research Project O+I
104

De-and Re-territorialising
the Classroom and Art:
Wochenklausur in School, Vienna, 1995-1996
Gerald Raunig
112

Jef Geys School Projects 1960-2005
116

three

Aim Higher Out of and Beyond school

128

Work as if you Live in the Early Days of a Better
society!
David Harding
130

We are 17
Johan van der Keuken
139

Shape of Ideas: Rolls-Royce Apprenticeship Training
Scheme with Tate Liverpool
Gillian Brent
144

15 seconds
Christian Dorley-Brown
153

Celebrations for Breaking Routine
with Flamingo 50, Venus and Exit 3
Anna Harding, Kristin Lucas and Marie-Anne McQuay
162

Kids of Survival
Tim Rollins
169

four

young people challenging museums and galleries
178

student reinstallation of a permanent collection
gallery, los angeles county museum of art,
june 2003-march 2004
michael asher
180

art inside out at the children's museum of
manhattan
deborah f schwartz
190

application: proposal for a youth project dealing
with forms of youth visibility in galleries
carmen moersch
198

play and nothingness the model for a qualitative
society, an activist project at the moderna museet,
stockholm 1968
lars bang larsen
206

a toe in the water: giving young people
a voice at the whitechapel art gallery
steve herne and janice mclaren
220

five

artists collaborate with young people in their community
228

siddiequa, firdaus, abdallah, soeleyman,
moestafa, hawwa, dzoel-kifi by joost conijn
230

isep, the laycock school and other experiments
236

creativity with purpose heads together productions
adrian sinclair
244

children make sculpture: the work of elizabeth leyh
248

magic me intergenerational arts
jan stirling
258

planet volco
a project by loraine leeson
266

contributors
270

credits and acknowledgements
271

All text by anna harding unless otherwise stated

magic moments

collaboration between artists and young people

'Magic Moments' occur when something special happens – something clicks, shifts, is triggered, an awakening occurs. A particular art experience can release latent energy, a belief in yourself and your own ability, confidence and clarity. American philosopher John Dewey considered the root of art as specific experiences, something set apart from the general stream of consciousness, something which seemed unrepeatable, unique, and nameable. My quest has been to identify situations where artists have offered such magic moments to young people, to identify how and why they have genuinely set off sparks. I have collected together projects from a variety of settings including schools, playgrounds, correctional facilities, galleries, youth clubs and apprentice training centres. I try to focus on how artists engage young people in processes of critical and reflective thinking and conceptual problem-solving, rather than on the making skills associated with art. *Magic Moments* is written primarily from the artist's perspective, in order to articulate what they see as the essence and potential of these collaborations; I am interested in how artists relate to young people in ways which might be different from other adults. I include young people's perspectives where I could access them, but these are unfortunately often poorly documented or overlooked, which makes this work suffer from an over-reliance on a narrow range of adult perspectives. I pay less attention to project organisers who are not front line delivery; where they appear they provide valuable illustrations of the preoccupations of various sectors.

I have organised the projects in five arenas which are by no means exclusive, and many projects cross between several arenas. The first section considers primarily artist perspectives, focusing on how artists rationalise their activity. The second section on schools presents artist projects which interrogate or expose prevailing education systems or propose alternative education systems. The third section looks at projects engaging with young people moving beyond school. A fourth category is museum or gallery settings, focusing particularly on projects which give young people a voice in these institutions. The fifth section presents projects which take place in community settings. Across these arenas, artists employ a variety of modes – such as observer, teacher, facilitator, mentor or role model, or instigator of critique. In each feature, while seeking out 'Magic Moments', I had a set of questions in mind: how and why did a project originate and evolve? What were the motivations behind it? What was unique or special about the context in which the project took place? What opportunities and constraints did a project contend with and how? What ideas, techniques or strategies were used? What did the project offer young people? Did the project shift from an original idea? What were the key dynamics pertinent to its success or failure and on what terms is this judged by different interest groups? What can we identify of value?

I use the term collaboration because it seems that artists, more perhaps than some other adults, engage in projects as equals with young people. Walter Benjamin's famous essay "The Author as Producer" of 1934 sets an important context in arguing for a radical, innovative, socially engaged art practice, for the emancipation of the proletariat. One route to achieving this was to defy the constrictions of individualist production in preference for artistic collaboration. Collaboration and modification of authorship has also been linked with the marginal or with counter culture in an alternative Modernist stream that includes Surrealism's collectively produced 'exquisite corpse' drawings, and Dada actions. A more recent context for the current proliferation of collaborative practice involving young people stems from viewer participation in phenomenological inquiries, incarnated in conceptual art works from the 1960s, in which collaboration was viewed as a version of the 'expanded field'. The divide between action and contemplation would be abolished and a convergence of spectator and environment would emerge through participation. Artists began to enunciate open-ended environmental propositions and hypotheses and took upon themselves new functions, more like those of an intermediary than a creator. Arguments for self-expression and creativity in education emerging in the 1960s were part of a strong cultural reaction against rationalism, in far-reaching changes that Raymond Williams called the "structure of feeling of the time", with the personal growth movement promoting individuality and authenticity. More recently, activist art practices and art in regeneration contexts have built on aspirations emerging from this late 60s art activity, often with a link through cultural studies, media studies or intermediate artists rather than specific knowledge of projects from this era, which were often poorly documented. While socially engaged art practice enjoys a renaissance, community learning projects surviving from the 1960s and 70s often became bogged down after facing years of bureaucratic red tape and inadequate resources. Seemingly new practices oblivious to this heritage appear to the initiated to be reinventing the wheel, often blissfully unaware of a wealth of experience from which they might benefit. This book attempts in some ways to bridge a generation gap.

Today a growing convergence between business and education thinking has surprisingly offered new roles for artists. Policy think tanks and management gurus have persuaded governments of beneficial links between artists' creativity and the world of work, seeing artists as uniquely gifted to nurture such things as creativity, motivation and increased self-esteem. The concept of 'Thinking

Outside the Box' was one widely used by management consultants in the 1970s and 80s. Daniel Goleman's best-selling book *Emotional Intelligence*, based on the work of psychologists Mayer and Salovey, *The Creative Spirit* (which was also a PBS television series), and Richard Florida's *The Rise of the Creative Class* are examples of the phenomenon of equating the creativity of artists with future business excellence.[1] Links between what is required for excellence in the arts and in business were made in the United States in the School-to-Work Opportunities Acts of the 1980s, in the Arts Education Partnership founded in 1995 as part of Goals 2000 (a national partnership of organisations exploring how the arts can transform American education), and in an examination of how arts learning can aid student achievement in the SCANS report (Secretary's Commission on Achieving Necessary Skills) entitled *What Work Requires of Schools*.[2] Set up by the Secretary of Labor, its remit was to determine the skills young people need to succeed in the world of work, to encourage high-performance, high-skill, high-wage employment and to help teachers understand how curriculum and instruction must change to enable students to develop those skills.[3] Business literature repeatedly emphasises building strong relationships through authentic experiences, perpetual novelty, creative spirit, transformative experience and freedom within the workplace. However, some critical theorists in education have cautioned that these qualities may not be so widely applicable to the workplace, for example in low skill routine work, and that this model is based on the experience of successful business executives.[4] Shirley Brice Heath has usefully demonstrated in her research that philosophies of creativity, collaboration and communication which mark out those who succeed in private profit-making enterprises are similar to the sense of agency gained by teenagers in after-school arts projects, where they can take on multiple roles and responsibilities that allow them to think outside given structures.[5] In such projects, artists can motivate children by giving them a platform in decision-making and project management, empowering them by listening to them, boosting their confidence and motivation and connecting school activity with the world around them. Contrarily, cynics have suggested that in fact the role model offered by artists is that of being out of necessity multi-skilled, continually refining and improving their practice with an eye to future opportunity purely for the sake of survival, which for most artists amounts to accepting short-term contracts, low wages and economic insecurity.

Many of the projects presented here from the 1960s and 70s could not happen today. Any whiff of excitement or risk can so easily get lost in funding applications, consultation documents, committee meetings and reports, or by a whole range of new arts 'professionals' who may not even notice the magic. With the growth of a 'professionalised' art sector, artists working with children on creative projects today are in danger of being swamped with bureaucratic regulation around health and safety insurances, and child protection legislation, and organisations shy away from being involved for fear of litigation. Creative freedom is buried with preordained targets and output-based evaluation, while in schools, emphasis on testing and accountability have had the unfortunate effect of stamping out activity which cannot be easily and quantitatively measured and assessed. Furthermore, in our consumer-driven culture, parents who try to boost their and their children's self-esteem through means such as designer labels and accessories, or who are obsessed with good exam results, fail to see the value of getting hands dirty and engaging in creative arts or simple creative play.

Management-based, profit-oriented targets offer an inadequate vocabulary for assessing the value and impact art can have. At worst, projects based on such criteria result in formulaic quick fixes, where the highlight for the organisers might at worst appear to be the photo opportunities of smiling multi-coloured faces engineered to satisfy funders. Artists employed to work in these situations often feel frustrated at their inability to make an impact under such constraints, and soon get fed up with being used as a salve like sticking plaster in short-term politically driven interventions rather than being allowed to engage in more profound ways or on their own terms. This book attempts by contrast to make visible some of the many artists who have achieved profound levels of engagement with young people in projects which have often made a difference to the lives of both young people and artists.

I note a particular propensity for projects to involve 'disadvantaged communities', culturally diverse with low wages and high unemployment, in acts where one class imposes its values on another. Matthew Arnold stated, in a famous passage about the civilising role of culture: "Plenty of people will try to give the masses, as they call them, an intellectual food prepared and adapted in the way they think proper for the actual conditions of the masses. Plenty of people will try to indoctrinate the masses with the set of ideas and judgements constituting the creed of their own profession or party."[6] While some practitioners may choose to remain oblivious to the larger cultural and political context in which they operate, the projects in this book often tend to be politically aware, if not politically motivated.

I have asked artists to express their own understanding of the value of their work with young people, with the aim to assist artists, teachers, galleries, policy-makers, funders and all those engaged with young people to consider how to work together in ever more fruitful ways, and to engage more fully with the potential that artists have to offer.

Artists' Perspectives on working with Young People

Artists are romantically perceived to hold onto core values that community arts organisations, schools, museums and galleries have lost touch with because of the political imperatives that constantly impinge on their work. Motives for engaging young people in their art practice vary. Some artists see young people as a refreshingly authentic or alternative voice, a liberating force, capable of spontaneous and direct expression, characteristics which the artist may themselves aspire to. Artists are sometimes considered child-like in their curiosity or playfulness: it is intrinsic to artistic work to constantly challenge and break rules, turn things on their heads and look at them from new angles. At the same time, making art is a demanding process which involves asking fundamental questions, being concise and articulate, combining generative and critical thinking. Artists are presumed to be more comfortable with open-ended experiences than non-artists. These are all qualities and skills which artists have a predisposition to recognise and value in young people.

Those featured in this book generally do not think of themselves as teachers and largely have little knowledge of education theory. They tend to consider themselves co-learners rather than experts; enablers, mentors, nurturers offering alternatives to the authority role so often adopted by parent or teacher in order to wield control, or to achieve specific outcomes or tasks. Artists draw on experiences (learned perhaps at art college), such as developing meaning through dialogue or creating knowledge, generating creative environments where participants find themselves engaged in a discourse between equals, together on a journey of investigation.[7] Mutual trust, mutual benefit and mutual respect are the basis of such approaches to working, which too often is not the daily experience of some young people, who may face prejudice, hardship or ill treatment. Such approaches empower young people by giving them permission and attempting to eliminate boundaries and hierarchies that often prevent a flow of ideas. Unsurprisingly, young people are more inclined to flourish when they are considered as intelligent and their ideas are valued, when adults have time to listen to them and encourage them, which our society often does not make time for.

In the past, artists tended to keep a distance rather than engage in a more hands-on way with young people. Helen Levitt's photographs of children playing in the streets of Harlem, New York since the early 1930s to the present day, show children transfixed in play, moments transformed by fantasy. Her work was informed by the preoccupations of the Surrealist art scene of Brassaï, Henri Cartier Bresson and Luis Buñuel, not by any desire to change the world or improve young people's lives.[8] James Agee noticed in her images of childhood "innocence... the record of an ancient, primitive, transient and immortal civilization, incomparably superior to our own, as it flourishes, at the proud and eternal crest of its wave, among those satanic incongruities of a metropolis which are, for us, definitive expressions and productions of a loss of innocence."[9] Her images convey freedom, a sense of space and musicality. She is imaginatively absorbed in the children's play, as though she were invisible. Small gestures, stage scenes, words exchanged on the wall catch her attention; she shares with fellow Surrealists an interest in the poetics of the chance encounter and the found object. Going into Harlem as artist-woman-flaneur-photographer, from a circle of artists seeking out the burlesque and the carnivalesque, her framing is lyrical rather than social commentary. Henri Michaux's poetry about the special primitive, transient state of childhood appeared contemporaneously in 1938 in volume one of *Verve*, which included images by Cartier Bresson and Bill Brandt.

Nigel Henderson saw his photographs of children in the East End of London as images of 'alternative culture'. One particular series of photographs from around 1950 of boys 'doodling' in the street on their bikes, he said summoned up "a certain delirium in which a boy may fantasise and divert himself... for hours on end". Street photographs showing children at play were for him a medium releasing "an energy of image from trivial data".[10] He took these photographs in the working class neighbourhood where he lived from 1945-1953 with his wife, the anthropologist and economist Judith Stephen, who was conducting a survey "Discover Your Neighbour".[11] Henderson remained a voyeur, from a class apart from the scenes he observed. While he never exhibited the photographs as artworks in their own right, they had an impact on artists, architects and designers of the day. His friends, the architects Alison and Peter Smithson, saw in his work the element missing in new towns being designed to accommodate families bombed out of London's East End, and sought to reclaim the potential for neighbourly association celebrated in these images in their designs by recreating residential streets in the air in a presentation at the CIAM meeting in Aix-en-Provence in

Nigel Henderson,
Gillian Alexander skipping,
Chisenhale Road,
c.1950-1952

1953 (Congres Internationaux d'Architecture Moderne) in which they included Henderson's photos. Henderson's interest in alternative culture also fed the exhibition *Parallel of Life and Art* which Henderson organised at London's Institute of Contemporary Arts in 1953 with Eduardo Paolozzi and the Smithsons, joint founders of the Independent Group, an exhibition which took the form of a collage of raw and grainy images such as blow-ups of micro-organisms, fossils and news photographs.

Allan Kaprow, the artist and writer at the foreground of 'Happenings', saw childsplay as a liberator. He was instrumental in involving other people in an expanded art practice. As a student he had been hugely inspired by John Dewey's book *Art as Experience*. In 1949 he scrawled a note in the margin of his copy: "art not separate from experience... what is an authentic experience? Environment is a process of interaction".[12] Dewey had complained that the capacity to have an aesthetic experience had become the purview of experts, and that art had become the exclusive site of aesthetic experience. He invited artists to pay attention to the aesthetic dimensions of everyday life, to restore the link between artworks and things that informed them, which could also be experienced for their own aesthetic qualities. In working to shift the site of art toward everyday life, Kaprow referred to himself as an 'un-artist', shedding conventions of art in order to have unfettered experiences of life. His assemblage *Rearrangable Panels* of 1957, consisting of nine panels, was designed to be rearrangable by its owners, curators or himself, an early nod at the participation of others which would become a central principle of his work.[13] His vanguard performances or Happenings in the decade following 1958 opened elements of everyday life or everyday technology to the 'strangeness' of the fantastic or poetic. Kaprow's three young children playing together became a key inspiration; he noted in their self-generated play how stereotypical roles from life were adopted. The hotly negotiated roles of mum, dad, teacher, etc., however, were too much like the stage, so eventually in place of roles he would assign the performance of common routines, tasks and choices to participants. The sociability of childsplay was a key influence – having playmates as opposed to competitive games, an attitude that he could imagine in adult forms, shifting from trying to 'play' to an audience to Happenings which involved actively seeking playmates, moving from writing detailed scores to proposing general templates for aesthetic experience drawn directly from life, montages of games, rituals, routines, exchanges, choices, conundrums, and jokes.[14] Photographs of Kaprow's tyre environment, *Yard* of 1961, in the back courtyard of the Martha Jackson Gallery in New York, show him with his three-year-old son, Anton, playing in the mound of tyres. The 'come out and play' invitation of the installation offered an alternative to the 'do not touch' injunctions inside the gallery. Curves replaced the harsh angles of the gallery and several large bronzes (Barbara Hepworth, Alberto Giacometti) in the sculpture court were wrapped, simultaneously protecting and erasing them, reinforcing a critical distance implied in the work's ancillary relation to the gallery. Kaprow was also inspired by Johan Huizinga's *Homo Ludens: A Study of the Play-Element in Culture*, which looked at the role of play in all fields of life, making a distinction between competitive gaming and play, seeing 'gaming' as work-ethical regulation of play in modern industrial society for the purpose of increasing the chances of optimising the outcome, for profit or victory.[15]

Stephen Willats has looked throughout his career at physical and psychic pressures which individuals in today's society are subjected to, and in certain projects worked specifically with children in examining these issues. At the Markisches Viertel, the vast housing blocks in Berlin where he worked in the late 1970s, he saw children's wall drawings as an expression of counter consciousness, symbols of resistance to the determinism inherent in the architecture and planning. He has looked at ways in which personal spaces can be defined within preordained structures and anonymous architecture, looking at self-organisational models used by young people within these circumstances. Having met a group of the children, his approach was to tape record an interview with them about their drawings, and then contrast the outcome with the reality of their parents' flat.[16] Fascinated by the complexity and proliferation of these children's drawings he produced a bookwork based on the children called *Ich lebe in einem Betonklotz*

(*I live in a concrete bunker*), and a series of works entitled *Berlin Wall Drawings*. In *The Kids are in the Streets* made at the Oval, south London in 1981-1982, he described the tensions and frustrations of 18-year-old Paul Rogers' life, contrasted with his involvement with skateboarding at a park nearby, a world constructed by Rogers and his friends, viewed by Willats as a manifestation of counter consciousness. At his studio, Willats directed a series of working sessions with Rogers over a six-month period, in which Rogers' photographic prints, found objects and reactions to the Brixton riots are presented alongside Willats' own photographs and tape recordings. Willats describes Rogers' work as "his own view of the hopeless future in store for teenage youth in today's inner city". Willats' work was important in bringing this subject matter to a mainstream art gallery arena.

Motives for collaboration between artists and young people have often been ill-defined and unclear. When Brit Art star Tracey Emin (famous for autobiographical works such as an unkempt bed, snapped up by the collector Charles Saatchi for £150,000 ($272,000), and for works about abortions and love affairs) worked with a school a few years back, confusion over ownership of the artwork ended in a fight. The value for a school of having a celebrity artist come and work with their pupils left behind a bitter taste when teachers realised that in fact Emin presumed ownership over their work. "A £35,000 ($63,500) Tracey Emin quilt – but worthless if school tries to sell it" was the headline news on *The Guardian*'s front page on 30 March 2004, when Emin demanded the return of a blanket made with eight-year-olds after the school tried to auction it. Her gallery, White Cube, warned that if the school persisted in trying to sell the work, its former artist-in-residence would refuse to authenticate the work as hers, sending its value crashing. Taking as her theme the title "Tell me something beautiful", Emin had invited pupils from two Year Four classes to come up with their ideas of beauty and then to sew words in felt letters on bright fabric squares. The bold patchwork, featuring words such as "tree", "sunrise", "dolphin" and "nan", was reviewed as an Emin work by critics, recuperating this collaboration as the work of an individual genius. Trouble hit when a teacher investigated whether the quilt could be auctioned to raise funds, after it emerged that an acrylic display box for the work would cost up to £3,000 ($5,500), which the school could not afford. A consultation with teaching staff, governors and a cross-section of parents produced broad agreement in favour of a sale, particularly given that Sotheby's auctioneers suggested a £35,000 price tag if Emin would authenticate the work as hers. The artist's response was to deny authorship, but ask for the blanket back. Art critic John Slyce said "They were lucky to have an artist of that stature spending that amount of time with them... the artwork should remain in context with the kids. Children's primary experience of art should not be as commodity." This standoff is a far cry from the feel-good nature of the original project and suggests a need for far more careful consideration of motives and ownership by all working in this field. Buying into the commodity status of the famous artist also had a downside and perhaps the young people's learning or motivation would have been just as enhanced working with a teacher given equivalent preparation time and resources. This can understandably be a source of resentment from teachers, who may be artists in their own right.

Confusion over attribution in collaborative work is being productively discussed in the legal field of intellectual property, with new Creative Commons licensing providing ways to ensure that each party's work is acknowledged while

Ecclesbourne primary school in north London was hoping to auction the quilt for £35,000 Photograph: Sean Smith

A £35,000 Tracey Emin quilt – but worthless if school tries to sell it

Lucy Ward
Education correspondent

First it was an unmade bed that plunged her into controversy; now Tracey Emin is engaged in an artistic tug of war with a group of school children over a patchwork quilt.

The Britart star, whose first experiment with bed linen was snapped up by Charles Saatchi for £150,000, is demanding the return of a blanket made with eight-year-olds as part of an art project after the school involved tried to auction it.

According to the White Cube gallery, the fashionable London art venue which represents Ms Emin, she is "extremely upset and depressed by the news" that Ecclesbourne primary school hoped to raise £35,000 for art projects by selling the blanket at Sotheby's.

The gallery says Ms Emin wants the quilt — currently packed up in an orange bag in the school's storeroom — handed back, sharpish. And in case Ecclesbourne persists in trying to sell, White Cube is refusing to authenticate the work as hers, sending its value crashing.

The gallery told the school in a letter: "Tracey is one of the country's leading contemporary artists and Ecclesbourne school should be proud to be in possession of such a historically valuable collaborative work ... but your actions suggest otherwise. In the light of this, Tracey has requested that the blanket is collected from the school as soon as possible."

The standoff, which reaches into the darker corners of intellectual property law, is a far cry from the feelgood nature of the original project linking artists with schools. Ms Emin went to Ecclesbourne in north London in 2000 as part of a scheme in the capital titled Art in Sacred Spaces, in which children's work created with 12 contemporary artists was displayed in places of worship in a week-long exhibition. Tak-ing as her theme the title "Tell me something beautiful", Emin invited pupils from two year-four classes to nominate their ideas of beauty and then to sew the keywords in felt letters on bright fabric squares.

The resulting bold patchwork, featuring words such as "tree", "sunrise", "dolphin" and "nan", was reviewed as an Emin work by critics including the Guardian's Jonathan Jones, who wrote: "She acknowledges the celebratory, incantatory function of art. You leave thanking the Lord that she has found a subject other than herself."

Trouble hit the blanket project only when Ecclesbourne teacher Chris Mooney investigated whether the quilt could be auctioned to raise funds after it emerged that an acrylic display box would cost up to £3,000.

A consultation with teaching staff, governors and a cross section of parents produced broad agreement in favour of a sale, particularly given

Sotheby's suggested £35,000 price tag if Ms Emin authenticated the work as hers.

The artist's response — denying authorship but asking for the blanket back — is contradictory, the school claims.

Henry Lydiate, professor of art law at the London Institute, yesterday suggested that a failure by art project organ-isers clearly to establish the terms of the collaboration at the outset could be to blame for the row. There were historical precedents stretching back to the studios of the Renaissance masters for artists to retain authorship of a work despite not having created every element of a piece themselves, he said.

However, while an artist might not sign an artwork to prove authorship, Sotheby's could still sell the piece, making clear its history.

But art critic John Slyce, who has worked on school collaborations with artists, said: "This is a horrific precedent for the school to try to set.

"They were lucky to have an artist of that stature spending that amount of time with them ... the artwork should remain in context with the kids. Children's primary experience of art should not be as a commodity."

Cover story, Education Guardian
guardian.co.uk/arts

Austin cartoon: WHERE TRACY EMIN SAT IN THE STAFFROOM. £200,000

The Guardian, front page, 30 March 2004.

also making it available to others for creative purposes. By applying a Creative Commons copyright license and (cc) to her work, an author invites the world to make certain uses of it without giving up her copyright, declaring 'some rights reserved', using a range of flexible, customisable intellectual property licenses available free of charge to legally define what constitutes acceptable use of their work. The origins of this principle can be found in the age-old idea of commons, with the idea that society and the economy are better off when certain resources are shared. An artist might, for example, agree to give away a work as long as no one is making money from it, but include a provision requiring payments on a sliding scale if it is sold. As participation in the Commons project increases, a variety of specific intellectual property license options will evolve in response to user needs, creating templates for others with similar requirements. Hopefully this may encourage clarification over motives and ownership.

Artists and schools: interventions in Education systems

In the 1950s, original artworks, generally prints, were loaned out to schools by enlightened museums and local authorities. Artists felt they were contributing to young people's education in this way, rather than considering that they themselves might step into schools.[17] The education sector has been gently persuaded over recent years that bringing in artists to work directly with young people is a good thing, yet we remain largely inarticulate about how engagement with artists really benefits young people and are only beginning to find appropriate vocabulary for this. Artist projects in schools are often still viewed as a special treat, perhaps for the summer term after more formal teaching and assessments are out of the way, but in today's climate, with a new government initiative in Britain offering funds to certain schools to work with artists, it is difficult to say no.

Brian Jackson's vivid writing on creativity, citizenship and empowerment is particularly relevant to our enquiry. "Human talent is like yeast: in favourable conditions it multiplies" he stated in a *Sunday Times Magazine* special issue in 1970, marking the 100 year anniversary of the struggle to emancipate education.[18] His short lifetime's work as an education campaigner, sociologist and writer addressed the dichotomy between what he identified as educated middle class values and working class culture.[19] Although the terminology has changed, these agendas are still central to debate around culture. Brian Jackson and Dennis Marsden's *Education and the Working Class* of 1962 asked whether the working class child must accept the present price of access to high culture, intellectual satisfaction and material well-being. Personal experience informed Jackson's work: as one of a crop of scholarship boys who benefited from a grammar school education, he knew first-hand that "you were expected to keep rules and customs that you had neither heard of, nor conceived of. You were expected to think and feel differently. You were expected not to be a working class lad – or if you were, to get busy with the camouflage."[20] Jackson campaigned against damage caused to children's self-esteem by teachers' limited view of what constituted talent – valuing written skills, speed, tidiness, and minimum error. In Jackson's view, "many of the most creative are slow and untidy; all of the most experimental chance many errors to gain one success." He felt that "creativity relies on the flow of ideas. This happens best in an atmosphere where risk is encouraged, playfulness with ideas is accepted and where failure is not punished but seen as part of the process of success…. Innovations come when existing knowledge is combined in novel ways to meet the demands of new circumstances." He never forgot what it was like to be a child "bombarded with information and instructions from grownups" and felt that "sometimes parents need to respect the invisible signs: Private: child doing nothing. Trespassers will be prosecuted."[21]

Working Class Life, embarked on by Jackson with Dennis Marsden in 1958 and published in 1968, captured a crucial moment in time when older working class values encountered mass media, asking:

[are we] moving in the direction of a society sapped by the poorest middle class concerns (such as those about personal status), the poorest mass media attitudes – those preoccupied with the packaging and not the packet's contents, and the poorest of all the old working class situations: a vast but enclosed community transformed into a passive, conforming audience? Or can the decisions, in an inevitably changing society, be taken differently? Can they lead to a fusion of middle class feeling for individual development, with multiplication of experience which mass media may offer, and those qualities of spontaneity and community?[22]

While Jackson's work has largely been overlooked, it could be viewed as a precursor to recent initiatives, particularly the work of Professor Ken Robinson.

Governments today increasingly look to art as a political tool in terms of its transformative potential in relation to the lives and aspirations of young people. In the United Kingdom, in Tony Blair's first Labour government formed in 1997, the new Secretary of State for Education David Blunkett appointed a National Advisory Committee on Creative and Cultural Education, a task group to explore links between creativity, the economy and education, bringing together leading business people, educators, artists and scientists. The committee was chaired by Ken Robinson, then Professor of Arts Education at Warwick University and, since 2001, Senior Advisor for Education at the J Paul Getty Trust in Los Angeles. The resulting report, *All Our Futures: Creativity, Culture and Education*, published in 1999, and Robinson's subsequent book *Out of Our Minds: Learning to be Creative*, which became a best seller in the business world, have both been highly influential in promoting the importance of creativity.[23] Robinson argued that young people's creativity and self-esteem are important for future economic and social well-being; he considered conditions under which creativity can thrive or be stifled. He promoted the need to reconnect feeling with intellect in meeting the educational challenges of the twenty-first century and has called for major restructuring of the education curricula in Britain and the USA, to put an emphasis on creativity and overcoming blocks on creativity, to foster self-esteem and to focus on projects that surprise, energise and enthuse pupils. Robinson bemoaned the fact that universities and schools are now run more like businesses, that a preoccupation with the bottom line is detrimental to the quality of education and that creative thinking requires the teaching not only of knowledge and skills, but also opportunities to speculate and experiment. Robinson's advice was instrumental in encouraging the British government to set up Creative Partnerships in 2002, a new organisation directly accountable to the Department of Culture Media and Sport and based at Arts Council England. Creative Partnerships is committed to the positive development of young people through cultural practice and creative learning, challenging where necessary conventional educational thinking and practice by forging new partnerships between young people and artists. The aim is to help develop the imaginations and skills of young people through meaningful and sustained cultural experiences in the formal and informal education sectors, to help schools to identify their individual needs and then enable them to develop long-term, sustainable partnerships with creative organisations and individuals. It is based on the premise that artists may be able to free up creative thinking and motivate in unexpected ways, which classroom teachers, schools and parents or carers often don't have the time, skills or resources to do. It forms part of broader policy aimed at cultural entitlement, citizenship and social inclusion and arts policy aimed at the 'professional development' of artists. Much of this policy stems from a desire to improve opportunity and aspiration through culture, but may be in danger of falling into traps of over-regulation as yet another government initiative for over-stretched teachers to contend with.

Aim Higher
Out of and Beyond school

The community photography movement of the 1970s offers an example of practitioners developing appropriate media and methods for engaging young people largely disengaged from conventional forms of learning; I offer an introduction to this movement and its often overlooked achievements. Grassroots photography projects, often with radical political aspirations, offered important opportunities for self-discovery for young people fortunate enough to find their way to such a project. Andrew Dewdney and Martin Lister's article "Youth and Photography" describes one of the many community photography projects to emerge in Britain in the 1970s which were important for young people.[24] Engaged in a quest shared by many of their generation for more relevant forms of cultural practice,

> in 1969… we carried with us, as we believe did a much larger group, a broad and theoretically unclarified conviction that a closer and clearer relationship between Art and Society was necessary. We were dissatisfied with the institutions of Art, which perpetuated a rarefied and mystifying view of the creative imagination. Above all we shared a deeply felt rejection of exclusive and elitist ideas about creativity being a special quality of naturally gifted individuals, usually white men, which was not shaped by history or culture.[25]

Rejecting "the incestuous cycle of art, produced by artists in art colleges with an attendant business of gallery contracts, exhibitions and exports", they evolved a practice using photography as a central tool in working with teenagers at the Cultural Studies Department of the Cockpit Arts Workshop (part of the Inner London Education Authority). Following Walter Benjamin, they questioned fine art's "autographic practice" and proposed instead the importance of mass and mechanical media in a new, popular, available yet serious art. They developed an approach in which social, economic and historical forces were made central to the analysis of cultural forms, legitimising popular culture as a field of study, firstly at undergraduate level, but eventually filtering through into schools and the teaching of young people generally.[26] Finding it hard to convince art teachers, art advisers and inspectors that the study and practice of mass media or study relating to the contemporary experience of young people was important, and depressed by the continuing presence of art school ideologies in a watered down version in most school art departments, they decamped to other subjects such as English and Social Studies which could accommodate an emphasis on society. They chose to work in film, video or photography in order to achieve currency with young people. Black and white photography was their preference due to its affordability, accessibility and ease of distribution, but also the view that it did not require a long apprenticeship to achieve reasonable results. The ability to recognise the potency of images and put them into circulation are skills which such projects, focused on democratising image-making perhaps overlooked, discounting the significance of aesthetic decision-making and praising participation over quality and impact of image. Dewdney and Lister admitted in retrospect to "a rather zealous adoption of theory" which could be accused of resulting in rather formulaic practices.

Another account of the burgeoning community photography movement in Britain in the 1970s is provided by Derek Bishton and Brian Homer's article "People Power?".[27] They describe how project workers, who generally did not use the name artist, largely saw the photographic act as directly political and their role as political activists. Again the empowerment of community members through the act of pressing the shutter and directing cameras at subjects relevant to them was of greater importance than quality of image in conventional fine art terms. Community photography offered positive alternatives to images generally in the public domain, as it established alternative voices:

> There are not many occasions when you see black people photographed at ease at home in their environment. The 'ghetto image' of poverty and deprivation is far more common. You can see therefore how important photos like these were within the community at WELD [Westminster Endeavour for Liaison and Development, one of the many community photography projects in Birmingham] and how they help establish an alternative identity...

Jon Stewart of WELD stated.[28] Art projects offering opportunities to represent alternative self-image and identity continue to be important in offering insight and empowerment to young people.[29]

Bootle Art in Action was one of the many grassroots, often isolated community arts projects that thrived during the 1970s, fuelled by the energy of passionate individuals. Margaret Pinnington, whose maisonette was the project's first base, described:

> Many of these youngsters had turned their backs on formal schooling and had little academic aspiration. Through photography they began to realise that they were not the 'failures' that the formal education system had labelled them. We attempt to take the youngsters out to venues displaying their work on opening nights and let them talk to people about their photographs; why they took that particular photograph and how they developed it.... The youngsters love this and are quite at home talking with professional photographers about their own photography. They have had the opportunity of meeting famous people in the art world and have the confidence now to articulate their ideas to them. In the early days, people visiting the project were very surprised at the quality of the youngsters' work, in some instances they did not really believe that youngsters without any formal or technical training in photography could produce such good photographs. What has become clear at *Art in Action* is that this encouragement of self-expression is fundamentally different from schooling. Although schooling involves the passing on of skills, it is always closely linked to particular aims – it is so much more teaching, rather than learning.... A good community photographic project can stimulate a natural and ordinary creativity, a desire on the part of all of us to participate in and comment on what is going on around us.... The photographs at *Bootle Art in Action* are as powerful as any advertisement hoarding, but that is not because they're clever, but because they're true.[30]

Some of the young people who grew through such projects went on to make significant contributions in these fields, such as artist and filmmaker Isaac Julien whose exposure to filmmaking came from Four Corners community filmmaking facility in east London, or Bob Long who moved from Camerawork in east London to set up the Video Nation series at the BBC in the early 90s, a ground-breaking series giving ordinary people cameras to make their own video diaries.[31] In this way the movement graduated as alternative identities filtered into the mainstream media.

young People challenging Museums and Galleries

Andy Warhol appreciated children as an audience – their responses, he felt, were often refreshingly honest and direct. In 1983 he made an exhibition especially for children at Bruno Bischoferger gallery in Zurich. However, generally young people have been considered by museums and galleries as a sub-category requiring a kind of second tier of programming. The art business is currently polarised into two positions: on one side is a privatised art world of exhibitions with expensive admission charges, sponsors and elite corporate and celebrity receptions, obsessions with branding and spectacle; on the other side is a tendency towards the democratisation of culture, brought about partly by governments seeing an instrumental role for culture and accounting for their spending in these terms. Many institutions struggle to find meeting points between a top-down and bottom-up view of culture and cultural entitlement and much policy is confused because the terms used to understand quality and impact of art swing between aesthetic and accounting terminology. Increasingly, rigorous demands for accountability for public funds have goaded art institutions to prove their worth through educational services which aim to engage and civilise 'new audiences', while a parallel new industry has grown up to evaluate these activities and prove their worth.[32] Working with 'disadvantaged communities' including young people today provides an important source of revenue for art institutions. How far these activities can be co-opted whilst perpetuating exclusive cultural space remains to be seen.

Museums, galleries and exhibitions play a pivotal role in the formation of the modern state as educative and civilising agencies. In this section, I focus on art projects which engaged young people with museums and galleries, particularly those exposing power relations at play within these institutions. The projects show institutions increasingly aware of their need to be not only accountable to young people, but dependent on them for a future. The creative potential of setting up dynamic relations between adult proprietors and youngsters can have profound implications, which so far are only entertained on a temporary basis, after which conventional power and control are quickly reasserted. The contributions in this section suggest benefits which such interventions can accrue and that a much more central engagement of young people in arts institutions, engineered by artists, has enormous dynamic potential for all parties.

Public museums and art galleries were often founded with education central to the 'civilising' mission of founding philanthropists, which forms the basis of their charitable status.[33] In the late twentieth century many museum displays were perceived to fail to compete with TV, computer games and shopping as popular entertainment, so museums searched for ways to reinvent themselves.

Techniques used for revitalising museums included blockbuster exhibitions, interactive displays, shopping malls and smart cafes and restaurants, reincarnating them as glamorous locations for corporate entertainment and, more importantly for this book, education and outreach programmes were developed to engage young people. Many education departments started out as 'docent' programmes, run by well-to-do wives to pass on a connoisseur's insight into collections to visiting groups. The enormous growth industry of museum and gallery education has more recently expanded, with artists working as guides to exhibitions, running workshops and taking on residencies in neighbourhood contexts beyond the institution, in school and community settings, primarily in order to ease the process of visits to the museum or gallery. Artists engaged in the 'democratising practices' of museum and gallery education have been involved in educating about the work of artists exhibiting in the gallery, following the traditional role of gallery education departments. Occasionally, as a thorn within the institution, they may aspire to change perceptions of art as an elitist activity. Within the arts economy, gallery education work for many artists is one of the few avenues of employment available making use of their artistic skills. It offers artists opportunities to work with people in contrast to the solitariness of the studio, and inspiring children can be particularly rewarding if you take away the pressures of assessment and paperwork surrounding teachers' lives and if it is not a full-time commitment (although attitudes are changing, some purists get concerned that too much work in this field and people will forget that you are an artist).

The growth of children's museums, starting in the USA, and shifts towards child-centred cultural programming, such as youth arts festivals and even a children's art biennale in Utrecht, The Netherlands, indicate an embracing in some places of young people as citizens and consumers. Art specially designed for children is another growth market, akin to the industry of children's literature. Children are also being looked to as artists in their own right with, for instance in the UK with the Artworks awards for young artists and a recent high profile conference at Tate Modern entitled "How old do you have to be to be an artist?" which celebrated artwork by children.[34] This section on young people challenging museums and galleries only touches on enormous changes being brought about in terms making arts institutions more engaging to youth, indicating how artists can be creatively involved in this process. Many institutions make the mistake of involving artists in these processes only once creative projects are planned in detail rather than engaging with their ideas more fully. I hope this book will emphasise the benefits of engaging artists at the earliest possible stage as the most profound impact is generally seen in projects where artists and creativity are central to their conception.

Artists collaborate with young people in their community

Artist David Cashman, who with Roger Fagin co-founded the Islington Schools Environmental Project (ISEP) in 1974, explained that five- to 11-year-olds have an inexhaustible supply of energy for playing, running and climbing: "A child cannot sit still for long unless the body is dulled and the energy held in check. Many artists have wanted to celebrate this energy, with the aim not to stand back, educate or raise consciousness of the forces which shape children's worlds, but to join them in mutual improvisation."[35] Artists and artist groups in this section focus on young people fulfilling roles within their community. While some projects may appear intent on improving people's lives and aspiring to achieve specific outcomes such as regenerating communities or breaking down prejudice, these projects demonstrate how funding initiatives and more 'professionalised' practice seem to fix thinking around tested formulas and achieving specific goals such as meeting curriculum objectives.

The latent energy of children was celebrated in an international movement for radical education flourishing in the late 1960s and early 70s, the Environmental Education movement, which focused on the interrelatedness of man, culture and surroundings and practices of decision-making and self-formulation of codes of behaviour concerning environmental quality.[36] Colin Ward's prolific output of publications, including *BEE*, the *Bulletin of Environmental Education* (later with Eileen Adams); *Vandalism*, 1973; *British School Buildings*, 1976; *Streetwork: The Exploding School*, 1973 with Anthony Fyson; and *The Child in the City*, 1978, are important in this field. *Vandalism* explored young people's motives and energies in a non-judgemental fashion, informed by the anarchist Bakunin's idea that the urge to destroy is also a creative urge. Five categories of vandalism are mapped out in this book by sociologist Stanley Cohen, on a spectrum from what society tolerates to acts that we are least able to accept, concluding that: "Rule breaking is a certain transaction that takes place between rule breakers and the rest of society.... It's down to the perception and definition by certain people that it poses a threat which is against their interests and that something must be done about it." He described the stereotype of the vandal as a working class male adolescent involved in what is generally considered wanton, senseless or motiveless destruction of property, usually public property of some kind. As vandalism could not be explained in terms of accredited motives such as acquiring material gain, it was considered motiveless. He saw that vandalism is "often motivated by impotent rage and hostility against authority" and that it might also be considered a way to relieve boredom or a conscious tactic to draw attention to a specific grievance, a "resentment of the rules of the game" in late adolescent boys who feel entirely powerless, and have a fairly realistic view of the limited horizons on offer to them. David Downes, in *Vandalism*, refers to an essay written by an East End boy: "The school was always trying to turn you into something you were not. It was a waste of time." Opportunities for excitement, autonomy, or, less ambitiously, a simple sense of action, are blocked. What the young person wants – or what the Message tells him he should want to want – cannot be reached. He doesn't have enough money to participate fully, and he doesn't have the talent, luck or contacts to really make it directly. Faced by leisure goals he cannot reach, with little commitment or attachment to others, and lacking any sense of control over his future, his situation contains an edge of desperation.[37]

Sociologists Ian Taylor and Paul Walton described activities around a park on a Sunday afternoon in Bradford in an article "Hey, mister, this is what we really do...." They saw children stacking pallets at different heights against a wall to create an elaborate chase game and roller-coasting in stripped down trolleys in a supermarket car park. Both groups avoided Bradford's park, which to them seemed to hail from a bygone era, with its Latin inscriptions in praise of profit and Puritanism. Six-year-old children were busy smashing a lock chaining up a rocking horse, not in their view an act of vandalism, rather they feel they have a right to play and don't understand that they are locked up as an attempt at keeping the children from danger. The park provides nothing of the adventure and risk which, the authors argued, was the core of their play.[38] Many sociologists identified these feelings preceding a "drift into delinquency", but could equally be deemed as untapped creative expression, a debate which continues, for example, with graffiti artists today.

In *Streetwork: the Exploding School*, Ward and Fyson called for broader links between school and surrounding environment, encouraging educators to explore the idea of the 'exploding school' which revolved around community contact, addressing community problems, a belief that pupils should leave school knowing 'how things are' in the local area and what s/he as a citizen can do about them, forming a bridge between school life and real life in Environmental Education.[39] Involvement in the locality of the school could provide endless resources from which to learn, rather than rare visits to the countryside or a museum. Ward suggested that children set up their own museums or local collections, which would be so much richer and more meaningful than any major museum collection. Simple local opportunities for breaking routine, he argued, offered more valuable lessons than one-off visits to remote museum displays. They stressed the need for greater relevance in subject matter in all subjects, particularly for 'under-achievers' who were more likely to become early school leavers.[40] The film *Kes*, directed by Kenneth Loach in 1969, presents an example of this, in which an English teacher released from a young boy his account of training a kestrel. The boy whose conversation had been considered of no consequence, when asked to talk about something concrete and of immediate interest, emerged with a flood of conversation.

Ward's ideas appeal today to artists who are called upon to work in social contexts such as regenerating communities. Practices from the earlier community arts movement which fell out of favour with funders for many years are being reinvented, but often with little knowledge of historical precedents in what is now being considered an increasingly significant area of art practice which can offer enormous rewards for both artists and young people.

1 Goleman, Daniel, *Emotional Intelligence*, New York: Bantam Books, 1995; Goleman, Daniel, Paul Kaufman, and Michael Ray, *The Creative Spirit*, London: Penguin, 1993; Florida, Richard, *The Rise of the Creative Class*, New York: Basic Books, 2002.

2 *What Work Requires of Schools: A SCANS Report for America 2000*, US Department of Labor, June 1991.

3 http://www.academicinnovations.com/report.html

4 Gee, Hull and Lankshear, *The New Work Order: Behind the language of the new capitalism*, Boulder, CO: Westview Press, 1996.

5 Brice Heath, Shirley, "Making Learning Work", *After School Matters* vol. 1, no.1, pp. 33-45, 2000.

6 Arnold, Matthew, "Culture and Anarchy: An Essay in Political and Social Criticism" in Stefan Collini ed., "*Culture and Anarchy*" and other Writings, Cambridge: Cambridge University Press, 1993, pp. 30-31.

7 Carnell, E and C Lodge, *Supporting Effective Learning*, London: Paul Chapman Publishing, 2002.

8 Phillips, Sandra S, *Helen Levitt*, San Francisco: San Francisco Museum of Fine Art, 1991, p. 27.

9 Agee, James, "A Way of Seeing", introduction to *Helen Levitt* exhibition catalogue, New York: MOMA, 1933, pp. xii-xiii.

10 *Nigel Henderson*, Anthony D'Offay Gallery London exhibition catalogue 1977, note 23, quoted in *Transition: the London Art Scene in the Fifties*, Barbican Art Gallery exhibition catalogue, London: Merrell, 2002, p. 102.

11 The research project "Discover your Neighbour", organised by the sociologist J L Peterson, required its tutors to live on site. The Hendersons moved to Chisenhale Road at the borders of Bow and Bethnal Green. As a form of "auto-therapy" in the treatment of the nervous breakdown he had suffered after being retired from the RAF in 1943 where he had been a bomber pilot, Nigel Henderson walked the streets for several years. "I just walked and walked and stared at everything." As an observant outsider, it was some years before he considered photographing "this sort of stage set against which people were more or less unconsciously acting". *Nigel Henderson*, Anthony D'Offay Gallery London, notes 21 and 26.

12 Kelly, Jeff, "John Dewey and the Ranch", in *Childsplay: the art of Allan Kaprow*, Berkeley and Los Angeles: University of California Press, 2004, p. 7.

13 Kelly, *Childsplay*, p. 14.

14 Kelly, *Childsplay*, p. 51.

15 Huizinga, Johan, *Homo Ludens: A Study of the Play-Element in Culture*, Boston, MA: Beacon, 1955.

16 Willats, Stephen, *Ich lebe in einem Betonklotz*.

17 The Leicestershire Museums Service in England was famous for this and held an exhibition of its art for schools at the Whitechapel Art Gallery.

18 Jackson, Brian, "Children of Gold, Silver, Bronze" in "100 years of state schools", *Sunday Times Magazine* special issue, 1970, pp. 13-14.

19 Jackson was a campaigner against the harm of selective schools and selective entry, he promoted equality of opportunity through a truly comprehensive education system, and almost single-handedly created the National Extension College in 1963, a model for the Open University, pioneering flexible part-time and learning opportunities for mature students. He was instrumental in founding the Pre-school Playgroups Association in 1961, a self-help initiative in the face of government inaction. See Kit Hardwick, *Brian Jackson: Educational Innovator and Social Reformer*, Lutterworth Press, 2003.

20 Jackson, Brian and Dennis Marsden, *Education and the Working Class*, London: ARK editions/Routledge, 1962.

21 Introduction to Brian Jackson, *Fatherhood*, St Leonards, NSW: Allen and Unwin, 1984.

22 This was part of the lively debate at that time about working class culture. Key publications were Raymond Williams' *Culture and Society*, London: Penguin, 1971; Richard Hoggart's *Uses of Literacy*, London: Penguin, 1969; Jackson's colleague Michael Young's *Family and Kinship in East London* London: Penguin, 1969; and Floud, Halsey and Martin's survey *Social Class and Educational Opportunity* London: Methuen, 1973. On television, Dennis Mitchell's *Morning in the Streets*, BBC, 1959, and *Saturday Night and Sunday Morning* by Karel Reisz, 1960, were part of a new interest in working class culture.

23 Department for Education and Sport, National Advisory Committee on Creative and Cultural Education, *All Our Futures: Creativity, Culture and Education*, 1999 and Ken Robinson, *Out of our Minds: Learning to be Creative*, Capstone, 2001.

24 By the end of 1978 nearly 80 such projects were running using photography in community work. Research by Paul Carter of Blackfriars Photography Project, which was set up in London in 1974, quoted in Derek Bishton and Brian Homer, "People Power?", *Ten: 8*, no. 1, 1979.

25 Dewdney, Andrew and Martin Lister, "Youth and Photography," *Ten:8*, pp. 4-13.

26 Key courses included Popular Culture Units offered by the Open University, the MA course at the Centre for Cultural Studies, Birmingham University and the Photography degree course at the Polytechnic of Central London.

27 Bishton, Derek, and Brian Homer, "People Power?" (Bishton was editor of *Ten:8* magazine).

28 WELD (Westminster Endeavour for Liaison and Development) was one of the many community photography projects in Birmingham at the time. Others included Sidelines, SPAM (Saltley Print and Media), Maypole Photography Project, CAWS (Community Arts in West Smethwick), Wide Angle, and Building Sights. For further details see Pete James, "Laminated in Time: A Brief History of Community Photography in Birmingham", *Source* 33, Winter 2002, pp. 46-49.

29 See for instance "Abiboyo" by Kamina Walker, in Norman Binch and Sue Clive, *Close Collaborations*, Stoke on Trent: Trentham Books, 2001, or Roz Hall, *The Value of Visual Exploration: Understanding Cultural Activities with Young People*, West Bromwich: The Public, 2005.

30 *Ten:8*, no. 21.

31 Rowbotham, Sheila and Sheila Beynon, *Looking at Class*, London: River Oram Press, 2000, pp. 173-184.

32 See for example Felicity Woolf, *Partnerships for Learning: a guide to evaluating arts education projects*, London: Arts Council England, 2004.

33 See Carol Duncan, *Civilising Rituals: inside public art museums*, London: Routledge, 1995, and Tony Bennett, *The Birth of the Museum*, London: Routledge, 1995.

34 "How old do you have to be to be an artist?", conference organised by Artworks at Tate Modern, 30 June 2005.

35 Cashman, David, "The Laycock School Experiment and Current Schemes", *Art for Whom?*, London: Serpentine Gallery, 1978 (exhibition curated by Richard Cork).

36 This definition of Environmental Education comes from the *Nevada declaration, International Working Meeting on Environmental Education in the School Curriculum*, Nevada, 1970.

37 Downes, David, *The Delinquent Solution*, London: Routledge, 1966.

38 Taylor, Ian and Paul Walton, in *Vandalism*, p. 95.

39 Ward and Fyson, in *Vandalism*, p. 88.

40 Ward and Fyson refer to Sir Alec Clegg's address on the 100th anniversary of the Education Act of 1870, where he reminded educators of the injustices and indignities that children, collectively known as John Robinson, suffered at the hands of the education system which, Ward and Fyson argued, "owes him most and offers him least", *Vandalism*, p. 56. See also Charles Hannam, Pat Smyth, and Norman Stephenson, *Young Teachers and Reluctant Learners*, London: Penguin, 1971.

artists' perspectives on working with young people

The accounts in this book are written in a variety of styles. Some result from conversations between the editor and artist, others incorporate a range of viewpoints on the same project (for example artist, young person, teacher, organiser). Some artists have been prompted to write accounts at the request of the editor, other projects have been written about by a third party. The different approaches are mixed here rather randomly, so that the reader may find themselves being tossed on waves from one approach to another.

The first group of artists give a sense that they enjoy being kept on their toes by contact with young people. Richard Wentworth is interviewed by artist colleague Ruth Maclennan in a conversation that opens our eyes to artists' ways of thinking and talking. Faisal Abdu' Allah describes keeping up to the moment in terms of cultural references as a necessity in his profession as a barber as much as in his art with young people. He is motivated by and encourages young people's ambition, while their preconceptions of artists are refreshingly disrupted when they realise that he is just a normal person. Bob and Roberta Smith involves his daughter as a sparring partner and engages young people in his own work to give it a playful edge. Autogena, Smith, Illingworth and Wentworth refer to their own childhoods, in particular recalling a child-like sense that anything is possible, everything can be challenged, qualities which they hold on to and seek out in young people around them. They are attracted to the idea that children have license to be mischievous, something which they seek in their own work. Shona Illingworth describes the significant distinction between engaging young people in the process of making her own artworks versus working as a facilitator in an art programme aimed at bettering young people.

The Jar of Sawdust and the
Lawned Sheep
Richard Wentworth and
Ruth Maclennan

Richard Wentworth: The period in which I grew up was a rather restricted one. My Dad imposed a lot of constraints because that's the way he was brought up, so he couldn't do anything else but pass them on. And then there's the whole genetic thing: no matter how you cover it up, it's going to go out there. As a child, I really just loved being around the making of the world. I loved seeing the world being put together, and taken apart. I had a few opportunities for this. There was a workshop – it was a sort of estate workshop, of my uncle's – and there was a sawmill, at least I think it was a sawmill, I remember a lot of sawdust....

There was one of those sort of can-do, factotum people, called Perry. Perry was a sort of rough diamond. He knew how to do things. I learned about the joy of knowing what lies beneath the surface of things. I absorbed his enthusiasm. He was someone who always had dirt under his fingernails. I think what I liked about him was that he could see beneath the surface of things. He would show me how a shiny car would be full of hot and oily stuff, which made it work. My son is like that too; he's an engineer.

My childhood was the product of a certain type of establishment. My education was very uptight, and there was always a right way to do things. I was saved by Perry and by a teacher, a potter. He was a wonderful character. He was different from the other teachers. He'd been to art school. And he wore different clothes. He did things in a different way from everyone else – I think he also made his own furniture. It was not so much what he did but the way he looked at things, and showed us how things could be. He could show you why a teacup handle worked, or why it didn't work. He was very eloquent about that. I think what he taught was about malleability, about feeling how the world is full of processes. He allowed one to pursue them, to make stuff, and figure out how the world is made. This man was very important to me. All these things are probably connected to grubbiness. The potter didn't have much feeling for literature, and I don't either.

But everyone has different facilities, or allegiances. And mine weren't to words. And nor were his. More to shapes and objects. You don't expect to be good at everything. There was something to do with his enthusiasm, his curiosity, his generosity. But he never did that in an overt way. He gave me the sense that culture was everything and it could all be interesting.

He probably saved me.

Ruth Maclennan: From what?

From all this airlessness of the establishment. Those empire culture ways produced an airlessness of behaviour and also a weight of class and tradition.

How were these things reflected in the way art was taught, or not, and how do you think things have changed?

I entered art school at a time when the Beaux Arts studio tradition was still in place, just. Where the basis of artistic activity was described by the space it occupied in the studio. Painting this size [arms open wide]. And just there, someone making a little thing, far away, you can see her. And maybe somebody working on the floor. And that more or less holds up as a studio until too many people start to arrive, and computers appear.

When did that happen?

Well, incrementally; I suppose it's quite recent. How do you get from the 1970s to now? In that time you move into smaller rooms separated by locked doors – the computer is always seen as holding vital information and needing to be guarded: so was the filing cabinet or the school secretary typing, but that wasn't precious in quite the same way. All the departments separate and become over-mediated. Why shouldn't a potter mingle with a video artist? They're only shapes. Instead you go around an art school and find departments multiplying, becoming the 'Public Ceramics Department'.

That seemed to me absolutely extraordinary: the ambitious titles and the narrowness of the focus. Most of our institutions are narrow, and are forced to meet targets. It's the docket culture. You don't get to speak to anyone in other departments. I suppose I'm the beneficiary of the last period and I feel advantaged by that.

What is the most important period in your own life? And what would you say motivates you in your work?

I think play is really, really interesting. Probably the most thrilling period in my own development was seeing my children play. Not in a very deep way, and certainly not in an organised way. They used to come to the studio a lot. And the studio at the time was a very self-consciously productive place. It was a real artisan working space. And I still like that. The children were unbelievably free. It wasn't badly organised, and pretty well all the tools were there, and they could use whatever they wanted. They would approach them in a very abstract way. You could mould, you could cast, and you could carve, and break, and crumple. You could make a Richard Serra if you wanted to. The children would completely abuse all these processes. They would use things that would be seen as quite dangerous: big drills, sledge hammers, presses and band-saws. I used to say, "go for it". It gave them an extraordinary confidence. I was always amazed at the sort of images they would make. They would get very thin brass shim and cut it with scissors, and spend an incredible amount of time using all the available nails to bang them through the shim into a piece of wood. There was a lot of quite close, quite focused detail.

Felix [Richard's son] was completely obsessed with making sawdust. He would saw for hours, and then assiduously sweep it all up and put it into jars. I've got rows and rows of sawdust. He saw sawing as a means of producing dust, which is interesting. But you learn later that dust is waste. All of this playfulness – they would be left alone – has clearly had a huge effect on what sort of people they are. What they did was not really pictorial, but physically pictorial. They would make something that looked like a dagger, made of chipboard. They would then maybe metal it, with brass shim. But it was made of chipboard for goodness sake! They were very invested activities. These activities didn't have to be finished. At school there isn't time for this sort of thing. They ended up with a studio of their own in a corner of mine, which they boxed off, and they'd spend hours there. I certainly wasn't suggesting what they should do. I remember this being done to me and it was terrible.

How did you become involved in teaching? And what are you trying to do at the Ruskin School of Art?

I don't know why I'm involved in it. I don't know any teachers I respect who have been taught to do it. I think in a good art school, you need people who are theoreticians, and historians. Then you need practitioners, people who've come straight from the studio, who smell of the studio. You need all these different levels. You need some people who don't practise at all, but who are extremely generous and who remember last week's conversation. It's all symbolic. They're all cherishing in different ways, and you bring them together in a school to make a demanding space, an infectious space. I'm struggling to say what I mean, trying really hard to say what I think. That's the condition of advanced civilisation.

Maybe what you hope for is that people get some experience that belongs to them. Left alone to play, that Swiss world authority says – and I'm not putting him down – "if you leave children with some elements: gravel, bird droppings, seeds, marbles, sooner or later they'll put them in a row". There are certain things happening of their own accord: like realising that if you press a pip in a certain way it will fly through the air. There are lots of impulses that are sometimes deeply buried, but they are there. Wouldn't it be nice if most people were allowed to discover that this slippery, dynamic, small thing could fly? That's all that play really is.

How would you describe yourself?

You can probably tell that I'm not a painter. I know a lot about architecture and design, but I'm not an architect or a designer. I find that kind of work too regulating. It hasn't got the intellectual space, or rather it's a different space, and mine isn't there. My work is something to do with my sense of materiality, with where materiality and meaning meet; so I'm probably a sculptor. There has to be some sort of physicality, even if I reduce that to a photograph. I don't like my photographs; I find photographs horrible things. But I'm interested in the physical content. You can feel that something was done. There's a sense of purpose, even if you don't quite get the purpose; you can feel that a human being was here and purposefully reordered the world in some way. I don't draw. I'd like to, but I don't. I write notes to myself, in words; and I take photographs.

The photographs are somehow found sculptures.

It's an illness. All the time that I've been sitting here I've been noticing two acorns on your blinds. The two acorns are hanging just like testicles hang. I love the fact that the chair is a microphone stand – the black wang coming off. It's worth a lot of Sarah Lucases. I say that to honour her, because when she's good, she's really good.

So what do you think can or should be taught about how the world works?

Everybody should know something about how the world is made. It doesn't much matter what technology you happen to grow up with, you still know it hurts if you fall, and you probably rehearse it quite quickly and soon realise that if you fall a long way you'll die. A huge part of finding out is working out states of mind in relation to the facts of the world as you encounter them. Probably because I'm getting older, I often think about what a brilliant invention the staircase is, and how brilliant it is to be able to transport yourself upstairs. I learned that. I can remember, in my uncle's flat, my ne'er-do-well cousin who could come down the stairs two at a time, which was terribly grown up. That was what big boys did. It's a process of internalising. I suppose it's a branch of sports: the way you can get these feet to talk to the stairs. Learning to deliver yourself to the bottom without hurting yourself is about visual competence, which is sophisticated. This goes back into architecture, and the processional, and ground and space.

It's funny that Hector [Ruth's baby son] doesn't know all this. Very soon, he'll be noticing things: such as that there's status attached to sitting on your own at the table, as opposed to being strapped into something.

He already does...

Maybe that's to do with wanting to become vertical. I'm sure there are lots of Swiss-German border books about this.

Can you say something more about the idea of wonder that you've mentioned before?

[Pointing at the home-made mobile hanging nearby for the baby] I can't not name every image. I love the fact that one is a cat and one is a fish. The worm is completely wormy. But it's amazing, these are just deposits of black on white and these [points at eyes] are doing damn all – they're as dumb as that camera is dumb – and yet the brain goes, 'owl', 'penguin', 'cat'. It still amazes me that that's what we do. I cannot un-worm the worm. What is that? It's a worm! Then I have to think, "It isn't, because a worm would be wet and viscous." That's wonder. That's bloody amazing. Hector will start insisting that something is something else. You'll be laughing because you won't be in that bit of the belief system. You'll say, "no, you're looking at that upside down".

There were things that Joe and Felix [Richard's sons] did that were so willed, to do with their desire, which is also how they used language. We were at our hut in France once, and it was the first time that there had ever been sheep there. It was May, and Felix was four, and we got out of the car and Felix said, "Oh look, they've been lawned." Jane [Richard's wife] explained something really complicated about a Tom and Jerry cartoon, where Tom ends up having his fur mown by a lawn-mower. Felix had never seen the sheep shorn before. That must be very close to Hector's will to see 'owl' [in the very schematic drawing on the mobile].

At the moment, we're also projecting meanings on to Hector's expressions. Undoubtedly, they don't mean what we think they do, but we read all sorts of emotions into a burp or a frown.

What's interesting about that is the sheer force of your speculation, and the fact that you share that with Hector's father. You probably talk of nothing else. These projections backwards and forwards on to this piece of humanity, are very formative and anthropomorphising. You don't do it with a cat – though children do. Children will a dog to be talking to them. That process of analysis, or speculation, of projection, is fantastically interesting. I can imagine some parents denying Felix the opportunity to make sawdust. In a technical sense, it 'wasted some wood', though they were no doubt scraps. And, of course, he increased the likelihood of cutting himself by doing it.

Can you talk a bit about the BBC (British Broadcasting Corporation) project we did together. I'm interested in the idea of trust and will – the will to do certain things which is enabled through the establishment of trust.

[In 2002, as part of the redevelopment of BBC Broadcasting House, Richard was asked to make a new work. It is one of a series of artworks commissioned by the public art agency, Modus Operandi, on behalf of the BBC. In addition, Richard was asked if he would do an educational project with children, using spaces and resources in Broadcasting House. At this point he approached me to do the project with him, whatever it turned out to be. The children were nine-year-olds from the Gateway School in Westminster. The project was hosted at the BBC Twenty First Century Classroom, around the corner from Broadcasting House, in the autumn of 2002. We decided that it would be interesting for the children to work with sound initially, as they were given access to the Broadcasting House radio drama studio, just before it closed down for refurbishment. Richard and I, separately and together, then led the children in several two hour sessions of what might be called constructive play, which we hoped would lead to the children's making something that was interesting to them, and to us. They had the use of video cameras and computers for editing. In the penultimate session we took the children outside to film, and to the RIBA (Royal Institute of British Architects) and then in the last session they tried their hands at editing. I also took the children's footage home – some of which was extremely beautiful and expressive – and edited a short piece that we called *On Foot*. The project as a whole was far too short – particularly as we missed one session because it was Eid and most of the children weren't at school. There wasn't enough time for the children or for us really to follow through with the ideas that we had started to develop. The Arts Committee of the BBC was enthusiastic about what we had started, and indicated that it would like us to take the project further. This may yet happen.]

The BBC project was quite a modern artist's thing. It's very like being seduced, where feelers are put out and you get drawn into something. Lots of curators do it: they sort of draw you in. "I'd really like you to meet so-and-so. I don't quite know which way this will go." It's often extremely attractive. Sometimes absolutely disgusting, and you have to say no. The artist's job is to recognise that and to refuse. There are times when you get brought to a threshold, which is quite tantalising, and you don't know what it is, but you know that in the transaction there is a hidden expectation that you'll know what to do when you get there. You don't usually have to sign a bit of paper saying what it is, though sometimes you have to write a proposal. But actually, nobody knows what the hell is going on. They broker some sort of relationship. Artists are good at getting caught in the cogs of these processes. Sometimes they do good work with it, but sometimes they just feel like they're caught in the cogs. Of course, the lubricant is that somebody says they'll give you 25 quid ($44); often I've done it when I really needed the 25 quid. More interesting things have happened when I haven't needed it.

When I was at the Royal College, it was an artisan sculpture department, so what you made when you were there was called a 'job'. As in "What job are you working on?" While I was there, the language moved to a 'piece'. Now people say, "I'm working on a project." That's something to be explored. It's rather like the open plan Beaux Arts studio turning into little boxes with locks on the doors and computers, with no sense of occupied space. This territory of the 'project' is moving all the time. People say, "it might develop into a bigger project". They don't really name what you're doing. It is quite flirtatious. If one were really to take the BBC project to pieces, I would say that we were interested – I was interested – in the sheer might of the BBC, its brand. It's far more interesting than being asked to work for the government. And of course the BBC is now damaged [because of the David Kelly tragedy and the subsequent Hutton Report]. "Would you like to work with the BBC, and a new 'unit' or whatever they called it, and some children?" It was like, "Have you ever had Japanese food before?" "Well no, but I hear sometimes you eat live fish. I'll try it." I think that that mentality is important. So we arrived there.

Then there was a second thing: you and I knew each other, but not very well; and I knew I was thrashingly busy. I knew I wouldn't be able to do it on my own, and that I wouldn't be that interested in doing it on my own. There was something that we did, where I went, "uh uh uh", and you went, "uh uh uh" [hand movements back and forth]. We sort of shimmied to a point where it was happening. I think you did more work than I did – I don't know how one weighs such a thing – but you did. In an unspoken way, we ended up finding ourselves in a very unfamiliar environment, which couldn't quite be described as institutional, nor was it commercial. It wasn't a Soho post-production house – that might have been more interesting. It was slightly self-conscious – probably with some awful name like an 'electronic learning facility'.

I think it was called the Twenty First Century Classroom.

Yes. That's not to say it wasn't well meant. Whether it was better for being over-designed rather than boffin-like with a wall with shelves and stacks of electronic equipment is a moot point. I think that that would have been a more interesting proximity for those children. It had the feeling of an applianced place, which goes back to what I was saying about the world as a plastic place you can feel your way around.

You and I were caught in two senses. We felt that the grown-ups were rather a problem, because they were frightened. They felt they had jobs to do, but they didn't know what they were. And we looked like amateurs. Even sort of, maybe, paedophiles – though that atmosphere hadn't got going much. I think there was a huge – not tension, but there were lots of agendas. I don't think they could have said clearly what they were; but they knew they didn't really believe them. You and I were moles or secret agents. But the truth is, we didn't know what we were doing either. It was like one of those processes that you sometimes see, in mass gymnastics, when two groups pass through each other, apparently without having any effect on each other. Our job was to get to the other side and somehow claim, in spite of all these bloody humans around, these other grown-ups, some territory that was workable for us. The motives were that we wanted it to be enjoyable for us but also, I think there was a big, not a do-gooding thing, but a public-spiritedness in it. There was a lot of generosity.

What did you think of the children?

There was a sense that the children were really wonderful and that we could identify with them very strongly. We were struggling to meet them, so they could sort of know us. We had an idea that there was something of collective value, which could be released. But we didn't know what it was, or how to do that – we're not trained to do that. We'd never been to primary school 'trust' classes. I think in a completely inside-out back-to-front way we somehow did amazing work. I was almost hysterically conscious that these were multi-culti children. I see those children every day on the bus, in the street, and I don't pay any attention. But there was something about that roomful....

There was only one boy who spoke English at home, I think.

Yes. They were amazing. I was disturbed later when I heard that they'd been picked, and others had been excluded. Even so, there was a very strong energy. There was also a sophistication that wasn't released at all, so when we played Consequences and they all wrote about shopping, you thought that their entire culture, or what an anthropologist would think of as culture, is based on shopping. That was all that they were able to articulate. That doesn't mean they don't do other things that they aren't so able to talk about, but the fact that those stories all focused on shopping was extreme.

Somehow, in retrospect, it seemed like a necessary false start, which we had to get over.

We felt we had to work against this inarticulacy. When we played Chinese Whispers with these children, who were pre-pubescent – partly because of their age (if you play Chinese Whispers with late teenagers, it's incredibly sexual, and very enjoyable for that) – there was a love, I thought, I don't often use this word, that was beautiful. I remember thinking at the time, and I hadn't thought of it before, of the word to confide, and the word confidence and that they are related and confide must be to do with faith, and of course trust. The way that they became intimate with each other was incredibly eloquent [here Richard mimes the way the children cupped their hands to whisper to each other]. The collective witnessing was fabulous: the way they were watching and half-trying to get it. They were still aware of being watched though not oppressively. By that time they just saw us as helpers. But they did think that there was a requirement to perform, because the teacher was still there, sitting in the corner eating her sandwiches.

It was a difficult situation for us. There was a sense of expectation. Everybody expected us to do something, but they, and we, didn't know what that was, what we were 'meant' to do. There was a sense of very high, undefined expectations.

That's a crushing condition, which we all have, and which never goes away with lots of grown-up transactions, some of them just social. Tonight, for example, I'm going to dinner and there's a bit of me that's wondering, "Why have we been asked and why are we going?" It's cruel, because they're nice people. There is something going on, because that's why we ask each other to dinner. It's not as simple as that we've made too much food and it will go off. In a way we do want to get it right.

I want to find a name for it, for that thing on the pavement, when you misread the other person's movements and you didge and dodge from side to side to avoid the person coming towards you. I think it's an incredibly beautiful moment. You can be intimate with somebody, which can be devastating, because of course you're mirroring, dancing, and you have to get past twice before it starts to get funny. It only happens four times a year perhaps, but it's very strong. I saw Jonathan Miller once, and he described how when you go into a room and find you've made a mistake and you're in the wrong room – it's pretty much an institutional experience with people who are having a meeting – you pull a ridiculous face. You do something because you know you already look like an idiot. You get hold of your idiot rictus, slap it on quickly, so they know that you know and that you're not really that stupid.

We know that we have expectations, which affect us constantly. The person who is begging can be remarkably similar to the person who used to take your ticket in the tube. They're often not dressed so differently, but you're meant to know. A lot of our anecdotes are based on our mistakes.

That was a digression. I think that weight of expectation was nobody's fault but was constricting. There was a need to lighten up a bit.

I would like to find a bigger pool of people to have conversations like this with, because that could generate a much better breed of curator, enabler, or whatever, who would understand more about brokering. On the whole it is only people who are very sophisticated with other people who can do this. There are two people who come to mind: Kaspar Koenig and Melanie Bloch, who both have an amazing way of making connections and introductions and making you feel,

"I am an important artist and I really want to do this." This is an incredibly helpful thing. We didn't have that, and all the people who were there doing the less glamorous part of the job, the teachers – everyone in fact – felt a bit oppressed. We felt we were the centre of attention and somehow, somewhere there was a piece of paper with a description of what we were meant to be doing, which we'd never seen because of course we were inventing it as we went along.

I wrote the ubiquitous, fantastical 'proposal'.

It is what you do when you have to write proposals, because the truth is that they are NOT proposals: they are – there is another word for it, they are pro-posals. 'Preposterous' means pre-post-erous. It's the cart before the horse. Isn't that fabulous?

You never fulfil it.

It is because it is not a proposal. If you had an idea, and woke up in the middle of the night and wrote it down, sent it to 50 people, that would be a proposal; but it's never like that. The thing is actually an artificial birth. They all are.

Can you tell me more about your teaching experiences?

Sometimes when you meet somebody you have not seen for a long time, who you remember as a painting student, and they say, "I am a counsellor at the Tavistock", you think, "you bloody well would be; it's fantastic; you would be brilliant!" The initial medium of being in art school is not a million miles away from a kind of psychoanalytic playground. It's a quite privileged set of freedoms, if you know how to play with them. If you realise, "I can do this and this, and I can relate here and un-relate here, and stretch here" – it is not surprising where people end up. As far as I am concerned, whatever people do at art school, it's cultural. It doesn't worry me if someone says, "I no longer paint." But some people respond in a tut-tutty way. You think to yourself: I didn't know that there were Soviet scene-painting colleges, where you were trained to do footwear.

Back to the BBC: it's funny because I don't suppose we'll ever meet those children again – but I think there were one or two of them who were incredibly creative. You didn't know whether (or how) their creativity was going to come out: whether they would be able to articulate themselves verbally or on paper, or pictorialise, or whatever. I did feel quite proud that we'd paid a lot of attention to them as individuals, which I'm sure is very difficult to do at school, because there isn't enough time to talk to children about their lives. I remember saying "What's an architect?" One of them answered, but she muddled up archaeologist with architect. That was a very interesting conversation. Then one of them said, "I live next to one of those."

This thing about trust and will is interesting. When we went out filming with them, and thought "Oh my God, we've only got half an hour left and we want them to have something to show for themselves", we all relied on our instincts. We responded to the moment and gave them just enough of a lead; they had the confidence to follow their own interests. The three groups of

five children were given a video camera and microphone and each had a simple task that they could interpret as they wanted. By now they had enough confidence to do what they wanted, not just what they thought we wanted – though that was always a consideration. However, the looseness of the brief meant that they had to interpret it in their own way.

I remember the arbitrariness of the decisions we had to make on the street. We said, "You're in charge of cars; you're doing the skyline; you're in charge of people." [One group was told to film the traffic and street, one to concentrate on people and another on buildings.] It's a funny way to slice up the urban scene. I thought it was interesting that they didn't balk at that: they saw those parameters as perfectly good ones. You can walk down the middle of the street perfectly successfully but in a codified way you're not meant to, it's where the cars go. But the middle of the street is not somewhere that won't support your weight or deliver you to where you want to go. What was funny, was that they accepted that codification, in the same way we accept that it's better to walk on the pavement. We can go and argue, "I'd rather walk in the road", and we sometimes do that for a bit. But when we said, "you do this, you do this, you do this", they all went "OK", as if they recognised or understood that this could knit up in some way; it wasn't beyond their imagination or trust.

They trusted there was some sense in our directions. [LAUGH]

There's a problem with curators… or rather with the librarians of culture, such as the Arts' Council, with the brokers, the docket people. They sign off the work. And it's done. I felt with our children's project that I only half got my studio sensation, I didn't quite get my art. It doesn't have to be that thingy but it has to be palpable in some way, inside me. Then I feel that I've worked. I feel that I only half worked with the children.

I feel as if it was just beginning to take off.

It's probably what it feels like when children are taken away from you.

There was a problem in the way it was framed, as if single-handedly the project was going to transform the BBC's relationship to children. There was so little time. We had very little room to manoeuvre, literally. We had to do it in that room, full of easy-to-use computers and branded projection screens and stacking chairs. And we had to do it in those few hours.

I would've been happier if it had taken place, for the sake of argument, here or in my studio. No amount of theorising, no amount of bad paragraphs that begin with the words, "best practice, blah blah blah", is worth the energy and particularity of a human: that person, who doesn't know what they're doing, who is in a studio or in a school or an art school at this minute, making waves.

      One of the things I do at the Ruskin School of Art is I run up the stairs – and I think I'm going to have a heart attack. I run up the stairs because it's really important to, because all forces are pressing upon me to walk up the stairs with a pipe, in a slow, dignified, ponderous way, and I say to myself, "I will not do that."

In fact I don't particularly want to run up the stairs. I don't mean to say that I always run up the stairs. It's me pushing against the building and the institution. There's something about making pace and energy and the possibility of proximity and absorption and, maybe at worst, mimicry. Mimicry is a bit sad. There's a time when you're growing up when you just copy someone perhaps because you have a crush. Absorption is more interesting because it's under the surface.

I was once giving a lecture on my work at an art school; and after the lecture a student came up and said, "I'd like to talk to you about your work, because I'd like to make work like that." How does one reply to that? It was very strange.

Yes, in certain circumstances, it could have been very complimentary, but it sounds as if it was banal.

Actually, it was somewhat unhinged.

But maybe in a few years' time, in a dozen years' time for example, that might be their hinge moment: "I don't know who she was, this person came, I once heard or I once saw...." Those are important moments, and they're unquantifiable. One can say: people need conditions; culture needs conditions. In order to do what we're doing, we need time. You've got to be in a culture that at least supplies sufficient time to let people do what we're doing. You can't then cross all the Ts and dot all the Is and say, this is what it will be like, which is what Demos [an independent political thinktank and research group, based in London], or perhaps not Demos, but what all the forces appear to be doing all the time.

There was a lovely thing that a boy at the Ruskin said: "You don't have to do it, but it's quite a good thing to do a foundation course; it sort of got me out of the A Level thing." It's a statement about another kind of space. It's a voice, a bloody voice.

creativity with purpose
Faisal Abdu' Allah

I like the approach of this book, looking more critically at what it means to the artist.

Someone once asked me "Why do you do workshops when you don't need to at this point in your career?" The perception of the artist in society has a certain ring to it; there's a strong preconception about the look, age, gender, race which an artist should be, so that when kids see me, they think to themselves "Oh, he looks like an ordinary guy!" This puts them on an equal footing with me, I'm not here as a teacher, I'm here to enable them to access the gift they have been blessed with. I say "you guys have a gift: your imagination". Immediately they feel special. I tell them that I do not have a monopoly on knowledge, or creativity. I'm here to bring them to the level that I'm at, and I do this through building a stable relationship based on honesty, engaging them with their space, finding what are the elements that they engage with. They giggle at first when we talk about Moschino, Evisu and other designer labels, but these are all things I also engage with. In my barber's shop I'm always engaged with contemporary culture. My nephew (who is also working in the shop) is on pirate radio now as we speak. I'm forced to engage with what's in, the moment is very important. To be an active participant in contemporary culture, there is a strong link with young people and that is where I commence. In some of the projects the participants come here, see where I reside, what influences me. When they come here it doesn't fit with their perception or expectation of an artist, which is of a warehouse, someone with an assistant, involved in a sterile art-making process.

In my work the rules don't change with different age groups. For example, at the National Maritime Museum workshops there was one young lady who was very in tune with ideas about the composition, light, etc.; she stayed with me and the ideas throughout the process. We also had special needs kids,

Faisal Abdu' Allah
group studio sessions.

some with Downs Syndrome, they all brought their ingredient to the project. I
have to alter my language by simplifying the rationale so that the younger kids
can plug in, but the outcomes of the young children are just as accomplished if
not more so than older people – they don't have to think about the consequences.
The older ones worry about what their friends will think, they shy away from
taking a photo home.

I worked with Stuart Slade, Education Officer at the Maritime Museum,
on a series of schools workshops with seven- to 11-year-olds over three months
following the opening of my exhibition in the newly opened Queens House in
2001. We ran four sessions a day, each with a different class group. In each class
of approximately 30 children, half worked with Stewart and half with me. I split
my half into three groups: roughly five becoming photographers, five as models,
and five looking at my exhibition, *An Affair of Honour*, as reference. A painting
of the *Execution of Lady Jane Grey* was the inspiration for this work. Costume
and role-play are always good starting points for young people to access and
play out some of their inner creative thoughts. I use the line "creativity is a gift".
I feel that the creative persona is suppressed in young people; this immediately
becomes apparent when working with them, when they ask "can I really do that?"
and I say "of course!" Then they begin to enjoy things, their humour and laughter
begins to work as they begin to own the idea. Working this way allows me to
extract some of that DNA matter, like a code under a microscope; it becomes
living testimony of who they are. The workshop format is a vehicle for us all,
it's like taking an escalator.

Gorillas on the Loose from
the *Image Conscious* project.

I always give the workshop participants a sense of ownership, so that they perceive it as being their work. I use a Polaroid back on my Hasselblad camera so that they can preview and adjust the composition; they compose the photos. I had become detached from working in a creative and fresh way with the model in my work, as you can see for instance in *Last Supper I and II*, 1995. This work, although it features young adults as models, was highly controlled. I'd been more rigid in my interpretations, with models all carefully posed. The work didn't allow any space for escapism, no room for a contemporary pose, whereas the workshops on the contrary allow me to reinvest something from today, something hand-held – like 50 Cent, or a girl's pose referencing Kylie Minogue. I realised that maybe representation is not so fixed, that's what I learned particularly from the Maritime Museum workshops. The workshop experience also made me conscious of audience – in the case of young people this would be about their concerns with what their friends would think, looking at the image. This really sharpened my focus rather than working with a vague notion of an art audience as I had done previously. Probably I'd lost touch, slightly lost sight of the word 'friend' as my primary audience, people who are not used to engaging with these types of artefacts. I think I'm inspiring these young people to make new work, to renegotiate things I thought I knew, to negotiate with this other space. Engaging younger minds is really important to me.

When I have shown my portrait of *Hassan* (from the *I Wanna Kill Sam* series, 1993) to young people, their interpretation is that this guy is defending himself, or another kid said "he's just posing, whereas at the time the newspapers criticised this work as promoting gun culture". I always find the best critique comes from kids.

In *Image Conscious Part II*, Little Red made a recording of some new songs and performed them at the 02 Centre, Finchley (part of the *Box 1* magazine project produced for Camden Arts Centre's Off Centre Programme, 2003). She still calls me and we have spiritual discussions about where she would like to take her career. This makes me take stock of myself, knowing that her generation are coming up behind me, that she is sticking by her guns. I need to reinvest that energy in my practice, and work with that energy and directness. This project gave her a good idea of what it's like to knock heads with people in an industry that requires things from you, such as punctuality, focus on outcome, ambition, etc.. She came away with a document, something which left a trace of her ambition, with her in the frame, getting an essence, having to do her own research, delivering the goods, understanding the legalities of ownership.

creativity with purpose

Little Red from the *Image Conscious* project.

Camden Arts Centre's only stipulation with this project was that they wanted a magazine. It was a strange process. I met each of the young people one to one, at the same Burger King in Camden in back to back meetings, and talked to them about what they were interested in. (The 14- to 16-year-olds were recruited through Camden's Youth Work Plus scheme, for young people who may be experiencing difficulties at home, school and socially.) One boy seemed quite hard to get through to and eventually dropped out due to health and family issues. When I asked "What do you like doing?" he would say "I don't know." But then I asked "What's your passion in life, what interests you?" His eyes lit up: "cars, sports cars" he responded, so we went to buy some car magazines, talked about cars, I got into his world. We decided to go to the McLaren car showroom to do a photo shoot. Unfortunately, this had to be cancelled as he was not well on the day.

I would question whether a mentoring system is really the right way of engaging with these young people. We have disengaged as a society from building on their strengths. I became much more critical of the whole education-youth service system through this project. Projects like this are a good indicator of our lack of understanding of the elements that motivate and drive young souls.

In my own practice I wouldn't have a remit, a fixed outcome in mind. My initial starting point would be to talk to individuals to see where their interests lie and allow that to shape a project, shape the medium. Something like this needs to be an ongoing thing, not just a six-week project. I would let nature take its course, not steer someone in a direction where they're not going to run. The world is built on communication, at some point they may reference this experience in their future life. They might see me on TV and remember it's the same guy. Art takes time, maybe 50 years, you never know. As long as I leave individuals with a trace, I've done my job as a practitioner. Failings are when you take it all away after. I always say to them "tell you what, get back to me". I leave the option open.

With Little Red I talk a lot about music, styles, what's in, we critique music. She also keeps in touch with the guy from the mentoring scheme and the guy who recorded her tracks; she kept us in the frame personally, so I would say a level of professionalism came out of this project. She's been let down in the past by adults. My message to these young people was "there's nothing stopping you achieving anything you want". On the same *Image Conscious* project we closed a fashion store for a morning to do a photo shoot with Aisha, who wants to be a fashion model. Women by their very nature are more curious than men, they are inquisitive, they're looking for outcomes, maybe that's why more girls than boys took part in this project – I feel it's encrypted on their DNA.

My philosophy is that the artisans are the shapers of social consciousness. Artists must be media savvy, be wise about how to spend money and have knowledge of business.

My current project I am sworn to secrecy about, but it's working with historical icons, it will take the form of large format portraits. These guys who I am photographing say "crime doesn't pay but the hours are good".

These are icons but they are also like kids – they're playful too, that's what I like. Life is a game to them. Their minds are young, they're always running jokes.

Bare Dust

shona Illingworth

Bare Dust is a video by artist Shona Illingworth, made working with a group of 12- to 17-year-old boys living on Trowbridge Housing Estate in Hackney, east London. It was commissioned by SPACE Studios and Hackney Wick Public Art Programme in 2000. A group of adolescent boys play football over the abandoned foundations of the tower blocks where they once lived. We see only their feet, which never seem to touch the ground. As they criss-cross these surfaces their fragmented voices break through a low, heavy continuous sound, talking of isolation, vulnerability and violence. Throughout the video, images of the enormous weight of the tower blocks repeatedly interrupt the flow of the boys' footwork, as they are blown up and collapse heavily to the ground.

The title Bare Dust is taken from a fragment of speech in the video, where a boy says: "it's just ground down, it's just dusty now, walk across there, it's just bare dust".

This investigation of place is an artwork using football as a vehicle to explore the boys' relationship to their estate. Shona distinguished clearly between engaging them in making an artwork and the alternative, which is working as a 'cultural representative' or as part of the support services. She was clear what she wanted to make and why. A level of respect had to run both ways and that meant her valuing the time the boys contributed to the work rather than demanding it. She believes firmly that art can present complex critical views, which may be provocative, uncomfortable and not necessarily shared, and that this makes the work engaging and honest for participants.

The tower blocks on Trowbridge Estate were destroyed in the course of a programme of regeneration, leaving behind empty spaces in which the boys on the estate now hung around. In a sense the tower blocks had indeed been reduced to dust and the boys now played football across the remaining footprints of the buildings. Trowbridge Estate is physically isolated in a semi-industrial area, an estate with a high proportion of children, pensioner households, single parents, semi-skilled and unskilled workers, unemployed people and residents living in poverty. The estate is bound on three sides by major roads and by a canal on the fourth, but the constraints which isolate the boys there are far from purely physical. I wanted to explore the often contradictory social, physical and cultural parameters that define spaces for young people, particularly within cities, and to make a work which examined the psychology of place in relation to architecture and urban location.

As an artist I often explore hierarchies of articulacy in my work. For instance in society, verbal and written articulacy are often prioritised and are framed within very specific conventions. There are many distinct forms of expression used by the boys that are part of a constantly changing language and culture, but that culture also restricts or circumscribes what the boys can talk about and how it should be discussed. The fragments of speech in *Bare Dust* are taken from of a series of recorded interviews I made with the boys. There is an economy of language in their struggle to articulate their experiences of the estate. Their difficulty in expressing views and their struggle to define emotional experience serves to further highlight their isolation and confinement within specific social and economic limits; limits which are perpetrated and sustained both externally and internally.

The boys were restless and did not find it easy to focus. They have complex and contradictory relationships to the place where they live. It's their home but it's also a place where they feel threatened and in turn are seen as a threat. It's tough to be different here, to openly imagine becoming anything, living anywhere else, yet there is little space for young people on the estate.

During the recording sessions the boys spoke of a friend who died, knifed in a revenge attack on a station platform close by; of someone jumping off the top of a former tower block, and of the inherent dangers within their environment.

> This estate's deep, on the stairs where they've been blocked off,
> bare little kids must have been playing there and said 'look up,
> look up here' and there's bare needles and everything….
>
> … and the dark alleys as well, junkies and everything, just
> inviting crime… get me, my sister's walking through there,
> I don't love that, you can't see nothing, she could get raped
> or something….

These stressful realities complicate and pressurise the relationships the boys have with their families and neighbours, with authorities and with their own emerging sense of who they are. They are affected by, involved in and framed by these realities. There is an underlying sense of futility; as one boy says: "… we just walk round in circles".

There are young people who are variously involved in violence, drug use and crime; however young people in general are becoming increasingly vilified both by the press and wider public, especially teenage boys living on inner city estates. There seems to be a growing tabloid fascination with the crimes of children and young people without any attempt to analyse or understand the context or underlying causes of these crimes. Understanding something of the lives of young people is essential in determining the role and activity of an artist working with young people within their social context.

In her article "The kids aren't all right", *The Observer*, Sunday 5 December, 2004, Maureen Rice-Knight examined the apparent increase in Britain's hostility towards its under-18s. She identified this trend as being significantly higher in Britain than in other parts of Europe. She refers to a study released by the Institute of Psychiatry in September 2003 which tracks the emotional health of three generations of British teenagers over 25 years, finding that:

> It showed a serious and sharp decline in their mental health, while behavioural problems, such as lying, stealing and being disobedient have doubled. Emotional problems, such as anxiety and depression, have soared by 70 per cent.

Examining the impact that changes in employment levels has had on teenagers from 16 to 18 years old she quoted Ann Hagel, a psychologist and research development adviser at the Nuffield Foundation:

> 16-year-olds used to be important members of society: they had jobs, money and an identity. Now, if you aren't interested in another two to five years of conventional education, you're a write-off. They're school children with no power or they're nothing.

In the 1970s, 70 per cent of all 16-year-olds were working and earning money. This number has now fallen to around five per cent. There are many young people who don't do well at school. 26 per cent of 16-year-olds leave school and don't go on to further education. For them there is perhaps access to vocational training, but little possibility of a job, and there is no income support. For two critical years they remain dependent on their families. For many they also remain confined in their estates. In Trowbridge Estate the boys wouldn't cross the road to use a nearby all-weather football pitch, as this meant crossing the boundary into another estate.

There is a class-based confidence which exists for those within a small sector of British society. For many there is always the sense that there are places where they don't belong, have no right to be, where their intrusion will be exposed. This subtly defines the city in a complex layering of social, economic and cultural divisions. For many young people living on an estate this takes on extreme proportions.

Young people have a highly tuned sense of these often conflicting parameters. They are going through a significant and intense period of transition and experience the changes in other people's responses to them acutely, as they try to create a position for themselves both within their peer group, in the wider community, and independent from 'family'. The shape and parameters of their area are changing rapidly as they try to establish status and territory. Young people are caught between childhood and adulthood; for example, their presence in the playground is suddenly viewed with suspicion, and yet they are not allowed into adult social spaces such as the pub.

In making *Bare Dust*, I wanted to articulate something located in the experience, site and context of the boys on this estate but which also had a wider frame of reference. Football is a major pastime on the estate. It's also a conscious source of vain hope, an unspoken fantasy shared across racial difference, a diversion from the constraints of the boys' everyday lives. Football is something they can do together as a group without being seen as a threat, where they can express frustration, pleasure and mutual support.

> Everyone round here wants to be a footballer.... You know it's
> not going to happen to you, but you've still got that little bit of
> doubt in your head.

This boy's statement in the video eloquently describes a complex and contradictory situation, knowingly self-defeating but allowing a brief suspension of reality, through a need to aspire to something that would bring attention, status and respect. This suspension of disbelief allows the boys, against the odds, to postpone thinking about the troubling future ahead.

> You've just gotta dream big, that's what I think bro'...

Football provided me with a vehicle to explore the boys' relationship to their estate. In the video they map out their area with a fluid and eloquent control of the ball, playing a game that has no end and where no goals are scored. The relative skill and synchronicity of their movement as they trace a route across the waste ground contrasts with their struggle to articulate their anxieties, frustration and vulnerability in a place that can be unpredictable, insecure and threatening.

In this transient and restless period in their lives the boys are isolated, and given little stake in their surroundings. When playing football however, everything is focused on the intensity of the moment, the continually shifting group dynamic and a briefly shared fantasy of the future.

The boys' descriptions of their lives on the estate were highly critical. The work does not attempt to offer a solution, nor is it a documentary; it is an investigation of a place. There are inter-relationships in the work between the collapse of the physical architecture of the tower blocks, the intermediate 'gap' in the continuity of the city left behind and the transient fantasy of football played out in the temporary spaces created where the blocks used to stand, which are open to a range of interpretations.

The boys' experiences of their estate surface throughout the video as fragments of speech that rise above the images. These fragments of speech are highly specific but do not form personal narratives. Instead they are pared down to suggest the violence, threat and pressures that exist for young people as ongoing and not confined to a set of incidents.

The boys' voices in the video are in my view disembodied and fragmented registers or reflective elements, floating over the ground where their feet move so fluidly, fragile between the heavy collapse of buildings.

In retrospect I associate aspects of my own childhood with *Bare Dust*. In a sense I was orientated to elements of the young people's lives and the place where they lived, and sensitised to aspects of their experiences. I think this contributed significantly to the relationship I developed with the boys in the brief period we worked together and to the strategies we employed to make the work.

I grew up in a disused early warning station, built and then abandoned in the 1950s, on the north west tip of the Scottish Highlands. My family moved to an empty shell there in the late 1960s. The site was very isolated geographically and we in turn were isolated socially from the local community who lived in a nearby village and the outlying area. We were classed as 'incomers', 'White Settlers'. Our family struggled financially as did a lot of people living in the area. The site was enclosed by a fence and entered through a gate and cattle

Shona Illingworth,
Bare Dust, 2000.
Five minute digital
video with stereo
sound shown
on a continuous
loop, front projected
onto a wall.

grid. It comprised a number of concrete Nissan huts, which were converted slowly into living accommodation and workshops and collectively became a 'craft village' in the late 1960s, early 70s. The army still used some of the huts as bases for field operations. As children we played in the empty buildings and on the footprints of buildings that had been removed.

I remembered this some time after I had made the video. I thought, too, of the sense of isolation and enclosure, of being socially marginalised, of constant money anxieties, of being afraid of being associated with where I came from, of being discovered, of being found out that I didn't belong, betrayed by the wrong accent, the wrong family name. I thought too of the concrete buildings. I also distinctly remember the complex experience of wanting to 'belong', to be located, but being identified as part of a constructed community that I did not want to be associated with. I did not want to be seen as socially excluded but I was also very angry and frustrated, battling with a conflict of status. As a teenager this is intense, and there are distinct vulnerabilities and complexities that emerge when individual identity is evolving so rapidly.

I consciously drew on some of these experiences when working with the boys, in an attempt to enter into a discursive collaboration on more equal footing with them. The decision to film only their feet and to present the image of the estate through images of them practising their football skills while having their voices create images of their environment came from a sensitivity to being negatively contextualised by others through assumptions about the place you come from.

I came to the group with ideas for a piece, but this had to evolve through the process of making the work and through working with the boys onsite. Originally, I had pre-planned to use a set of 'workshop' processes to structure the filming and recording. These, thankfully, were quickly abandoned. Though the group tolerated this form of rather patronising 'facilitation' it was clear that it created an artificial divide.

Working with a group of young people who are defined as 'disadvantaged' or 'socially excluded' within a frame of reference defined by funding and commissioning agencies can implicate the artist in a highly problematic chain of associations. It can place the artist in a position of patronage via the institutions that support them, a privileged visitor sent to 'improve' the lives of individuals who have been grouped by a specified set of criteria.

Often the implication is that the artist will service the group by instilling a 'sense of community' and 'increase self confidence' through facilitating 'creative expression', while at the same time maintaining a position of cultural authority. This in the first instance defines the group within a limited frame of reference while denying the complexities of the social and economic conditions that impact on their lives by offering art practice as some form of palliative.

By setting these parameters and agendas, both the funder and the commissioning agency limit the artist's capacity to critically engage with the young people they are working with. By employing an artist primarily to facilitate these agendas there is a danger that real working relationships between artist and young people cannot develop and instead, dialogue or activity is filtered through idealised notions of adding quality to the lives of those who are 'disenfranchised'.

To encourage challenging or provocative work is risky if the desired outcomes have already been defined. It must not be forgotten that art can present complex critical views and that these may be provocative, uncomfortable and not necessarily shared. Idealised and generalised representations of both art practice and community can both patronise and further alienate all of those involved.

There is a deadening weight of privileged philanthropy which requires a grateful and happy subject as the successful result of its investment. But I would argue that to engage critically with your environment and the context within which you live, to engage in a more equal discourse with an artist, to work with an artist as a professional individual rather than a 'cultural representative', where there is a process of inquiry and risk involved, is more demanding and in the end rewarding.

In my work I'm very interested in the psychology of place and in how we locate ourselves. I was genuinely interested in how the boys related to, experienced and understood their estate, and they responded very directly to that genuine interest. I wanted to articulate the fragility and transience of their lives and respond to the isolation and enclosure I sensed there. There was no obligation for them to work with me and I was clear about what I wanted to make and why. There was a level of respect that had to run both ways, and that meant me valuing the time they contributed to the work rather than demanding it.

One of the most important things for young people is respect and there is a very problematic 'respect' culture growing, I believe, out of the increasing isolation of young people, which is exacerbated by complex social and economic conditions and fuelled by increasingly negative press. 'Respect' culture has been around for a long time and if someone isn't shown respect or doesn't give respect, then the alternative is disrespect, hence the practice of 'dissing' someone. Understanding how this operates is important. Many young people are seen as a problem, and yes they can be very difficult to work with, but essential to working with them is respect for their time, their space and themselves as individuals.

I was very much supported by Danny Brade, a lead Youth Worker at the Youth Centre on the estate who had worked there for many years. He had gained respect and trust from the young people and children on the estate who valued the continuity of his presence and investment in them. Not all of the boys were easy to work with but quite quickly the group developed strategies themselves to contain any disruption from individuals to allow filming or recording to go on.

As an artist I am not part of the support services infrastructure; I am not a therapist or a social worker, and I am not trained in these fields. It is clearer and more direct for me to work as an artist who will be there for a short space of time to make a piece of work. The wider positive effects of this for the young people involved are difficult to measure and may not be immediately apparent. But they should not include false promises; too many young people are promised things by outside authorities and are let down.

There is much scope for developing commissioning programmes for artists who are interested in making their own artwork within a particular social context, instead of employing the artist as a facilitator or 'cultural ambassador'; to create programmes where the agenda and development of the artwork is defined by the artist working within that particular social context rather than being pre-determined by the organisation.

Each artist will bring something to that place according to who they are and what their practice involves. This includes their specific areas of interest, their working process, and how they define outcomes. As in much art practice, the work may change in the process of development, it may create unexpected results, it may invite controversy, may be critical or subvert an established order. It may involve a lot of pleasure and little material outcome. It may seek to redefine or challenge existing ideas of what an 'artwork' and 'outcome' might be.

Short term projects with artists can have real value, but they often result in closure once the project is over. Commissions may be long or short term but it is the commissioner, not the artist, in my view that should be responsible for continuing the relationship with the community or groups that it's working with if a social difference is intended. While an interaction between a young person or group of young people and artist can have a positive and even inspirational effect in both directions, an organisation is in a stronger position to address pragmatic needs, such as working with other agencies, to create opportunities for young people longer term which could make a real difference.

These issues should be considered in advance so that the artist isn't parachuted in and out with no consideration for the potential effects of this. The Hackney Wick Public Art Programme and SPACE Studios who together organised this commission are a case in point. They took a longer-term strategic view of working with communities within a given area while allowing artists much freedom to realise their commissioned work. Both SPACE Studios and Independent Photography – an organisation I have also worked with in south east London – carry on, with impossibly small budgets, to establish continuity with communities through programmes of artist's commissions that have taken many forms. This has both built on existing relationships and dialogues with communities and through that process opened up more opportunities for artists to make engaging and diverse work. These commissions allow artists to make work without 'dumbing down' the art or patronising the communities.

Through my preoccupation with the relationships between physical architecture and landscapes and the psychology of place I have worked with a diverse range of people across a variety of different sites. This has also included working with young people in a range of different contexts. In all instances it has been important for me to work as an artist in a direct and straightforward way, and not to attempt to package ideas or processes to disguise them as something else. Conversely, by trying to mediate art practice through some 'social education' formula, two things occur: the 'social' group or individuals are patronised and the art process is mythologised, made precious and remote. In my view it is a mistake to think that people don't have the capacity to engage or contribute to complex ideas in a work and it is also a mistake to calculate the accessibility of a work by the number of people who like it.

Video and sound are ideal media for working with young people, who often have a very sophisticated understanding of the media and are open to experimentation and discussions about complex issues such as the position of the viewer, fragmented narrative, constructed realities, differing perspectives, identity, stereotyping, ambiguity and interpretation, as well as abstract notions such as atmosphere, space, time and orientation. In working with video and sound, it is understood that there are many different ways to say something.

These are also media that lend themselves well to involving members of a group in many different ways, so that individuals are not exposed or required to do something they don't want to or feel unable to do. In my experience, strategies for making work involving other people evolve out of developing strong working relationships with them, based on mutual respect. This may not mean visibly 'working' all of the time, it may mean 'hanging out'. Here a level of flexibility is needed, as is establishing a dialogue that is direct and open.

Bare Dust was initially shown as a large outdoor projection onto the three-storey white wall of the Victoria pub on the Trowbridge Estate in April 2000. A reception was held in the pub for all the residents of the estate and an invited audience. It was screened alongside another projected work developed by artists Rachel Garfield and Heather Libson. The boys were delighted to be in the pub for their event and to have such a good turnout for the work. *Bare Dust* was then screened in May 2000 at the Royal Insitute of British Architects (RIBA). I insisted that the boys arrived by taxi at this imposing building in the centre of London; they watched the video which was shown on a loop in the large lecture theatre at the RIBA at least five times and then we all went to McDonalds (their choice) for lunch. *Bare Dust* was then installed in the RIBA galleries for Architecture Week 2000 and amongst other subsequent screenings has been shown in an exhibition in Gallerie Arteves Kosoves, Prishtina, Kosova in December 2004.

Bob, Roberta and Etta:
the Art of collaboration

Bob and Roberta Smith was introduced to the art world at an early age by an artist father, who would take the family to the National Gallery and stand drawing from a Poussin painting for 45 minutes. While these trips enabled father to pursue his passion in art, the kids hung around. As an art child in the 1960s and 70s, openings at the ICA and Happenings were central to Bob Smith's childhood. Smith continues this tradition today, placing children at the centre of his art world and involving daughter Etta in a collaborative art practice.

Inspired by a photograph taken by tutor Bill Culbert of a light bulb switched on against bright sunshine, with his kids milling in the background, Bob and Roberta described this as the kind of sculpture that he wanted to cultivate. The first project to implicate children was in Sunderland at the Northern Centre for Contemporary Art in 1996, which provided templates for large toy cars that children could use to build their own customised vehicles, which were then displayed in the exhibition. A second child-friendly project involved children trying to sail concrete model boats in the Serpentine boating lake in London. The children were soon frustrated, declaring the boats "rubbish" as they would not float, while adults watched enjoying the perverse existentialist joke, a send-up of child participation which is a game continued throughout this work.

Smith's daughter Etta made her art debut as a baby carried in a sling on her father's chest at the Serpentine boating event. Over the years, Etta became increasingly involved in this art production and evaluation, creating an "alternative position", unwittingly from her side, knowingly from Bob and Roberta's.[1] Bob and Roberta incorporates Etta's phrases in the titles and content of artworks. *When Jimmy comes to my House* and *Winter then Autumn then Winter again!* are two 'collaborative' paintings apparently based on Etta's phrases. Incorporating Etta into the work might seem a declaration of an absence of good or bad taste in the tradition of Marcel Duchamp, who explained

Etta, photograph by
Bob and Roberta
Smith, 2004.

left: Bob and Roberta Smith, *Car*, Northern Centre for Contemporary Art, 1996.
right: Bob and Roberta Smith, *Make Boats*, Serpentine, London, 1996.

his work after 1912 as an attempt to escape the rule of taste by the use of mechanical techniques and the recycling of ready-mades, shifting the concept of taste from the expressive action of a uniquely gifted individual to a situation where the title of a work, for instance, became very important and the role of language in establishing the significance of the artwork was tantamount. The language would quite deliberately avoid employing a vocabulary of aesthetics, in a gesture of visual indifference.[2] *Make Your Own Damn Art* is a slogan painting painted for an exhibition in Barcelona in 1998 with the words in Catalan. Bob and Roberta delight in the irony of a photograph showing the child's serious art-going expression as she looks at the work whilst oblivious to the meaning of the text. A photo of Etta with the painting *You are Not My Brain!* shows her accusatory finger pointing out towards her accomplice father, apparently annoyed with him making material through photography of their art relationship. This is one of a series of photos showing them making work together, supposedly 'authenticating' the democratic nature of their collaborative working process. This co-production involved making editions of cast concrete panels of slogans decorated in a variety of colourways. They are made by rolling out a slab of clay and then stamping letters in reverse – a procedure which takes some adult thought. The letters are arranged in an Etta-esque style, although it is of course never clear how far this is her own hand. A plaster cast is taken and then a rubber mould made, from which the panel paintings are cast. Some spelling interventions and suggestions are made when it is felt to be necessary; in other places the quaint idiosyncrasies of childish misspelling require a hands-off approach. The final colouration of these multiples consciously adopts a 'child-like' eye. One of the series entitled *Pork Beef Lamb*, sounding like a quaint old English chant, is their special song for supermarket trips, deciding which meat to buy for the weekend. Some of the slogans are Etta's, some could be Bob and Roberta's in the style of Etta; the degree of collaboration is deliberately enigmatic. Shared authorship tends to cover all sorts of production arrangements, which are generally only unpicked at moments of dispute, however the power obviously lies in who is authorised to do the calling, and how a work arrives at the point where the convention of art can be bestowed on it.[3]

An anti-aesthetic is introduced through other people's narratives. In the exhibition *My Dream Studio* at the Arnolfini in Bristol, children were invited in a workshop to contribute to the installation with *My Dream House*, which became intrinsic to the show. At GAK in Bremen, Germany, the exhibition *Do All Oceans Have Walls?*, 1999, Bob and Roberta added a sandpit in which children could play, open to 'surprise outcomes' – in this case a series of Barbie dolls were cast

Artists' perspectives on working with young people

in concrete by children and added to the show – the sort of surprise outcomes that Smith enjoys. In *Improve the Cat* at Galleria Carboneto, Turin, 1998, plaster cats with their heads knocked off were provided along with a range of materials from which visitors could build new heads. Setting up these tableaux where the audience collaborate in making the work is an attempt to deploy the "aesthetic as subversive", a calculated risk which is inspiring and liberating, allowing the artist to stand back and let the music play, opting out of responsibility for closure. Such carefully judged irreverence would seem to be exactly what the art market can cope with. *Family Art Show* at Kunstakademie Dusseldorf, and Türkü, 2000, included crayons and sweets, the sweetener idea borrowed from Felix Gonzalez Torres at the Serpentine Gallery, with sweets being handed out, again bringing in a notion of play to send up the gallery space.

Slogan painting in Catalan with family at *The Other Britain*, Tecla Sala Barcelona, photograph by Bob and Roberta Smith, 1998.

Videos attest to further collaborations with children: *Make Concrete Vegetables*, shown in 1997 at Chisenhale Gallery, London, featured Bob and Roberta's mum teaching Etta how to make vegetables in the style of a children's TV show. *Silent Video*, 1997, exhibited at the Virgin Megastore in London's Oxford Street showed Etta making carrot aeroplanes. *Gang Warfare* at Independent Artists Space, London, 1997, included a video with children wielding power tools. These child-complicit works may on the surface appear accessible, but are shrouded with knowing jokes and ironic *double entendre*. The paintings, in particular, also maintain reasonable price tags in an art market reliant on authenticated single-author statements, something which tends to pose ongoing challenges in terms of market differentiation for artists interested in social engagement or collaborative practice.

The relationship between art and popular culture set up in the work shares a commonality with much Young British Artist (YBA) art production. In the theorisation of art as part of everyday cultural practice and the emergence of

Bob and Roberta Smith, *Carrot Aeroplane*, 1997.

a notion of culture as discursive practice, critic John Roberts refers to "In poor taste: Notes on Pop", a 1983 essay by Dick Hebdidge which argued that the best of Pop Art produced a consciousness of the pleasures of the popular and a commitment to the rights of the non-specialist spectator, renewing claims to 'truth' and 'authenticity' – a current in art since Romanticism.[4] The 'popular' spectator is judged to hold at bay the 'corrupt' professionalisation of art, and in Smith's work self-mockery disguised as child's work is a regular tactic. Roberts identified Pop's juncture with earlier conceptual art being in its attentiveness towards popular culture as an infinite source of readymades, as material to be reinscribed ideologically. Association with the non-art persona of the child provides a useful counter culture position.

Roberts also suggested that YBA attention to constructions of identity and notions of otherness, offered to them by postcolonial theorists such as Homi Bhabha, Trinh Min Hah and Gayatri Spivak as well as queer theory, raised ideas such as difference as articulation and performance-as-identity as means by which the everyday and the popular might be negotiated.[5] In Smith's work, the aping

Bob and Roberta
Smith, *Family Art
Show*, 2000.

of forms of attention customarily associated with children's art is a way of pulling strings behind stage, like a Punch and Judy show, a kind of ventriloquy. Collaboration with Etta is part of this strategy of problematising authorship – which may empower, or alternatively embarrass viewer-participants into engaging with the work. If we fail to play the game the illusion will not work.

The next phase for Bob and Roberta is to make family artworks in China, the modern art family's way of coping with the demands on artists to travel and work internationally. Is such work purely playing with the *idea* of social engagement or is there a higher goal of democratising the art-making process? Does Etta's collusion in shared authorship perhaps reflect ironically on a parent's desire for their own child to be a creative genius (or fashion accessory)? Either way, Etta insists that when she grows up the last thing she wants to be is an artist.

1 Mattick, Paul, *Art in its Time: Theories and Practices of Modern Aesthetics*, London: Routledge, 2003, p. 122.

2 Duchamp, Marcel, "Apropos of Readymades", in Michel Sanouillet and Elmer Peterson, *Salt Seller: The Writings of Marcel Duchamp*, New York: Oxford University Press, 1973.

3 Mattick, *Art in its Time: Theories and Practices of Modern Aesthetics*, p. 125.

4 Hebdidge, Dick, "In poor taste: notes on Pop", *Block*, no. 8, 1983, p. 56.

5 Roberts, John, "Pop Art, the Popular and British Art of the 1990s", in McCorquodale, Siderfin and Stallabrass, eds., *Occupational Hazard: Critical Writing on Recent British Art*, London: Black Dog Publishing, 1998, p. 54.

sound Mirrors
a Proposed Artwork
Involving secondary school Pupils
in Kent and in Dunkirk, France
Lise Autogena

The Sound Mirrors project is a proposed artwork originally conceived by Lise Autogena in 1996 for Folkestone, Kent. The concept of the commission is the basis for an education project with secondary schools in 2003-2005, which considers how the mirrors project can be an inspirational learning tool, involving local experts, scientists, artists, government departments and partner schools in France. This essay consists of conversation extracts collected by Anna Harding during the project's development.

I've been working on the project for six or seven years. It started out as a proposal for regeneration in Folkestone. They wanted artists to be involved, to do some small sculptures. Unfortunately, they asked me and I suggested a very, very big sculpture. My response was to think about regeneration of the area, as a foreigner, to look at how I thought regeneration could be approached from a cultural perspective in a different way than making a sculpture for a park. I wanted to create something that would have a real impact on Folkestone, that would create a communication channel, an invisible link across the sea. I wanted to see what an invisible bridge could look like and what impact that could have in terms of connecting communities.

I wanted to do something geographically specific to the area and coming from Denmark I was amazed by how much the Second World War was still present in that area, along the coast. I came across the sound mirrors. They were designed originally to create a defence system, you would have listeners standing night and day with inverted giant ears to listen out to the sky for enemy aircraft. In the beginning there were dishes on the ground, they would listen for amplified sounds from the sky by listening to the ground. There was a rumour that they were used for listening for the sounds of digging – they thought there were attempts to build a tunnel underneath the ground, which I think is extraordinary! There were all sorts of experiments taking place, for example carving dishes like giant ears into the chalk cliffs, the kinds of things that appear in *Tin Tin* books – the sound mirrors appear in several *Tin Tin* books as defence technology.

The idea behind the original sound mirrors was to create a whole network of listening devices along the coastline. Some of the sound mirrors would be good for listening really far away and some would be good for listening to quite specific sounds in particular areas. They might hear a strange sound and could ring the post office and activate the war defence mechanism. It was very sophisticated. A guy would be standing there night and day with a stethoscope attached to his ears, attached to an ear trumpet, listening for sounds in the dish. The stereoscope would then be attached to an ear trumpet to detect the direction from which the sound was coming in. But one problem was that they could never tell how close the aeroplane would be. You could listen apparently to sounds 50 kilometres away. But, unfortunately, it might not be real aeroplanes but things like milk floats. In a way it was quite sweet, like a failed technology.

Some of the children in our group have grown up next to these mirrors, which are amazing. There is a series of mirrors near Dungeness. It's like coming across something part ritualistic, part NASA, part outer space. These mirrors are just being restored. They were built between the two world wars. They built bigger and bigger ones. The nine metre mirror is the model that they hoped would be developed. Then radar was invented, which put a stop to the whole project. They have been standing here ever since. The absurd thing is that they were built in quiet places and they are all standing in what are now quite noisy places now – next to an airport, in a military shooting ground, next to a busy road.

When I came across them I thought that these were amazing visual images of sounds, standing in spectacular places, looking out to France as if they were waiting to hear something. Not many people know about them but for some they have become a bit of a cult thing, some people travel far to go and see them. They are a bit like radio telescopes, listening out to space for distant sounds or distant life. When they were built they were a secret technology and some people thought they were used to listen to sounds of French conversation, like a Big Brother system. Dr Tucker, the man behind the mirrors, was you might say a 'failed' scientist who in the end ran away with his treasure of notes.

I've been working with an engineer in America who specialises in dome technology, and we are planning to build a new mirror on each side of the channel. The previous mirrors were just used for listening out for environmental sounds from the sky. The new mirrors will combine the old acoustic technology with new technology. You are going to be able to climb up into the mirror, into a sound space. What you will hear are the sounds from the Channel itself with the two mirrors facing each other across the Channel, aligned for transmission.

When you come up into the sound space you won't know if anyone is over the other side, you may just be talking to yourself, but you will also be listening to the sounds from the Channel. With the old mirrors, the sound was purely acoustic. We will mix the sound of speaking transmitted across, creating a sound space around the listener's head, a multidimensional, binaural sound space. If it is really bad weather you may not be able to speak to someone. We are looking at microwaves and ways of making the sound mirror interact with the physical space between the two mirrors. You will really be able to climb it and come up into a private space while at the same time in a very mysterious way you will be talking to someone across the sea. We have also tested whether we can create sound spaces in front of the mirror, where sound is projected out, in a controlled sound space, making a performance possible within the mirror. We will be able to commission artists to create particular sound pieces, site-specific commissions by musicians, poets and all sorts of things. There are a lot of possibilities for this project. It is meant to a platform for everyone to use, to have a voice.

I am interested in how you can make something exist that is not actually physically there, which is just an image in your mind. Sometimes if things are not physical they are more open. I am interested in how the concept can be used as a platform for future projects. The idea is for kids to develop their own use for it, to create space within it.

There is a huge range of related research; for example a musician Richard Scarth is interested in how bats navigate, also with bats' relationship to radar; it also connects to people developing hearing aids and navigation for blind people. There is a man in nearby Lydd with a great knowledge of spying equipment, enigma coding and secret documents relating to the mirrors. A woman in Lydd, England's first holiday camp owner, was interested in getting them listed. There is a man living by the Dungeness mirror, a neighbour of one of the children we are working with, who was told he could buy the mirror for a pound ($1.75). But then English Heritage wanted to know how he would restore it, how he would take care of the hairy moth, the medicinal leech and other such conservation issues. I became very attached to the area, and to fighting for the survival of the old mirrors, some of which were about to collapse. Some people misunderstood and thought that money was being taken from conservation of the old mirrors to spend on my project, so there was some suspicion, but now I am close to the researchers and campaigners for the old mirrors. It's a fascinating process of research which I want to get the children involved in, and the kids being part of that community know many of the stories first-hand.

I gave presentations on the project to hundreds of children and felt so much reaction and excitement and personal connection with things they knew. Looking at how kids can be involved in the project, I am interested in their fresh thinking – for instance, how they might make links across institutions if an approach is made by kids, at what point will they be taken seriously? Maybe I'm being naive and Utopian. If the kids are really excited, they will take it on board, feel ownership over it, in the sense of finding their own way of dealing with it, pursuing it, interpreting it. Maybe they can make grand things happen which normally only grown-ups are associated with. We have given them a budget to commission specialists. It's hard to know if we will give them enough space to feel excited about it, and if we will be able to sustain excitement in research when there may be no tangible end product. Children need to know that there is a real response to what they are doing, that it means something. The question is how responsive are we prepared to be, at what point do we hand them power? This demands letting go.

I feel like a kid doing this, I have this approach to life in general, dealing with things that you know nothing about. I like to think I can encourage kids to be fearless, to have so much access to institutions that they feel they can ask them really obvious, stupid questions without feeling intimidated. Not enough people do ask stupid questions and kids are very good at it. My interest at this point is to see if it's possible to change relationships, to make things more human.

My own experience of school in an experimental class in Denmark was that I was encouraged to question systems of power and to encourage more female values. It was a very respectful approach. Here I see mistrust, fear, teachers allowing less chaos to make their lives easier. I suppose if you don't have the time to deal with individuals, this is the best way to survive when your job is out of proportion in terms of workload.

At the moment we are just working with one UK secondary school, primarily with a group of children aged 11 to 14. I would like to be there with the children as much as possible and would like to connect more with them, to have a more fluid brainstorm. It's great placing this project across the curriculum, supported by different teachers' expertise. Personally I am most interested in the fluidity of excitement, of personal dialogue with the kids, I need to find ways of communicating with them individually. I really need to work with the kids for two years, there's a lot they need to know about the project. I have no idea of how they will work on it, or with the kids in France. Hopefully they will find tools to brainstorm together, to overcome the language difference.

New children have now joined the project who are a bit younger. The original group are going into exams so the school wanted to pull them out of the project. The original group gave talks to other classes and got new kids to send in applications if they wanted to join. We had to fight for time with the school. It's difficult for a school because it's not about immediate outputs but the process of developing larger ideas. We need commitment from the school as to how they will support the project, we need the school to be much more involved. They can see that the children have developed a lot, especially in terms of self-confidence, but there are many different outcomes that are hard for them to see; it's more a way of thinking, thinking much bigger than your immediate surroundings. Now we are about to produce a website and involve a sound artist.

It's a natural progression for my projects always to grow. I like projects not to finish, I like how ideas grow, become something else, evolve into other things over time, see how others can use them. When working with young people it's important to me that the kids can take some ownership of the project, I'm disappointed when they refer to their work as "helping me with ideas". Now they are beginning to see that it is also about them realising their own ideas. It has taken them a long time to understand that. It confirmed what I already thought, that they have brilliant ideas and that if taken seriously and given the right channels of communication these can become brilliant projects. I don't believe in working with young people as a practice for myself, I wouldn't base all my ideas around children; rather I start with ideas and if it makes sense to work with children I would do it. Here they are adding value to the project.

The Sound Squad team of young people involved in the Sound Mirrors project made a presentation at the Department for Culture, Media and Sport:[1]

They are wearing their school uniforms and are looking very excited. They get their badges at reception and hustle off to the bathrooms to put on the new Sound Squad T-shirts that they have designed. They are brought into a large, high ceiling conference room that has a screen and projector set up. There is tea, coffee and water but no juice. Some of the DCMS representatives begin to arrive. There are six in all. The group of young people organise themselves: "If you do this, I'll do that…." They look out for each other, making sure that each person is doing what they should be to make things happen. They appear calm and professional whilst obviously pleased and a bit nervous. There is a real sense that they have a job to do and they want to do it very well.

There have been many issues to do with legal aspects of the building of the Sound Mirrors both in the UK and France and there is a real need for

UK institutional influence to win over key players in local authorities in France. The Sound Squad introduce themselves: Bradley, Dominic, Nick, Flora, James, Sian.

Sian: One day Lise Autogena turned up at our school and said she needed some help with her project. The people that showed most interest in their application and the people who put their hands up most were chosen. About two weeks later Mr Atkin, our headteacher, called us to his office, there were 20 people hoping to join the team and we were chosen. The name Sound Squad was created by myself, Sian Hannigan, and during the naming process everyone chose a name that they liked or made up – i.e. Listening Ears. Our logo was made by Dominic who came up with the idea when he was doodling and we all loved it.

James: *Sound Mirrors* – a history. They were built on the south east coast to detect the sound of incoming planes between 1916 and the 1930s. They were called the Listening Ears. They were designed by a man called Dr Tucker who joined the army after making a name for himself as a scientist. They are extremely large and some are bigger than others.

Dominic: The project is all about sound and communication. Lise's aim is to communicate with France with the brand new mirrors. If we can do this we will be able to perform concerts to the French people. The project is also about learning about communication. So far we have been learning about the old mirror and about Lise's mirrors. We have also been to the old mirrors and visited the site for the proposed new ones. Since we started the project we have been on many trips such to Denge, Folkestone, Dunkirk, Lille and Sangatte. When we visited the acoustic mirror in Folkestone we took pictures of it and studied it. We did the same at Denge. We went on a trip to meet pupils in France to find out more. We went to Lille for a cultural visit to see some artwork. We went to visit La Coupole to see where V2 rockets were launched. We went to visit Sangatte to visit the Napoleonic tunnel and the site where Lise wishes to build the new mirrors.

Sian: We've done many visits on this project – one of them was to Dover Museum to interview a man called John Iveson who is the curator there. He told us a lot about the mirrors and all that he knew. We saw pictures of a man with planes he wanted to make and lots of motors and parts that went into planes which helped us to see how much you have to work to get a good result.

Nick: In this project we have had many ideas and seen work by other artists. We have been visited by sound artists. They showed us what we could do to make sound more creative, that sound could be art. In this project we have learned many skills and one of these is filming. We have been filmed all the way through so in the future we will be able to show people what we have done. We have also done some filming ourselves with mini video cameras. We have been designing a website with Paul Farrington, he has shown us how he linked sounds to the site, and how to play around with sound and make your own pieces of music. The website will include a historical archive, information, resources, games.

Bradley: To try to publicise our project we need people to find out about the project. We have had many ideas for this, including a bus in which we will present the idea to primary schools. We have also come up with the idea of having an exhibition of the suitcase of Dr Tucker. If we were to get hold of this case we could extract information, which the curator at the Dover Museum is very interested in, and we could put it in an exhibition at the Museum. We hope that the mirrors will improve the relationship between England and France. We are currently making relationships with pupils in a French school. We could also perform to each other – local bands and school bands. This will build the confidence of young people wanting to make a career by singing or playing an instrument.

Dominic: We think that one of the most important things is helping Lise along the way, giving her ideas and inspiration. We like to be treated like adults, people are listening to our ideas and taking them seriously. We won't forget the old mirrors though as they are the foundations of the new ones. The main reason we have stuck with this project is because it is interesting. We have learnt a lot from it, for example, working as a team and being creative. Will Lise be the new Dr Tucker, the creator of the mirrors?

Bradley: We think the mirrors will be good for our school as our school is a performing arts school. We could create music or sound art from one side of the channel to the other. This could be the basis of our performance and we could show it to our French friends.

James: Every one of us has found out something new and looks at life now with a different perspective. We've met loads of new people who have a unique art – sound artists, filmmakers, graphic designers and lots of other artists. We have learnt many practical skills and improved in our confidence in talking to adults.

Bradley: Considering that the Entente Cordiale is ending this year, we thought the project would help form a relationship between France and England as it makes links with France, supports communication and is a cultural and arts project that links with subjects at school – English, French, science, geography and ITC. We have a voice and we are listened to, we can make things happen, and make a difference, the project is a real world outlook. Because us young people don't have many opportunities to be introduced to important people we were wondering if young people would actually be able to meet important people.

Nick: Can you support us with resources? For example, we'd like to develop a *Sound Mirrors* bus with an exhibition, interactive activities and sound games, to have a base for the project and set up a *Sound Mirrors* museum with information about what we are doing, the history, etc..

Paul: I don't know if we might be able to give you some support in terms of mentoring. We can help you make business connections/plans as I think you'll understand we can't just make up a number and hope it will work.

Juliette: Creative Partnerships have funded the education programme through to the end of the spring term and the group have their own ideas about what they want to do. It has come from them, so mentoring the children to come up with business plans for these ideas would be helpful.

Alan: Can I ask you about your visit to French schools? You talked about the bureaucracy, but what has the reception been like, has it been as enthusiastic as yours?

Sian: I'm the only one in the team who hasn't been on a French trip. When they came over here they went into a French class and were asking us questions. We were really really nice but when they came over here, some of them were really horrible to us and we couldn't see why.

Flora: They didn't seem to know as much about the mirrors as us.

Lise: In a way the connections have been made between the children themselves, I'm going over there to work with the school in a few months.

Paul: It strikes me that the success of the French side will come out of this kind of enthusiasm, the same kind of enthusiasm we see here and the bureaucrats will sort themselves out, otherwise it will seem like a bit of England over there and not something that they own. I have a couple of questions for you, Sound Squad. Adults like to talk a lot and what is really nice is to come into a meeting where we don't have to guess what people of your age want. You have made an effort to make this presentation for us and it does make a difference and you put some of us on the spot and its not very comfortable but don't stop doing it because it is a way to get what you want noticed and its important to keep on doing that and I hope that whatever little bits of encouragement we can give you can help. Really, to say thank you. Have you thought about sponsorship?

Nick: I thought we could try and make it a tourist attraction so that local businesses like hotels and restaurants could give us money and we could advertise them.

Paul: I think you are right though I don't know how much that will compromise your vision Lise? I think this is a fantastic documentary. Have you approached any of the broadcasters to get more sponsors involved?

Lise: It feels a bit like the artist Christo who tries to wrap buildings and sometimes it takes years. It can be problematic if you are an individual with an idea that is of public interest to get projects realised. I would like to know how can individual artists be enabled in this process?

Students from Anne Frank School, Dunkirk met with pupils from St Edmund's Catholic School, Dover to discuss what they would do with the Sound Mirrors. Here are some of their ideas:

> You could play music and see if the other person likes it.
> You could use it to amplify rock concerts.
> If the weather is good in England and bad in France you could reflect the sun back to France.
> The French and the English live next door to each other but the only reason the English go to France is to get booze.
> When you get sun in France you get rain in England. When you get rain in France you get rain in England.
> Instead of being pen friends you could be mirror friends – sound friends and arrange times to talk.
> Mirror marriages – though the French won't get married without seeing the other person.
> You could fight verbally rather than physically.

Juliette Buss, Project Co-ordinator: The boundaries for this project are deliberately very wide, and the outcomes are completely open-ended. What we do depends on the direction the children want to take the project. The remit is about challenging and raising expectations, and about giving children some responsibility for their own learning. We're looking at ways of supporting the children in developing ambitious ideas themselves, and giving them the skills they need to see them through. As well as generating ideas, which the children are great at, it also involves more complex skills such as being able to compromise and negotiate ideas as a team, so that initial concepts progress and move forward. Alongside this, we've also asked them to present at conferences and work in very adult contexts – like boardrooms, with all sorts of professionals including artists, designers, curators, and the Department for Culture, Media and Sport.

The children are fully involved in the project, working closely with Lise to advise, think and learn about the mirrors. They've undertaken extensive research, including interviewing acoustic mirror specialists and artists, visits to the sites of the old and the new mirrors, to Tate Modern, Lille, the Victoria and Albert Museum in London and the Dover Museum. As a result of all this, the children decided they wanted to find ways of telling their peers, friends, and family about the Sound Mirrors project. With Lise they have appointed a sound artist and designer to help them create a website for their work, and much more ambitiously, they have ideas for an interactive travelling gallery that they want to take to schools across the UK.

There are six children in the Sound Squad, but we and they are keen to get other pupils involved. We've just recruited two more groups of children. The

Sound Squad will be commissioning the new groups to work with a sound artist to make some kind of artwork – possibly for performance, the travelling gallery, or maybe the website – they have yet to decide. We've also been working with children in France, visiting them at their school in Dunkirk and talking about the mirrors.

We hope to help the children to be more independent thinkers in a system where there is a danger of being spoon-fed because of the need to get through exams. We recognise that this is a lot to ask and involves a lot of risk taking. The strength of the project has been that it straddles different subject areas, and doesn't sit within one area of the curriculum, but it has also made it problematic and more difficult for teachers to embrace. I think Lise has perhaps struggled with this side of the English school system. I worry that perhaps the children won't be able to cope with so much freedom. I do think children need to have clear boundaries, so that they can push against them. Lise's ideas can seem quite extreme in this current education climate, so my role is to temper them by ensuring there's a clear context. But we are lucky artists are able to try things out that teachers can't, to take risks and experiment with new ways of working. Artists have the luxury of being able to get away with things.

What has been amazing is seeing the children build this unique and mature working relationship with Lise and countless other artists. You can see that they are actually beginning to question things, take control, organise themselves, and have huge confidence in their own ideas.

1 People present at the DCMS meeting, Trafalgar Square, London, 14 July 2004: James, Bradley, George, Nick, Flora, Sian, Dominic – the Sound Squad; Paul Bason, DCMS Culture Online, examining the use of new technology for arts and culture; Mike Downs, International unit of DCMS, involved with coordinating the Entente Cordiale commemoration; Jo Turner, DCMS, joined to deal with online initiatives and international policy and Culture Online; Charlotte Collingwood, DCMS, arts education team, music dance and drama policy and overseas arts education initiative for young people; Julie Cabrole, DCMS, works with the international branch; Alan Simpson, DCMS, Arts Online, international branch; Kieran Renihan, geography teacher at St Edmund's Catholic School; Juliette Buss, Project Co-ordinator; Lise Autogena, artist; Tim Rolt, filmmaker documenting Sound Mirrors; Caoimhe McAvinchey, project evaluator – who also transcribed this discussion.

Artists and schools: interventions in Education systems

Unique educational projects developed within the public school system are presented in the work of Jef Geys, who ran an art project for 25 years in a middle school in Belgium. Room 13, set up by Rob Fairley at Caol Primary school in Fort William, has provided the inspiration for a crop of pupil-run Room 13s across the world. The account of Room 13 is based on an impromptu e-mail question and answer session which demonstrates the fluency, confidence and forthrightness which Fairley has cultivated in the pupils who manage Caol Primary's Room 13. The project has been such a success that it has been replicated in schools internationally. Martin Krenn and WochenKlausur have developed projects that consist of observations about schooling and proposals for improvements which they have developed in collaboration with young people. Dias & Riedweg and O+I display the sensitivity to articulate young people's hidden motivations and sensibilities, which they find are not tapped into in education provision. Their work attends to qualities in young people expressed outside of academic and examined subjects, which they consider largely undervalued.

Dias & Riedweg describe a sensitising practice which moves between intimacy and public space. Their projects with street kids in Rio de Janeiro, a young people's correctional centre in Atlanta and a new school building at Riem near Munich, provide visibility to subtle and often unspoken children's perceptions. O+I identify moments of motivation in their research project across 12 Southwark schools, aimed to enable the Department for Education to consider how to avoid high drop-out levels from school in poor and multi-cultural areas. Their research project detected motivation in Physical Education, drama classes or the playground, and looked at encouraging children's articulacy and verbalising skills to gain confidence and understanding through talking about what they have made rather than focusing on making activities.

Ben Sadler provides us with comical, cartoon-style commentaries based on his experiences of working as an artist in schools.

From a certain perspective a child's perspective can be somewhat complex

Ben Sadler

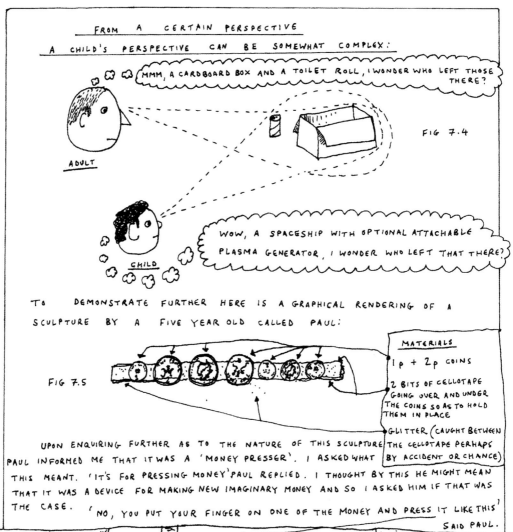

...**THIS:** 'THE CITY' AND ITS COUSIN 'THE TOWN' ARE MADE UP OF MANY 'STREETS' AND 'BUILDINGS'. SOME OF THESE 'BUILDINGS' ARE CALLED 'HOUSES'. UNITS CALLED 'PEOPLE' LIVE IN THESE 'HOUSES'. SOME OF THESE 'PEOPLE' ARE SMALLER THAN OTHERS. THERE ARE SOME OF THESE SMALLER 'PEOPLE' WHO ARE CALLED 'CHILDREN'. THIS IS HOW I UNDERSTAND IT TO BE.

N.B. NOT TO SCALE — THE UNIVERSE → THE SOLAR SYSTEM → THE EARTH → THE COUNTRY → THE CITY → THE TOWN → THE STREETS → THE BUILDINGS → THE HOUSES → THE PEOPLE → THE CHILDREN

FIG 7.7   (YET TO BE BUILT)

WHEN ASKED TO MAKE A DESIGN FOR A WALL IN A BUILDING I WORKED WITH SOME CHILDREN. THE EQUATION WAS SOMETHING LIKE THIS:

FIG. 7.8.
$$\text{ARTIST (NOT FROM AREA)} + \text{CHILDREN (FROM AREA)} = \text{DESIGN FOR WALL IN NEW BUILDING}$$

NOTING THAT I WAS NOT FROM THE AREA, BUT THAT THE CHILDREN WERE, I WAS ABLE TO MAKE THE FOLLOWING MATHEMATICAL LEAP:

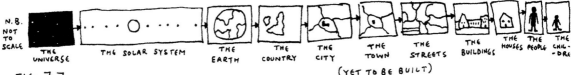

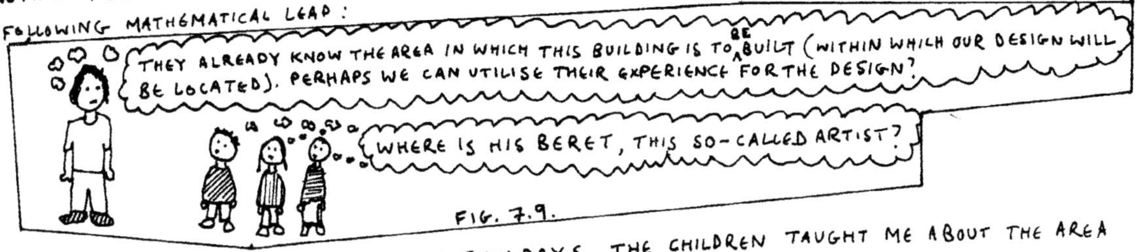

THEY ALREADY KNOW THE AREA IN WHICH THIS BUILDING IS TO BE BUILT (WITHIN WHICH OUR DESIGN WILL BE LOCATED). PERHAPS WE CAN UTILISE THEIR EXPERIENCE FOR THE DESIGN?

WHERE IS HIS BERET, THIS SO-CALLED ARTIST?

FIG. 7.9.

AND SO OVER THE COURSE OF A FEW DAYS THE CHILDREN TAUGHT ME ABOUT THE AREA IN WHICH THEY LIVED, FROM THEIR OWN UNIQUE PERSPECTIVE. HAVING LEARNT A LITTLE FROM THEM (AND THEY PERHAPS FROM ME) WE THEN THOUGHT ABOUT HOW THEY MIGHT CHANGE THEIR AREA.

THE RESULT WAS **MADTOWN**, A TOWN THAT OPERATED WITH ITS OWN UNIQUE LOGIC AND REVEALED MUCH ABOUT THE WISHES OF THESE CHILDREN. WE MADE THE TOWN AS A MODEL FROM BITS AND BOBS OF EVERYDAY JUNK AND THE ALL IMPORTANT PIPE CLEANERS.

FIG. 8.0

THE FOLLOWING IS A ROUGH ARTISTS IMPRESSION OF MADTOWN. BEAR IN MIND IT CONVEYS LITTLE OR NONE OF THE TOWN'S ACTUAL BEAUTY.

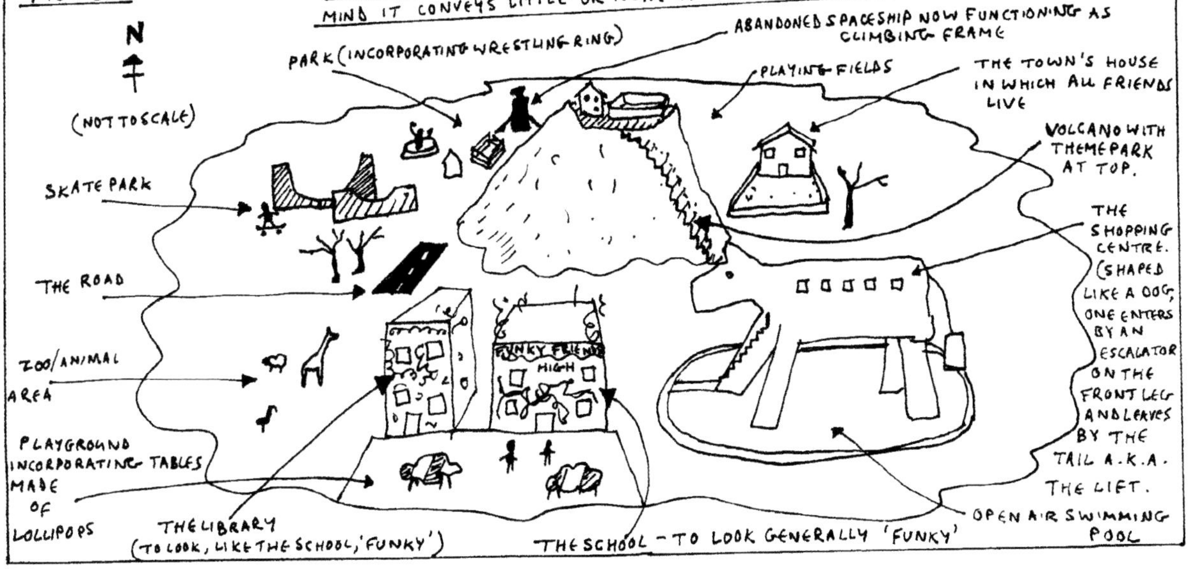

N ⚊ (NOT TO SCALE)

PARK (INCORPORATING WRESTLING RING)

ABANDONED SPACESHIP NOW FUNCTIONING AS CLIMBING FRAME

PLAYING FIELDS

THE TOWN'S HOUSE IN WHICH ALL FRIENDS LIVE

VOLCANO WITH THEME PARK AT TOP.

SKATE PARK

THE SHOPPING CENTRE. (SHAPED LIKE A DOG, ONE ENTERS BY AN ESCALATOR ON THE FRONT LEG AND LEAVES BY THE TAIL A.K.A. THE LIFT.

THE ROAD

ZOO/ANIMAL AREA

PLAYGROUND INCORPORATING TABLES MADE OF LOLLIPOPS

THE LIBRARY (TO LOOK, LIKE THE SCHOOL, 'FUNKY')

FUNKY FRIENDS HIGH

THE SCHOOL - TO LOOK GENERALLY 'FUNKY'

OPEN AIR SWIMMING POOL

From a certain perspective a child's perspective can be somewhat complex

A PORTRAIT OF THE ARTIST BY YOUNG MEN

AN ARTIST'S BEST WORK IS MADE DURING THEIR A-LEVELS. FROM AFTER THIS POINT IT IS A DOWNHILL SLIDE INTO WILFULL OBSCURITY AND RANDOM SYMBOLISM. SOME EVEN FORGET TO USE PAINT. SOME EVEN PAPER!!!!!!

FIG. 20.4 CAREER GUIDANCE TO CUT-OUT AND KEEP

SOMETIMES I HAVE IDEAS THAT AT THE TIME SEEM SO EARTH SHATTERINGLY BRILLIANT THAT I AM ALMOST KNOCKED UNCONSCIOUS BY THEIR SIMPLE ELEGANCE. THERE IS THEN A SUDDEN DROP BACK TO REALITY. THE PROCESS IS DEMONSTRABLE AS THUS:

FIG. 20.5

A. THE SLOPE OF INGENUITY
THE PINNACLE OF BRILLIANCE
B. THE VALLEY OF SELF AWARENESS

A. IS THE SAME AS B. ONLY WITH A LITTLE MORE INNOCENCE.

ON ONE OCCASION WHEN THE ABOVE OCCURED MY UNCONSCIOUS BRAIN FURNISHED ME WITH THE FOLLOWING NOTION:

HAVING WORKED WITH THIS GROUP OF GCSE ART STUDENTS FOR A WEEK (IN WHICH I HAVE SHOWN THEM MY OWN WORK IN DETAIL FROM A-LEVELS TO THE PRESENT DAY AS A PART OF IT) PERHAPS IT WOULD BE INTERESTING TO ASK THEM TO GIVE THEIR OPINIONS ON MY WORK, PERHAPS IN THE STYLE SUCH THAT THEY ARE TALKING TO ONE WHO IS UNFAMILIAR WITH MY WORK AND SUCH. YES!!! I'LL GET THEM TO TALK TO THE VIDEOCAMERA ONE BY ONE FOR AS LONG OR AS SHORT AS THEY LIKE. OH MY LORD! IT'S BRILLIANT! OH MY, I FEEL FAINT.

AND SO, AFTER REGAINING FULL CONSCIOUSNESS ON THE DOWNWARD SLOPE, I PUT THE IDEA INTO PRACTICE. ADOPTING THE STYLE OF AN ELEVEN YEAR OLD CHEMIST ONE CAN EXPRESS THE PROCESS, NÉE EXPERIMENT AS THUS:

MATERIALS
IS GCSE ART STUDENTS (MALE, GRAMMAR SCHOOL STUDENTS TO REPRODUCE THIS EXPERIMENT COMPLETELY ACCURATELY)
VIDEO CAMERA
PROCESS
TURN ON CAMERA, PRESS RECORD AND LET STUDENTS INDIVIDUALLY SAVAGE/PRAISE/EXPRESS INDIFFERENCE TO YOUR WORK.

CONCLUSIONS FROM THIS 'EXPERIMENT':

1. GCSE STUDENTS SEEM HAPPIER, GENERALLY, _AND INITIALLY_, TALKING ABOUT PAINTING AND DRAWING RATHER THAN VIDEO, PERFORMANCE, INSTALLATION ET AL.

2. THEY'RE QUITE HAPPY TO TAKE ON BOARD NEW IDEAS BUT A BIT RETICENT TO PUT THEM INTO PRACTICE (NOT ALL OF THEM THOUGH).

3. MY WORK IS 'A BIT WIERD. NOT WHAT I'D CALL ART'

4. MY WORK IS 'SOMETHING DIFFERENT OTHER THAN OFFICE WORK'

5. MY WORK IS 'ALRIGHT I 'SPOSE'.

PHOTOGRAPHICAL DOCUMENTATIONAL VIDEOGRAPHICAL STILLS EVIDENCE:

| '...it's pretty decent...' | '...it's more like symbolism than art...' | '...it's...quite...wierd...' | '...it's alright I spose...' |

SOMETIMES I FORGET THAT MY WORK MIGHT NOT MAKE PERFECT SENSE TO EVERYONE. MAKING THE VIDEO I HAVE DESCRIBED HERE REINFORCED THIS FOR ME. IT ALSO SHOWED ME THE OPPOSITE. PEOPLE CAN PERCEIVE THINGS IN YOUR WORK THAT YOU NEVER IMAGINED THEY WOULD.

THE TEENAGERS IN THE VIDEO SEEMED TO ALREADY BE IN THE SWAY OF GENERALISED PERCEPTIONS OF WHAT ART SHOULD BE WHILE STILL HAVING TRACES OF THE CHILD'S OPEN, ECLECTIC PERCEPTION. EITHER WAY, I GOT THE HELL OUT OF THERE BEFORE THEY BECAME VICIOUS AND STABBED ME WITH SPEARS. I TOOK THE CONCH WITH ME. IT WAS HORRIBLE WHAT HAPPENED TO POOR PIGGY. THEY WERE LIKE ~~~~~~

CUT-OUT N KEEP NO. 137 - REMNANT OF THE JOURNAL

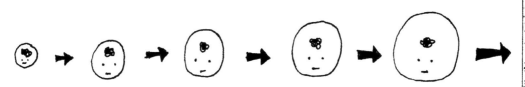

FIG. 20.6 DIAGRAM ILLUSTRATING THAT WHILE THE HEAD MAY EXPAND, ITS CONTENTS MAY NOT.

FROM a certain perspective a child's perspective can be somewhat complex

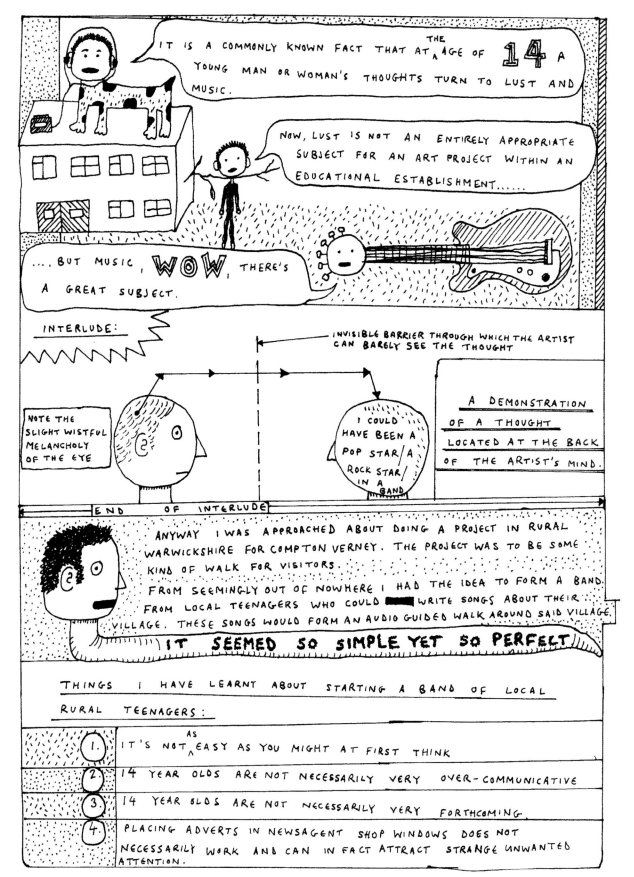

REVELATION: A GOOD PLACE TO FIND A CONCENTRATION OF FOURTEEN YEAR OLDS IS A SCHOOL. THEY HAVE THERE, IN FACT, A WHOLE ASSORTMENT OF AGES AND SIZES. THIS WAS THE BREAKTHROUGH I NEEDED FOR MY PROJECT.

INTERLUDE:

ARC OF VEILED REALISATION

A NEW-SPRUNG DESIRE TO FACILITATE THE DREAMS OF OTHERS

MOMENT OF HOPE AND DESIRE

PAST HOPES CRASHED UPON WAVES OF RESPONSIBILITY

(FIN D'INTERLUDE)

EVENTUALLY I FOUND A BAND FROM STUDENTS AT KINETON HIGH SCHOOL. THEY WERE ALL ALREADY IN BANDS BUT CAME TOGETHER TO FORM A NEW BAND.

THEY HAD COME FORWARD AFTER I WENT TO THE SCHOOL, SPOKE ABOUT MY WORK AND TOLD THEM ABOUT THE PROJECT.

FROM THERE THERE WAS A PERIOD OF SONGWRITING AND REHEARSING LEADING TO A SERIES OF SESSIONS IN A PROFESSIONAL RECORDING STUDIO, THE RESULTS OF WHICH BECAME A 10 SONG ALBUM AND GUIDE TO THE BAND MEMBERS' EXPERIENCES OF THE VILLAGE.

HERE IS THE BAND:

BAND FACTS:

1. THE BAND IS CALLED 'CIRCA '88'. THIS IS DUE TO THE FACT THAT AT THE TIME EACH MEMBER WAS 14 OR 15 AND THUS BORN AROUND THE YEAR 1988.

2. THERE ARE 8 MEMBERS OF CIRCA '88, ALTHOUGH ONLY 7 APPEAR ON THE PHOTOGRAPHS. THE 8TH MEMBER HAD A DENTAL APPOINTMENT ON THE DAY OF THE PHOTO SESSION.

3. ALL THE SONGS ON THE ALBUM ARE NAMED AFTER LANDMARKS IN THE VILLAGE OF KINETON, E.G. 'THE CHIPSHOP', 'THE PUB', 'THE CHURCH', EXCEPT FOR 'WAIT FOR THE ANSWER', A LOVE SONG WRITTEN BY GUITARIST/VOCALIST JASON. IT SEEMED TO BE A GOOD SONG TO FINISH THE ALBUM WITH.

4. THE ALBUM IS AVAILABLE BY CONTACTING thebeesaddler@hotmail.com

5. AS I STATED IN THE ALBUM SLEEVE NOTES 'I COULD NOT HAVE WRITTEN THESE SONGS. I'M GLAD THAT CIRCA '88 STILL CAN.' INDEED, CIRCA '88 WROTE ALL THE MUSIC AND I THINK IT'S VERY GOOD.

SO THERE YOU GO. A PROJECT THAT CONFIRMED FOR ME HOW REWARDING IT CAN BE TO WORK WITH, AND ALONGSIDE, YOUNG PEOPLE ON A CREATIVE PROJECT THAT CONFLATES BOTH THEIR AND YOUR INTERESTS.

AN ASIDE: WHITNEY HOUSTON STATES 'I BELIEVE THE CHILDREN ARE OUR FUTURE' AND THUS THAT BY IMPLICATION 'WE' ARE ■■■ OUR PRESENT AND 'THE OLD' ARE OUR PAST AND THUS THAT 'THE CHILDREN' ARE AVANT-GARDE.

From a Certain Perspective a Child's Perspective can Be Somewhat Complex

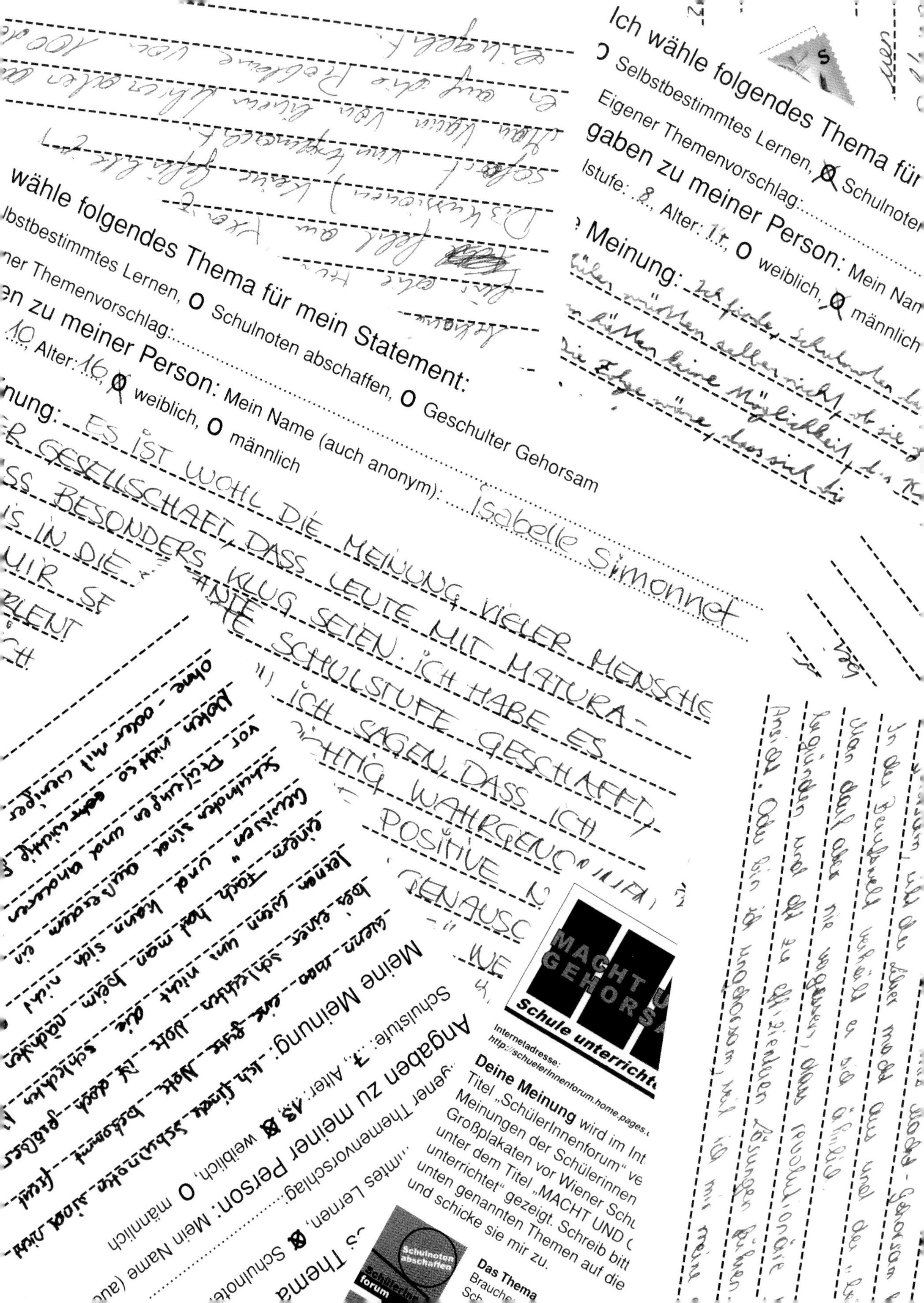

Ich wähle folgendes Thema für

O Selbstbestimmtes Lernen, Eigener Themenvorschlag:...... Ø Schulnote
gaben zu meiner Person: Mein Nam
Istufe:..8, Alter:.1r, O weiblich, Ø männlich

Meinung: _Ich finde, Schulnoten_

wähle folgendes Thema für mein Statement:

lbstbestimmtes Lernen, O Schulnoten abschaffen, O Geschulter Gehorsam
ner Themenvorschlag:......
en zu meiner Person: Mein Name (auch anonym):...... Isabelle Simonnet
10, Alter:16, Ø weiblich, O männlich

nung: ES IST WOHL DIE MEINUNG VIELER MENSCHE
ER GESELLSCHAFT, DASS LEUTE MIT MATURA-
S IN DIE ____ BESONDERS KLUG SEIEN. ICH HABE ES
UIR SE ____ NTE SCHULSTUFE GESCHAFFT,
LENT ____) ICH SAGEN, DASS ICH
CH ____ RICHTIG WAHRGENO (VILA)
____ POSITIVE N
____ GENAUSC
____ WE

Meine Meinung:
Schulstufe:... Alter: 13
Angaben zu meiner Person: Mein Name (au
ener Themenvorschlag:......
mtes Lernen, Ø Schulnoten O männlich

MACHT U
GEHORSA
Schule unterricht

Internetadresse:
http://schuelerInnenforum.home.pages.

Deine Meinung wird im Int
Titel "SchülerInnenforum" ve
Meinungen der Schülerinnen
Großplakaten vor Wiener Sch
unter dem Titel "MACHT UND C
unterrichtet" gezeigt. Schreib bitt
unten genannten Themen auf die
und schicke sie mir zu.

Das Thema
Brauchen
Gr

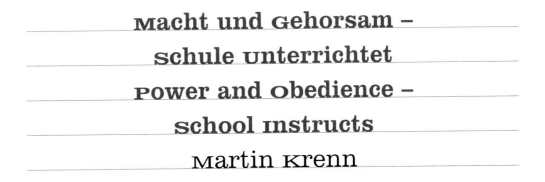

Macht und Gehorsam –
Schule unterrichtet
Power and Obedience –
school instructs
Martin Krenn

This project, developed from 1997-1999, consisted of an Internet project, a students' forum, a poster series and an exhibition presented at the Passagegalerie-Künstlerhaus in Vienna. It is an art project that I developed on my own initiative, not as contracted work, with the financial support of the Austrian Federal Curator for Visual Arts, who at the time was Lioba Reddeker. As an artist, I attempt to raise sociopolitical themes in the public domain and in art institutions. In my projects, which are usually developed over a long period of time, I examine particularly the ways that power mechanisms function. This often leads to collaborations with people active in the various fields of investigation.

At the outset of the project my question was: "Why do so many people unquestioningly accept the status quo of power relations which dominate and subordinate them?" School offered me an ideal arena to investigate power mechanisms at work. In my experience, we learn to accept inequality as children, arranged in rows according to height, or grouped by success in exams. We accept this as necessary and learn to internalise methods of control and subordination. As outlined by the theorist Michel Foucault, power lies in structures, in the organisation of space and the structuring of time, it is not only tied to individuals or groups and institutions; power does much more than just censure and negate; it effects us.

I had been involved with an alternative model of schooling through a part-time job at the Schülerinnenschule (Students' School) at WUK, a cultural centre in Vienna. I taught four to 12 hours a week from 1990 until 2002 in order to finance my art studies. 30 to 40 students aged 11 to 15 attend the school. The Students' School, managed collectively by students, teachers and parents, was founded as a childcare centre. It borrowed its basic concept from the Glocksee School in Hanover, a school where students evaluate their own progress rather than meeting formal exam requirements, earning equal rights at age 15 to continue into further education as pupils from any other school. Student self-evaluation

Power and Obedience – postcards from the exhibition.

consists of a report that they write at the end of the school year about their own achievements. Originally parents were the teachers; after several years they hired teachers. An integral part of the school is project-based instruction, which has also become popular in state schools in recent years. In meetings that take place several times a week, students decide together with the teachers on the design of the school day. All important decisions are made here, for example new admissions, changes in the school and teaching concept, schedule, and design of the school. Students, parents and teachers also share the cleaning and cooking.

Sometimes there's a misunderstanding that the 'alternative schools' are part of the Waldorf Schools which also call themselves 'alternative'. But our school had nothing to do with a school based on Rudolf Steiner's Anthroposophical ideology.[1] Instead of following esoteric ideas, we aimed to develop a constantly transforming school system led by a grassroots democracy, which consciously avoids orientation towards a particular ideology. It presents a counter model to most other forms of private and state schools.

State schools can be viewed as an ideological state apparatus, an effective means for the state to steer and control the reproduction and legitimisation of society. The idea of the ideological state apparatus was coined by Althusser, a Structuralist Marxist who explored the relation between state and subjects, asking why people are obedient, why do they follow laws, why isn't there a revolt against capitalism. In these terms schools, like prisons and army barracks, can be used by the state as a means of domination, with which it attempts to achieve its interests. The different ways that power functions in state schools can be seen, for example, in school policy: written, prescribed regulations attempt to design the school day as smoothly as possible and to maintain a school hierarchy which relegates pupils to the lowest level. Schools divide children and teens into groups according to their age, 'achievement', and 'talent', and their mastery of learning brands them either as successes or as failures. Grades express the degree of social conformity achieved.

The students are meant to deliver as 'work' the result of their subordination. The payment from the school system is doled out in the form of grades 'excellent' to 'unsatisfactory' or 'verbal assessment'. Good grades are meant to assure an appropriate position in the state's social hierarchy. This aims at an abstraction from one's own needs and interests and an internalisation of given behavioural expectations, goals, values, rules and regulations.

Through the alternative school's restructuring of the curriculum, other aims are pursued and hierarchical power structures are questioned rather than reproduced. In keeping with this, I attempted to develop a project concerned with power in schools from the perspective of students, collaborating with interested students from the alternative school as well as state schools.

I contacted teachers in state schools in Vienna and those interested invited me to their lessons, where I led discussions. These meetings took place during school lessons. We introduced 'power structures in the school' as a theme in classes ranging from psychology to German to religious studies. After the discussions, the students were invited to write statements on postcards – either anonymous or signed – on three themes: school grades, power/obedience, and self-determined learning. These statements, along with others sent by internet, were published on the home page "Schülerinnenforum" (http://schuelerinnenforum.t_or.at).

It became evident that many students have a sophisticated understanding of school systems. Many identified with the school, but expressed the need for reform. For example, Max M, 17 years old at the time, at a Realgymnasium (Comprehensive secondary school), wrote on doing away with grades: In the current school system, I think it is just as senseless to keep grades as it is to simply get rid of them. Almost no one really works better under pressure, but without grades, relatively lazy students like me, would do absolutely nothing in subjects that don't interest us so much. I agree that we should concentrate on individual students in the evaluations, even though I can't think of any good way to do that at the moment. Self-evaluation discussion could contribute, where a teacher talks separately with each student about their achievements.

An 18-year-old student in the final year of secondary school made an anonymous statement: Yes, I believe that there is an extremely powerful structure of obedience in the school. When it comes to decisions about the school, you clearly recognise that you have the shortest stick and have almost no say in the matter! Naturally, that also influences your personality. I think that it makes people depressed, that you stop having your own opinion about things and don't learn to take any responsibility for yourself. It is difficult to look forward to the school day if you know that... you are treated like a small child that has to do what she is told. School should be more relevant to life. For me, friends, responsibility, and strength in one's own opinion are the most important things!

Sergeja K, 15 years old: Students should decide for themselves whether they want to learn for their later lives. Additionally, they should choose and attend all of the subjects that are really important or interesting to them. If someone really likes a subject, it doesn't matter how strict the teacher is or how difficult the material is, because he or she is interested in it. Learning should be for you and not for teachers or parents. You determine your life, not them!

Veronika D, 13 years old: Self-determined learning: stupid! Reason: if students are able to decide what they want to learn, then we would only go to the movies, watch television, and have free time.... Apart from that, there would be no orderly time-table and consequently, only half of the current subjects would be taught; which the students would probably be in favour of.

This study, in which more than 200 statements were collected from postcards and emails, forms the basis of a video. The video concept, *alternative school students interview state school students*, was developed collaboratively with a group of young people from the Schülerinnenschule and shows the discussions that they had with students from regular state schools.

Excerpts from the video alternative school students interview state school students; *interviews carried out by pupils Paul Leitner, Nina Mangel, and Quilla Mederos from Schülerinnenschule WUK:*

What was your experience in primary school?

Ilona, Bundesrealgymnasium (Comprehensive secondary school), 15 years old: I was always at odds with my primary school teacher. She thought that I couldn't write neatly. So almost every day she made me write my work out over again. It really didn't matter to her if the work was correct or incorrect. Once, for a maths exercise, I really pulled myself together and wrote out everything neatly. She was really pleased, the only problem was, half of the answers were wrong. But she didn't look at the content, only at how it looked on the surface. I think that is idiotic.

Vinzenz, Sporthauptschule (secondary sports school), Güssing: I was rather aggressive during my primary school days. Every time I hit someone, the teacher hit me. I always yelled at her, and that's why she hit me. Then two years later I went to the Güssinger Hauptschule (secondary school). There, the teachers weren't as aggressive towards me, but they had big mouths and actually hit other children. Our biology teacher was particularly bad. We had three Yugoslavians in our class. One of them said something out loud and the teacher immediately started, "We don't need any foreigners mouthing off. Get lost and go home!"

How do the other students react when a teacher makes such racist remarks?

Vinzenz: They did nothing; they all just sat there quietly and looked stupid. Afterwards he completely denied it.

Was no one willing to testify to the incident?

Vinzenz: No, no one was willing to do that.

What are the power structures like at your school?

Ananda, Sporthauptschule (secondary sports school), Güssing: Often, someone has to write out the school rules during break. Also, sometimes as a punishment you might have to write out something from the Bible!

What is the hierarchical structure of school like?

Daniela, class representative, AHS (general secondary school), Salzburg: I think that the school simply wants to prepare people for society and society doesn't want people to do things that are completely out of the ordinary… Students should get used to the idea that there are authorities whom one should not question or criticise. Like in a company, there you also aren't allowed to say anything against the boss. In school you shouldn't protest. You should simply learn how to get on in life!

Artists and schools: interventions in Education systems

Power and Obedience – subway station poster.

How does democracy work in the school?

Daniela: Well, sometimes it is quite difficult. There are attempts. There is a school-community committee. But I really must say that it isn't organised fairly, because students have three votes, teachers have three, and parents three. But sometimes parents are also teachers. Usually there is a united front against the students: parents and teachers usually have similar opinions. It is very difficult for parents, who are never there, and don't know what is going on in the school, to have a say. And then, the headteacher sits in. Although he can't vote, it really stops you from saying what you think. As a class representative, if you want to say something against a teacher, that is very difficult because you're going to be graded by them. School needs to be individualised so that everyone can decide for themselves what they do.

Independent learning?

Daniela: Definitely! What's most important is to give each student the chance of not having to do everything the same. It has to be more individual and personal. It's much better to have smaller schools than monster schools with 3,000 students.

Was there any kind of dress code in the convent school?

Marlena, former convent school student: You had to wear a jacket, a blue one, and keep it buttoned up. The girls weren't allowed to wear wide jeans. They had to wear Levi's and a plain sweater and then a coat over that.

What were the consequences if you didn't dress like that?

Marlena: When you dressed like a good girl in the convent school, you got a red bow pinned on your sweater. If you didn't, then you got a black bow.

What did it feel like to have a little bow like that?

Marlena: You feel stupid. I was one of the only ones that always got a black bow, so the others always gave me this stupid look.

What are the structures of power and obedience like at your school?

Marie, BRG-7 school, Rahlgasse: Being bad in this school is relative. You aren't allowed to say anything. For example, teachers think that I am bad. I don't know why, except that I don't let anyone tell me what to do. That is simply how I am. It doesn't matter to me if they tell my mother or not… I say I am going outside (out of the school, during class time) and I really go outside. Yesterday I was outside! I'll go out again today, too. There is no other way that anything will change in this school. There are so many people here that just keep their mouths shut. That really bugs me.

Do you feel like you are a part of the school?

Marie: We are actually just like furniture. Just placed there, simply meant to be like that. That's just how it is. You come in, sit at a table, and every day is the same.

Who has power in your school?

Group of teenagers, BORG (State academy for music and art), Hegelgasse: Definitely the teachers. No… actually, the headteacher!

Student: I don't understand it, every student says that the teacher has power…. It's just that he is partly a teacher, and partly an employer. We have to do what he says. He prepares the work and we have to take the work, simply accept it. We can't do anything else.

Do you think that's good or bad?

Student: I don't know what good and bad is because I am only used to one type of school….

How should school change?

Student: I would like to have a different grading system. I would like to grade myself, or be graded verbally by the teachers. I had that in primary school. In the first two classes it actually worked quite well. I also think that I can grade myself quite well. I would be honest with myself. I wouldn't grade myself so high, with all As or anything. I think that it is good when the students can decide for themselves.

*Power and Obedience
– video presentation.*

During the visits to the schools and the work on the video, it was possible to make contact with students from various state schools who participated in completing the project in their free time. After several meetings, a core group formed (Neue Schule) comprising eight to ten students from alternative and state schools. Together, the group selected students' statements for the posters from among those on the Internet, worked out the layout and discussed the concept for the exhibition. A design for a new school was worked out and was shown as a diagram on posters and at the exhibition.

The posters hung for a month on billboards at bus stops and in the subway stations in Vienna. Positioning of the posters in busy public spaces ensured that they were well read.

The exhibition *Power and Obedience – School Instructs* showed the opinions and positions of students in conjunction with found objects such as rule books, school brochures and reports, from which it is possible to recognise

Power and Obedience
– video still.

the school's power structures. The exhibition was divided into several areas, each area taking a specific facet of school and education as a theme. The exhibition showed the video, found objects and all of the postcards with the students' statements. Participating students photographed sites in their schools, revealing what they consider to be problem areas. The exhibition enabled visitors to gain insight into classrooms, the school system and associated power structures from the students' perspective.

KRÄTZÄ, a children's rights group from Berlin with whom we had email contact, visited Vienna. In the exhibition, they presented documentation of their activities, publications and a little "school house" representing the constricted space in classrooms.

Through the posters hung in public spaces, many people were motivated to visit the exhibition and website. The media reported extensively on the project, especially the Austrian daily paper *Der Standard*, and we were frequent guests on Austrian Public Radio (ORF) where we held live phone in discussions. Towards the end of the exhibition, the group Neue Schule disbanded. The video has been shown in the context of further exhibitions.

My own perspective on schools was expanded by the opinions, discussions, and co-operation of a new generation of students. I found it particularly interesting to carry out discussions with student groups and teachers during sessions that we held in the exhibition. Here it became evident that in Austrian state schools a fossilised, hierarchical system still dominates. Attempts made in recent years to create more open structures in schools unfortunately have often led to capitalist-oriented ideas, stressing concepts such as 'life-long learning', 'flexibility', 'teamwork', and 'self management'. The attempt is made to teach children and teenagers how to meet demands that have spread through the globalisation of an increasingly unrestrained capitalism. Rather than just taking orders, people are expected to participate in a self-controlled manner, apparently determining their own needs, in a society based on competition. 'Social learning', developed in alternative contexts in order to learn social competences, is replaced by 'team work'. As a group, the team no longer deals with learning how to handle the contradictions of social existence, but instead, how to fulfil responsibilities and tasks as efficiently and quickly as possible and deliver results.

Recent developments in Austria, which have led to an increase in unemployment and the privatisation of state institutions, are also being expressed in microcosm in various alternative schools in Austria. Thus, some parents act like the teachers' employers and demand services that contradict the concept of the alternative school. Their children also sometimes behave like paying customers who simply want to consume.

These contradictions to the actual ideas of an alternative school should not conceal the achievements that have been made over more than two decades. Alternative schools still represent a different social model, a model that demonstrates that it is possible to live and work together in a grassroots democracy. Through *Power and Obedience*, in addition to articulating criticism of power mechanisms through the example of school, I attempt to offer insight into possible ways of interrogating these mechanisms.

Radio talk with students.

1 Rudolf Steiner underwent at the age of 36 a "profound spiritual transformation", after which he thought that he would be able to see the spirit world and communicate with celestial beings. These ostensible supernatural powers became the origin of Anthroposophist beliefs and rituals. In 1923 Steiner founded the Anthroposophical Society as "an association of people who would foster the life of the soul, both in the individual and in human society, on the basis of a true knowledge of the spiritual world". The Anthroposophical Society still define their schools as "schools for spiritual science".

creativity with purpose

ROOM 13: one Artist, 11 years, one school

Room 13 started life at Caol Primary School in Fort William in the Scottish Highlands, where it was set up by local artist Rob Fairley. It provides a blend of pupil autonomy, artistic and intellectual freedom, and curriculum enhancement that is not usually found in schools, giving pupils the intellectual skills they need to fulfil their potential in years to come. Attendance is voluntary; older pupils can go at any time during the day to work in the studio as long as they are up to speed on their classwork. Pupils take responsibility for their own learning and for the running of their arts studio. Mr Fairley says: "I give them critical feedback every step of the way, asking them difficult questions to make them think analytically about what they are doing. I treat the work here like any other piece and give it the analysis that I would of Guernica. It is the integrity of the work that I am looking for." Due to the success of the project, which is constantly evolving, a network of Room 13s has now been developed, each with their own identity, in schools in Britain and even in an orphanage in Kathmandu. For this book, Room 13 at Caol Primary were asked to contribute artwork in response to the theme of Magic Moments.

Anna Harding: What is Room 13?

Pupils: Good question… you would really need to visit one to see! Nobody really understands unless they visit. They are art studios run as a business by the students who use them. The business side helps with all areas of normal school work, the art side lets us talk about stuff which we would not otherwise get a chance to do.

How does it operate?

They work by each studio having a management team who raise all the money for stocking the studio by running a business… we, here in Caol, take photographs and sell them, make T-shirts, Christmas cards, postcards, design brochures, mouse mats… all sorts of things. The studio operates like any professional studio… maybe busier? The whole project is run by a small group here in Caol, supported by all the studio MDs.

How do you describe Room 13 in terms of your overall activity?

Fun.

Where does the work take place – what type of school?

It can take place anywhere. We are organising a piece which will be made from clouds which we are going to gather on Ben Nevis… but the work will be made in the studio (probably). All the studios in the UK are in normal state schools.

What's unique, special about this context?

Nothing really… though when Danni and Eileen were at a conference in Orissa in India they came back saying that it WAS unusual for such a long running student led project to exist in a state school. Actually somebody has just pointed out that it is pretty unusual for 12-year-olds to go to conferences in India!

Room 13 seems to be unique in being long-term as opposed to a short intervention like most art projects in schools. Can you say something about the long-term nature of the project?

Room 13 has been going in Caol for 11 years and is run by us. It started just in Caol but now we have studios in Lochyside Primary and Lochaber High School (also here in Fort William), Sacred Heart Primary in Glasgow, Hareclive Primary in Bristol, The Helpless Children's Mother Centre orphanage in Kathmandu, and Arasavanangkadu School in Tamil Nadu in India, and Hayley and Nikki are going out to Johannesburg at Easter to open one there. We are also going to start our own art college here in Fort William. The long time it has been running is good because everyone understands how it works and it means that long ideas can be done… some works we plan could take years and years to make.

It's perhaps not a coincidence that the project was set up in Scotland. Do you think this fact is significant?

Have to ask Mr Fairley because we don't know!

Mr Fairley: It probably is. It was Plato in his *Republic* (Book VII) who suggests that art should be the basis for all education and also wrote that a teacher should "avoid compulsion… and let your children's lessons take the form of play. This will also help you to see what they are naturally fitted for." George Davie in his classic account of the generalist tradition of Scottish university education *The Democratic Intellect*, writing about university education 150 years ago, says:

> The importance of [the] system was that it afforded a method of instruction well suited to enliven and bring home to the students the cultural and general content of the courses. The practice in fact was to supplement the lecture hours, in which

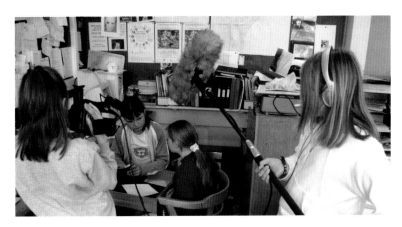

> the [teacher] had the class at his mercy, with examination hours
> in which, without detriment to his authority, he met the students
> more on a level, and, in the course of questioning them round
> the class on the subjects of the lecture, might himself become
> involved in argument....[1]

This is precisely what Primary Seven [the final year of Scots Primary school]
in Caol and Room 13 are doing.

Room 13's headline-making successes have all been in the visual arts
but even here we cannot claim to be particularly innovative, but are putting into
practice tried and proven thinking. In 1931 the Scottish artist William Johnstone
was appointed as full-time assistant art teacher at Lyulph Stanley and
Haverstock School for Boys:

> The effect on the children some initially difficult and disinterested
> (sic), was impressively swift, for his teaching was unlike
> anything they had come across before. More importantly it
> was unlike the accepted form of art education in elementary,
> secondary, and grammar schools at the time.... He would win
> their confidence, and keep his own work alive, by teaching them
> not as a teacher but as an artist, as though in his studio inviting
> them to paint, as artists, with him and on art of their own time
> and their own making.

Room 13 differs not one jot!

So, yes... you can say that Room 13 is basically Scots in philosophy...
but it works worldwide.

What opportunities and constraints does the context present – e.g. time, space, and expertise?

Mr Fairley: Time is easy – there is never enough. Our P7 class can use the studio
when ever they want as long as we keep our classwork up to date – which means
answering emails like this is not a problem... we just come and do it. When Rosi
and Ami made their Channel 4 TV film last year they were hardly EVER in class but
still kept up.

Space depends on the studio... Lochyside is probably the best space out
of the UK studios... it is bigger with lots and lots of sinks and good light. Caol is
getting cluttered with all the canvasses we use.

Expertise? Each of the studios is really good at something different. We
are good at painting, digital imaging, video and filmmaking, Lochyside are good

at sculpture and our website was made there, Lochaber High School's Room 13 is a multi media studio and Hareclive is mostly a painting studio. Sacred Heart in Glasgow is a music studio and they have a composer in residence! We can always swap artists/composers in residence when we want. We are thinking of putting an actor in residence into one of our next Room 13s!

The opportunities Room 13 offers are huge because everything we do is for real. Nothing is done because a teacher thinks it is a good idea or a good lesson... if we make a film it is aimed for being on TV (Rosie and Ami's was shortlisted for a Grierson Award so it must have been OK), when we write articles then they are meant to be published and when we make artwork the pieces we make are meant to be shown in galleries and have to mean something to us. It also allows us to travel, which is good... from Easter to Easter some of us will have been to Kathmandu, London, Glasgow, Delhi, Bhubeneswar, Calcutta, Varanasi, Agra, Inverness and Johannesburg.

Money is the biggest constraint and until we can set up the project to be self-funding it always will be.

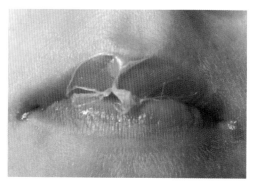 

Is there a key idea?

No... other than it is a studio that we run by ourselves.

Mr Fairley: It also does not patronise and operates at a high intellectual level (certainly undergraduate level).

Whose idea was it?

Nobody's... it just slowly grew.

How and why did it start and develop?

Two P6 girls eleven years ago started it when they asked Mr Fairley to come in and work with them. He said he wouldn't unless they paid him... so they did.

How did it change from the first idea?

It hasn't really changed, just got bigger and it is pretty cool to be able to have a network of Room 13 artists from all over the world to work with.

How long has it been going on for?

11 or 12 years.

Has Room 13 had to adapt or develop?

Yes. Room 13 in the High School is different… each Primary School studio is different, and the ones in other countries are very different, but the main idea is the same.

What do you feel Room 13 offers young people – e.g. permission, ways of thinking, being?

We have had a big discussion about this. We think it offers different things to different people. Some people want to just run the business side and others just want to make artworks. Some people just come into the room for peace and quiet to read a book and others come to listen to music and to talk about stuff. It certainly encourages everybody to think in different ways and to look at things in new ways. It is good for allowing us to control our lives in school rather than always just having to do what we are told with no explanation of why.

Mr Fairley: It gives us freedom.

What are the dynamics which make this project succeed?

O gosh I don't know. Don't know what dynamics is! Have looked it up so… one of the things which upsets adults but we think is fun is that the criticism in the studio is really really fierce. The artists in residence are quite likely to tell you that your work is rubbish unless you can say why you made it that way but that means you can ask them the same things… so we are always discussing and arguing.

Also respect, the adults totally well respect us and we respect them. We are all equal really, as they say they learn from us as much as we learn from them.

What does the work do to/for young people/adult artists?

In Room 13 there is no difference between adult and young artists. We are all just artists.

What do you think is the value of Room 13 for you?

We will ask everybody in the room…. Rachel, in the film, said it was like a home to her, so it will be interesting to see what everybody thinks.
Anne: an interesting place where your brain can run riot.
Katelyn: A peaceful room and a good place to sit and think.
Eilidh: A place where you can be yourself.
James: It can be annoying because of the noise but mostly it is quite fun.
Chloe: It is nice and relaxed.
Nicole: It's fun AND relaxing.
Lucy: (this year's MD) It's better than class because you can do your own work

your own way, and I got the chance to visit Tate Modern in London, and I really like taking photographs.

Rebecca: It's a fun and creative place to be. We can learn about philosophy and do all sorts of interesting things.

Mark: You can paint in it and you find you don't mess about as much as in class – you sort of concentrate better.

Mrs Innes (parent and classroom assistant): It keeps my children out of the house and at school!

Codie: Don't know... fun, good place to paint.

Hayley: I have got the chance to go to South Africa and I find it good even after school.

Amy: I got the chance to go to Tate Modern in London and you learn all sorts of different things.

Jamie: Because it's a place where you can paint and you are allowed to make a mess!

Laura: Because you can do what you want.

Alan: I like it because you can have a lot of fun and paint big big pictures.

Mrs Smith (P7 teacher): Freedom.

When do things work well/ less well and how can they be best supported?

We think the more we can run things the more easily it works. People are always saying we don't want to learn but actually what we want to learn is not always what we are taught, Room 13 allows us to learn all the stuff we do in class but in a different way.

The project can be best supported by trusting us.

Mr Fairley: Money is the way we can be supported best!! We always need more and the more money we can put together, the more Room 13s we can open.

What do you consider the key success (or otherwise) of Room 13?

We have been arguing over that one for ten minutes. Don't think there is a key success. Depends what you mean. The thing that made people notice us was winning the Barbie Prize... but that was just work from that year and we had been running the studio for years before that. Rosie and Ami's film being shortlisted for the Grierson Award was even bigger because the Barbie was just against other schools while the Grierson was against all other arts documentaries on TV. Winning three Artworks awards was important too. [The Young Artists of the Year awards scheme is run annually by the Clore Duffield Foundation]. The key success to the whole project hasn't happened yet... it will be when people really REALLY start to take us seriously.

What is its value for artists/young people?

It lets us be ourselves.

Mr Fairley: It allows us to be more creative than would otherwise be possible and gives us the chance to make new forms of artwork.

How do you measure the success?

Jamie suggests we use a successometer! Or you could measure success with a ruler but its size would depend on what font you printed it out on.

Seriously we don't know. Miss Cattanach (our headteacher) has said she can see the difference in the whole school but we are not sure how she means. We think that the constant attention from other schools wanting to join the Room 13 group is a sign of success. Room 13 teaches us that we have to take responsibility for our own actions.

Has the project changed?

Only very slowly... but each MD has a different way of doing things and of course each studio is different.

1 George Davie, *The Democratic Intellect*, EUP, 1961, p. 14.

Artists and schools: interventions in education systems

Finally Not Fully under control…
Notes on subjectivity and social
politics in the collaborative
Art praxis of Dias & Riedweg
Dias & Riedweg

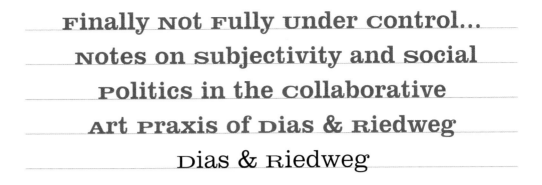

We, Mauricio Dias & Walter Riedweg, have worked together since 1993 developing collaborative public art projects in the fields of visual arts and contemporary performance. Our work varies from documentary to elaborate fiction, with a formal accent on video installation. It investigates how private psychologies affect the constitution of public space and vice versa, having as a main characteristic the involvement of an audience in the execution of each project and often a focus on sensorial aspects. We aim to question the boundaries of public and private space, and the public perception (including our own) of the mechanisms that affect and give form to public space. Rather than attempting to directly change things, we like to meet people and situations, always trying through these encounters to question and review perceptions of each context or situation encountered. These encounters take the form of 'sensorial workshops' or of 'staged encounters', that allow different people to slowly develop a dialogue that focuses on certain issues that relate a particular group of people to society in general. Although there are obvious differences between a work produced as an intervention in a train station or school building to one produced and exhibited in an international art biennial, we work in both contexts, trying to respect and at the same time challenge the frames of these institutions or events, always maintaining the motivation to reconnect people involved to the general public and vice-versa through artistic praxis. Our work is very much process (and therefore performance) oriented, but it also achieves a level of representation, most often in video installation. These videos are not meant to be a final product or result of each project, but a further step in which the dialogical form of art which we seek to develop is taken from its original audience to a broader sphere of resonance with the general public.

Dias & Riedweg,
Inner Services,
Shedhalle Zurich,
1995.

Operating across different arenas involves many different particularities in the process of working. The problems of carrying out an artwork within a prison or the public school system are definitely very distinct from those encountered in making such a collaborative artwork for a museum or a biennial. The challenge of making art in a dialogical form is frequently problematic and misunderstood in both arenas. The Modernist idea of the artist being a creator of poetry does not ever match the perception of these collaborative practices, in which the artists appear more as a repository of different speech and a stimulator for poetry as an accessible experience. We believe that poetry and eroticism are found in every life context, independent from economic conditions.

Our projects try to open spaces where the natural polemic that comes with poetry and art make the singularity of each individual visible, making visible the dignity of each person who shares the space where we live. Our work investigates how private psychologies affect and constitute public space and vice versa. We understand art as a subversion of culture, in order to create a field of action where the meanings and the state of things are constantly revised.

We operate in direct activist situations in public space and also in art events. We consider it important to do both and as often as possible directly connect these fields of artistic activity. The experiences and levels of dialogue raised in these two methodologies of bringing people together increase the level of perception and understanding among the involved groups, as well as extending the levels of reflection and production in contemporary art.

Below is a description of four collaborative projects with young people: one within the public school system of Zurich, Switzerland, focusing on identity and acquisition of language among immigrant kids, 1995; one with and about street kids in Rio de Janeiro, 1994-1997; one within two penal institutions (one for teenagers and the other for adults) in Atlanta during the Olympic Games, 1996; and finally one Art in Architecture project in Riem, Munich, in Germany. These four different projects illustrate the different methods and forms of operating collaboratively with youth in specific contexts, without leaving out our own doubts and fragility, which we consider to be important tools to communicate with people, especially young people.

inner services
Public art project and video installation, 1995
Swiss Public School System and Shedhalle Zurich, Switzerland

To complement the exhibition *Foreign Services (Aussendienst)* held at Shedhalle Zurich, which gathered artists working with foreign cultures as a subject for their art, our project *Inner Services (Innendienst)* was conceived to work in the gallery with about 280 children and teenagers who had recently arrived in Switzerland, all enrolled in the 'integration classes' of the Swiss public school system.

Workshops were held in each one of 25 classes spread throughout several public schools in Zurich during one month, in which certain perception exercises of smell and memory were introduced, departing from a repertoire of everyday objects and odours, like chocolate, toothpaste, deodorant and coffee among others. Games and questions were proposed in order to stimulate the memory of each participant, to make visible for them the existing connections between things and names, between memory/imagination and objects/odours. Afterwards, the students were invited to take part in an exhibition to include elements that they themselves would bring to the exhibition when coming to visit. The exhibition at the Shedhalle took form as the children's visits took place.

Dias & Riedweg,
Inner Services, Shedhalle
Zurich, 1995.

We asked each student when coming to visit the exhibition in the following month to bring four things with them: two objects or images that he/she associated with his/her homeland and two that they associated with Switzerland, the country to which he/she had immigrated at that time. Also two small glass bottles, each one containing a different odour: one that reminded them of the past in their country of origin and one that they associated with their present in Switzerland.

When arriving at the exhibition, the students saw a kind of classroom set-up inside the gallery, using real school furniture but arranged in a different way: the blackboard covered the whole perimeter of the space; the desks were placed in two rows in a corner and were covered with hundreds of small glass jars containing smells, small images and objects; in the centre of the space was a video camera, a microphone, a TV set and chairs of different heights. Each group of students sat around the camera that they operated themselves. One by one, they documented on video the process of workshops: each person described with eyes closed the smells and objects they had brought, the associations they made with their country of origin and their present life in Zurich. These descriptions formed video drawings of their individual memory and imagination, together forming an outline of their immigration process. The videos were kept permanently running in the room with the bottles of odours, objects and images, so that visitors could make their own connections through the project.

These daily meetings with groups of students at Shedhalle can be seen as performances or as single documented encounters. What matters is the description of each student in relation to his/her chosen objects and smells, a true memory, a battle of the senses with the need to speak, to express oneself through language. It is also important to notice how the immigration process is able to transform the identity of a person through the acquisition of a language which itself brings along a new system of meanings and, therefore, a new identity. These moments were often charged with extreme intensity and frailty – the need and the challenge of expressing oneself from the inside out – we were providing an inner service.

In order to record these moments, the students were invited to write with coloured chalk, in any way and in any language they wanted, on the gallery's walls, transforming them into a blackboard. These might simply be word associations with the smells they have brought or suggested by words written by others, such as coffee – cup – table – kitchen – mother – Turkish. By the end of the exhibition a single, large network of words in over 40 languages and several alphabets, whose meanings were interconnected, could be read around the perimeter of the gallery. By the exhibition's close, over a thousand small bottles and small things had been brought to be seen, opened and felt. After the exhibition, the objects were given back to the classes. (We don't keep objects or props, just the digital documentation of these elements in all the projects, with the exceptions of *Question Marks*, where the license plates were given out to the public in street performances during the show, and of *Devotionalia*, where the plaster moulds and wax castings forming an installation were donated as permanent exhibits to the National Museum of Fine Arts of Rio de Janeiro).

Devotionalia
Public art project and video installation, 1994-1997
Streets, favelas and the Museum of Modern Art, Rio de Janeiro

Devotionalia began as a mobile studio for street children and teenagers in Lapa, a downtown neighbourhood of Rio de Janeiro. The inclusion and collaboration of several social workers and NGOs, who work permanently with street children and teenagers, allowed the work to be extended through 1995 to 18 localities of Rio. Over 80 hours of videotape were used to record the making of 1,286 ex-votos – white wax copies of the feet and hands of over 600 children and teenagers who participated in the project. The metaphor of the ex-voto was chosen as its meaning was widely recognised by the young participants (a great number among them carry some kind of amulet or object they believe to bring luck and protection to their lives). While the ex-voto, in its religious tradition, is a symbol of gratitude for a granted grace, the amulet expresses a desire, a dream, a request and also a need. Each participating child made a copy of his/her own foot or hand with clay, plaster and paraffin wax as the basis for their ex-voto. Each ex-voto carries a personal wish, which was documented on video. The objects and videos formed an installation, a great collective ex-voto deposited in an art museum instead of in a church – not for God, but for Society, which is critical in the context of a Christian country such as Brazil. The displacement of these ex-votos from religious to cultural territory seeks to open new paths for reflection on social policies and artistic experiences.

From January to March 1996, *Devotionalia* was exhibited at the Museum of Modern Art, Rio de Janeiro. Approximately 3,000 people attended the exhibition's opening and at least half of them were from slums and poor communities where we had worked, mostly children and teenagers, entering the space of an art museum for the first time. The exhibition generated a public debate among well-known agents of culture and social work in Rio de Janeiro. After this, *Devotionalia* was exhibited in Europe in five venues: Museum of Modern and Contemporary Art, Geneva; Kaskadenkondensator Experimental Art Center, Basel; Lucerne's Medieval Market – Kornschütte; Stroom Center of Contemporary Art, The Hague; and during UNESCO's fifth International Conference on Adult Education in

top: Dias & Riedweg,
Devotionalia plaster casting,
Lapa neighbourhood,
Rio de Janeiro, 1996.

bottom: Dias & Riedweg,
Devotionalia installation,
Museum of Modern Art,
Rio de Janeiro, 1996.

Hamburg 1997. In each of these exhibitions, European children and teenagers responded to the ex-votos and videos made by the children in Rio de Janeiro with new videos and objects produced or brought in during workshops and debates.

Two years later, back in Rio de Janeiro, with the original material plus the new objects and images made by European children, we tried to find the same children and teenagers who participated at the beginning of the project. Many were dead. Many rejoined the project. New meetings and workshops were held in the original 18 localities. *Devotionalia* was concluded in 1997 with two simultaneous events: a final exhibition at Salão Negro, the main entrance to Brazil's National Congress building with the presence of several deputies and senators, and a happening under the Arches of Lapa, attended by more than 1,000 children.

From the exhibition's opening in the Congress to the date of the concluding event in Lapa, a daily series of video conferences were held via Internet between 18 federal deputies and senators from the National Congress in Brasília, and children and members of communities and voluntary organisations in Rio de Janeiro who took part in the project. These video conferences connected virtually, two territories in reality entirely apart. In the concluding event, the federal government announced a grant for a programme of a hundred permanent scholarships from the São Martinho Foundation to benefit 100 young people in Rio de Janeiro, in exchange for the donation of the art piece to the Ministry of Culture. Unfortunately, the government cut the scholarship programme six months later; the work is in a storage facility of the Ministry of Culture waiting to be placed in a public collection.

Question Marks
Public art project and video installation, 1996
Conversations at the Castle, Atlanta Arts Festival, USA

Question Marks was a project about communication and art conducted by two groups of prisoners who didn't previously know each other: a group of ten adult prisoners serving long-term sentences in Atlanta's Federal Penitentiary (one of the USA's largest maximum security prisons) and a group of 30 teenagers who were in a detention centre, the Fulton County Child Treatment Centre. For three months a communication process between these groups was developed through regular exchange of videos created in a series of workshops designed to sensitise them towards their own situation. From these videos, two installations were developed as well as some street performances aimed to communicate the project to the public at large.[1]

To get access into the Federal Penitentiary of Atlanta, the only possible way was through the psychiatrist of the institution who managed to persuade the warden to involve a group of ten prisoners in the art project *Question Marks*. The director of the youth detention centre agreed to the children's participation in the project based on the belief that this interaction between the groups could increase the level of self-criticism in both groups, especially among the youngsters. Guards and cameras were present at all times in these workshops.

Every day we held perception workshops with the prisoners of both institutions. The sessions were based on exploring associations between the senses of smell, touch, hearing and the body with memory and imagination. For the first workshop on smell, we brought jars filled with familiar smells such as after-shave, honey, disinfectant, shoe polish, earth, lime, cocoa butter, yeast,

Artists and schools: interventions in education systems

soap, toothpaste, mint, herbs, tobacco and cinnamon. We asked the participants to close their eyes and smell the jar without knowing what was inside. In order to stimulate their memory and imagination, we asked them to associate the smell with a place or situation, encouraging individual descriptions and images. The results formed drawings, sometimes connected to the memory of a lived situation, sometimes to imagination. They made drawings without using paper or pencil, visual descriptions that expressed texture, colour, size, light, situation, temperature, etc., that surpassed the limits imposed by the lack of visual and plastic material inside the prisons.

The second workshop came from theatre and performance exercises relating to space and the use of the body. These exercises, mostly done collectively, had the side effect of developing trust and understanding between the participants and also with us.

For the third workshop we brought tape recordings of daily life sounds and based on these, participants described places and actions on paper, such as: washing dishes, using the bathroom, a radio playing, birds, dogs barking, a door bell, a phone ringing, cars, someone singing far way, children, a door slamming, keys, footsteps on sand, footsteps on the sidewalk, footsteps inside home, as well as an 11 minute tape of waves breaking on a beach. While listening to this tape, the participants drew the rhythm of their pulses with their eyes closed.

For a workshop on touch we brought 15 cardboard boxes, each containing a different material. The boxes had a hole through which the contents could be touched without being seen. We asked the participants to touch and then associate the content of each box to a part of his neighbourhood, and then describe it. The materials in the boxes were feathers, satin, earth, sponge, jelly, ice, plush, tree cork, sand, vaseline, dry leaves, flour and metal. Again, sensations were followed by complex visual descriptions stimulating each participant's memory and imagination to increase self-awareness and the understanding that artistic activities may be a means for political and personal expression.

In parallel to these experiences and descriptions, participants made a series of floor-plan drawings of the places in which they spent their lives. Each one tried to remember and to draw whatever they could: the room, the house, the neighbourhood, the tribunal, the prison, the cell. While drawing, the participants narrated stories and facts about these places:

> (the room): individuality, privacy, desire.
> (the house): family, the past, childhood.
> (the neighbourhood): community, relationships, friendship, love, drugs, the Other.
> (the tribunal): crime and sentence.
> (the prison): imprisonment, crime, society, justice.
> (the cell): communication, art, present and near future.

These drawings created a larger context for communication and debate between the two groups of prisoners, revealing possibilities for both groups to reflect and express themselves through video. The relation between 'I and the world, I and the Other' was regularly revisited and discussed in each prison, and these conversations were taped and brought to the other institution. In this way, the two groups learned little by little about each other, which triggered an exchange between the groups that has become the project's main axle.

Dias & Riedweg,
Question Marks
license plates,
*Conversations
at the Castle,*
Atlanta, 1996.

The teenagers were invited to write down some of the questions brought up by the debates and to paint them on car license plates. The idea was to identify whatever mattered most from the conversations, choosing questions that would be brought to society by hanging them on cars. Instead of licence plates with numbers, we brought 350 license plates that were empty apart from a white frame indicating the name of the project and the two participating institutions. The plates were brought to the teenagers empty, like blackboards, for them to write questions they wanted to raise with society in their own handwriting. In Georgia, cars carry only one official license plate, placed on the back, which allows the front space on a vehicle to be a potential space for publicity. Each plate used by the teens to paint their questions was later fixed on the front of a car and circulated around the streets of Atlanta. Another connection is that the official license plates of cars for the whole country are made by prisoners through a system of forced labour in State jails. The fact that the teenagers painted on license plates, an object the American general public normally associates with prisons, was a critical allusion to the sad reality that 75 per cent of the teenagers in detention later in their lives become prisoners.

License plates could in this way personify the prisoners and bring the questions of young people and prisoners to public space in an open and investigative way. The painted license plates were given out on the streets. Here are some of the questions:

Are you who you say you are?
Whom should I fear?
Am I bad or what?
What do you want to know about me?
What do you first see when you open your eyes in the morning?

artists and schools: interventions in education systems

Each one of the 350 plates painted during the workshops contained an issue raised during the discussions. Each issue is a question mark, a non-answered critical question from a prisoner to society, a prisoner as a member of society claiming to recover his place within it.

Along with the drawings and the plates, a gigantic nest was made as the conversations took place. The nest was a metaphor for home. It was the nest of an African weaverbird, known for sharing a large nest with other birds, a collective nest made by several birds at the same time and containing subdivisions scientifically known as cells. During six weeks, participants wove coconut fibre and strips of shiny acetate over a large metal structure to make the nest. On each acetate strip was written a question for society. The nest's final shape resembled a jack-fruit, golden, gigantic and hairy. The nest formed part of the installation *Question Marks* in the exhibition *Conversations at the Castle* in Atlanta, 1996. It was hung from the ceiling, the floor was covered with water reflecting the nest's image, and the public could see in only through a small food hatch. Slides were projected on the outer wall with questions written by the teenagers:

How many times a day you can enter and exit your room?
Do you have kids?
Are you patient?
Does your mother make Christmas cookies for you throughout the year?
Sometimes do you also feel guilty?
Did you put me in to leave me out?

The impossibility of directly seeing the real nest aimed to suggest the difficulty of seeing the reality of a prisoner. It represented the distance between society and prisoner, the darkness this situation provokes. From the outside one could only see a reflection, a projection of its reality.

A second slide installation was made of the license plates and of the floor plan drawings and the video from the workshops and conversations among prisoners of both institutions.

During the exhibition, three street performances were held to distribute and hang car number plates on the cars of Atlanta. The first one happened on the street in front of the *Castle* during the exhibition opening. The second took place in one of the city's poorest neighbourhoods, from where many of the children in the Treatment Centre originally came. The third and last place was Piedmont Park, Atlanta's main public park, where the city's inhabitants come on their weekends.

Dressed as garage men, we spread the plates on the ground and approached people passing by, explaining to them the project and proposing to fix a plate on their car. 350 plates were distributed amongst Atlanta's inhabitants, some on cars, others on bikes, and some were sent by mail to addresses given by the prisoners. These plates turned out to be effective means for transporting messages out of the prison back to society, beyond the territory of art. From objects of art they turned into political/poetical marks in public spaces, questions for all of us. Provocations. Complaints. Question marks.

Kenneth L Rogers, one participant in *Question Marks* and for 18 years prisoner number 18224-008 of the Federal Penitentiary of the United States of Atlanta, wrote the following:

I believe Art is an essential reflector of Culture. I also believe that the several forms of artistic expression allow me to experience a vast field of emotions, both conscious and subliminal. They allow me to celebrate the excellence of human creativity, of which I feel myself as a vital part. Art serves to educate and/or make me sensible in face of the foreign. It works as a conductor, connecting me to both tangible and not universal elements. Art is a transcendental vehicle that obliterates political doctrines, territorial borders, religious dogmas and ethnical exclusivity. Art helps me to remember the power that exists in the manifestation of positive and creative energy.

marble and iron break

Public art project in Kunstprojekte Riem, Munich, Germany, work in progress

This is a long-term project begun in January 2002 with the invitation of the curator Claudia Büttner, to work in collaboration with architect Jan Spreen, responsible for the construction of the new Centre for Special Education of East Munich. After having visited the area and seen the architect's plans, it was proposed to work with the children and teachers of Riem's public primary school, soon to be merged with this new Center for Special Education. Many children and teachers working with us on this project would move into the new school in 2005.

A series of sensorial workshops was developed with children and their teachers in which everybody involved tried to connect smells to memory, images and objects, provoking associations with their own experiences and senses. Later, they each brought objects and images that they had chosen connected to a personal story. In this way around 500 objects and images were collected which were digitally photographed, to be set in under-floor lamps to light the entrance and playground of the new school, starting on the pavement outside the new building and finishing in the inner courtyard where the children have their playtime. We decided to work solely in the floor and not on the walls, because children very often walk looking to the floor. This intervention starting on the street and going to the inner yard, will signal the way to school.

A second intervention complemented this and consisted of words, phrases and drawings from their stories made directly on blackboards, digitally enlarged and then sandblasted onto the window facing the playground, fragile drawings and words of the children in their own handwriting. The glass surface remains transparent, revealing only now and then a fine opaque line that constructs a word or drawing. The children's individual world finds a sanctioned place in the fabric of the school.

The whole process of the sensorial workshops with the children's stories and the process of construction of the new school were videotaped and edited into a final DVD installed in the school library.

Collaborative Art Projects with Young People

In the early 1990s, we both worked as teachers in the Swiss public school system to pay our way as artists, and therefore were very much interested in creative and interactive praxis with children and young adults. What made us actually connect our careers as artists and our careers as teachers was, on the one hand, feelings of dissatisfaction that we often experienced within the boundaries of possibilities to develop creativity in the school system; on the other hand was the constant feeling of dissatisfaction that we had within the art system. The daily contact with youth at school was vibrant and essential to challenge things. We conceived the *Devotionalia* and the *Inner Services* projects very much based on these needs; these projects mark the change in our formerly separate careers as artists. It was equally important for us to develop our interactive praxis with youth to develop our artwork. We searched for an open territory where we could start some alternative examples of art and education that could free us and free the kids – from the school institution and from the art market, from the direct goals of education and the competitive and repetitive methods of the art world.

Our first three projects dealt with youth as collaborators (the third was *Question Marks*). Due to the surprisingly receptive reaction that these three projects got from the media, from the art world and other social categories, we soon felt trapped again in the category of art educators. We denied this reading of our work and tried to get rid of the often-used adjectives used by critics and institutions to define our praxis, such as helpers, healers, ex-teachers and even activists. We insist on our position as experimental artists working with collaborative methods, with no defined goals. The goal is the experience itself and what each one gets out of it, artist, collaborator, children or adults. It is not definable by anyone, certainly not by ourselves. The attempt to separate subjectivity from politicisation is an old hypocrisy of the intelligentsia, which is smoothly beginning to be unmasked through continuous experimental praxis in interdisciplinary fields worldwide today.

We believed then, and still do, that the power of these experiences lay exactly in the fact that every participant is free and responsible to judge if he/she wants to take part in it, and what he/she will get out of it. We have observed a huge range of difference in the levels of participation and satisfaction that people feel, which we always try to respect. This is one possible criterion that we use ourselves to evaluate these collaborations, although we try always in parallel to consider the criteria of how the experience of this group will be perceived by others. The real evaluation we consider the most important is the dialogue between the participants and the society which includes/excludes them, we try to make this visible in every art collaboration we design and co-execute.

1 The project was documented in the book *Conversations at the Castle*, Homi Bhabha and Michael Brenson, Cambridge, MA: MIT Press, 1997.

adaptation for change:
The southwark Educational
Research project O+I

The Artist Placement Group (APG), one of the most radical experiments in art history, was founded in London in 1968 by the artists John Latham and Barbara Steveni. In 1986 APG was renamed O+I (Organisation and Imagination) and has continued to seek societal change through the medium of art. Within their practice, art is seen as a strategy to define and use an independent position within national, regional and local structures responsible for shaping the future. These include government departments but also educational institutions and commercial organisations. O+I re-evaluate the relation between art and society through working in collaboration with other artists on researching and developing sustainable concepts and tactics. The aim of the Southwark Educational Research Project carried out between 1989 and 1990 was to establish a critical reflexivity within the Inner London Authority's Education Department. This project took place at a key moment in time, when responsibilities for education were gradually being devolved from a London-wide body to the new Local Education Authorities while introducing a new National Curriculum. Negotiated between the Inner London Education Authority (ILEA), O+I and the London Borough of Southwark during the latter months of 1989 it was piloted in Southwark, a typical contemporary inner city borough. O+I were asked to address the structural changes within the education system from the perspective of contemporary art, its role and function in education and its relevance to motivation and learning in general. In particular O+I were encouraged to engage with the issues identified in ILEA's report *Education for All*, such as the big fall-out of pupils from further and higher education.

The Southwark Educational Research Project set a precedent by providing a prototype for artists engaging with government departments and their decision-making process. It demonstrated how artists' propositions and suggestions can not only be taken forward but also effect change, in this

Inner London Education
Authority meeting, County
Hall, London.

particular context, in the future delivery of education as a whole. Over many
years O+I has undertaken a series of such 'placements', in which artists are
placed within industries or government institutions, accessing and intervening on
all levels of management. Maintained through all O+I projects is a methodology
rooted in context and based on an open brief and a series of negotiations. The
artist is paid through O+I with money from the host organisation, has access
to the organisation at boardroom level and is not obliged to make a specific form
of work in the first instance. These principles were outlined in the Whitehall
Memorandum negotiated by Steveni with the UK government in 1972, in which
a bilateral interest was agreed between artist and government activity. This
represents one of the greatest legacies of APG. When APG first evolved their
concept of placement in 1966, there was nothing similar with the exception of
the Gregory Fellowships at Leeds University, where an artist would be invited
to make art in a studio at the university with the intention of broadening both
art and other academic disciplines. Placements differed substantially from what
are now conventional residencies run on subsidies, without financial commitment
from the host organisation – which in O+I's view absolves both sides from
responsibility and significant engagement. The change in name of their
organisation from APG to O+I was to distinguish themselves from this emerging
version of placement known as 'residencies', which APG considered a certified
soft option, with reduced impact potential.

The idea of redefining art by changing the terms of reference, by
opening up new possibilities for the role of arts was not a new one. The Federal
Art Project in the USA, one of four cultural schemes of Roosevelt's Works
Progress Administration during the Depression, employed many politically
engaged artists keen to use art to promote social change. In Britain, the Council
for Encouragement of Music and the Arts (CEMA), established in 1939, forerunner
to the Arts Council of Great Britain (now Arts Council England), promoted
a similar vision of art's role in maximising popular participation in a cultural
democracy, an example of its activities being a series of concerts in factory
canteens. In the USA, at Bell Laboratories in the 1960s, artists were invited to
accelerate the possibilities of new innovations at a point where space travel and
computer interaction were transforming science fiction into reality, and at the
same time they sent scientists out into the workshops of artists through Billy
Kluver's new institution EAT, Experiments in Art and Technology. But what
set APG/O+I apart was in defining the artist as carrier and not exclusively as
maker of product.

The Project

Below are extracts from interviews with Steveni and Latham at their homes in Southwark, and a video interview, which comes from a series of interviews with teachers that formed part of the research project, which is held in the O+I archive:

Steveni: This project was unique in relation to the accepted idea of artists in schools, in terms of the way it was set up, how we worked across the schools, with the inspectorate, with the teachers, with six primary and six secondary schools. Our approach is to shift the received language-based thinking, to look at problems not even as problems, but to consider what the issues are from this different language base.

　　　We were operating in the field with the decision-makers, performing joined-up government in practice by linking children, teachers, education services as well as policy-makers. Margaret Thatcher was Prime Minister at the time. I went to the opening of a Henry Moore exhibition at the Royal Academy and Thatcher gave a speech in which she commented on Moore's wonderful, sensitive hands. I remember thinking, "Who writes her speeches?" I wrote a letter to her afterwards, dated 5 October 1988, commenting on her unexpected presence in an art arena and drew her attention to the fact that UK artists had set a world precedent by working in government departments with a newly-defined role, and asked her to recommend us to the relevant government agencies at Secretary of State level, offering a list of appropriate departments including the Department for Education. Through this route, our idea was taken up by the Secretary of State for Education and in discussion with them we decided to work with ILEA, this last Labour stronghold, at a time when it was being dismantled.

One of the key projects within the Southwark Educational Research Project was John Latham's *Recycle and Discuss*.

Latham: We felt we had something to offer, that we could ask them questions which most teaching staff could never get to. I introduced a routine, a practicality that could be put through any school. My instruction to the children was simply to go away and bring back five pieces of rubbish that are of no use any more. Bring them in and we'll put them in a pile. That brought in immediately the idea of rubbish, thrown away things, this was freedom to them, getting away from learning things. It raised the children's level of interest a lot. I remember one of the schools. I had two mornings with them. The first was to make something, the second to get articulate about what they had done. My interest was: how do you get to the beginnings of children's life, when they don't have responsibilities? What happens to their motivation when they are directed into things that they have to do in order to pass exams? Then they've lost something, something was very seriously different as soon as they had to think and belong to a body of behaviour, a body of understanding about a subject, which you had to conform to. It was very obvious that the secondary school mentality was a training in getting to think like the people they would have to compete with in the world of work, to do something worthwhile that they could get paid for – values that you felt were killing their creativity; they lost the fun of play.

In this project I feel that my imposition came in too quickly, the question of "What do you think you've done?" or "What do you think went on?" It was a very sophisticated question, which embarrassed them. They said the first day was the best day they had ever had at school, and the second day was the worst. I was saying they would have to be articulate about what they made for pleasure, and they had to speak in front of the rest of their friends about what they thought they'd done. It annoyed the teacher, because they'd had such fun in the first day and she thought it was a real downer to have to talk about it. It's a moot point. To be articulate is a great advantage. We need to have a language that makes sense. We are never given it. The originality factor has got to come across in the language. Only then is the person in full possession of their originality. Unfortunately, with *Recycle and Discuss* we didn't have the length of time it would have taken to develop the difference between verbal creativity and just making things.

Physical Education
(PE) class.

When going over the work that the groups had come up with, some of the kids were extraordinarily original. There was a black student, a black youth who made what I would recognise as African art, it was amazing that he chose things that had a kind of surprise element in them, objects with a haunting quality. It was amazing to me to find somebody living in England who instinctively came up with such a magical approach to objects. He got a lot of praise from me for doing a beautiful thing. At the other end there were people who made tanks. It was all from the pile of junk that had been brought in, they each took stuff from the pool and put it together to see what it suggested. They were provided with string, sticky stuff, I got access to all kinds of materials that could join things together.

There was a science course that I went to and played the *Recycle and Discuss* routine on them, and they got the hang of "How do we make it useful again?" I think it was more difficult to get them to do anything because they were already settled on some fixed idea. I could only classify it as 'clever', they wanted to be profoundly clever. What they needed to do was to forget usefulness, just to develop the look, the appearance of what could be done. The question came up of whether the activity was in fact technology, which meant 'not art'. It's like the school league system where schools are rated according to exam results, it frightens children into feeling that there is something that they ought to do which they don't understand and wouldn't understand, that only the grown-ups do. I think it's grown-up pressure.

Steveni: The inspectorate's preoccupations were with how to deliver a National Curriculum within a Borough where they were dealing with a high level of poverty and a lot of racial tension. We didn't know how we could contribute, but I guess they had nothing to lose by working with us. What I think we offered was new ways of identifying motivation, things that could keep kids motivated, which might keep them in learning – for example in *Recycle and Discuss*, we asked what they did and why they did things, why they put things together in certain ways. We also focused on observing, documenting and plotting the courses of motivation in existing classes such as drama and PE, using photography and video recordings, or for example making sound recordings of children's playground games.

What we did was about joining up what teachers were up against and students were up against. When we first went on-site the schools' headteachers on the whole had a preconceived idea of the role of artists in schools, as had been promoted by arts authorities, about introducing people to the making processes of artists, to bring out the possibility that children could make something. All this in spite of an announcement sent from the schools inspectorate that spelt out the difference of our approach with great care. So there was quite some negotiation to be done to overcome differences of expectation of what artists could offer, and we equally had to change our perceptions of teachers. The inspectorate sent out a form to the schools, then we visited each school to follow up, we had to build relations with teachers and see which teachers responded. In some schools it was a science group, not necessarily art classes, it depended on each school's inclination where and how they could bring us in. In some we worked with physical education – gym; some schools just wanted us to interview teachers. We appeared to get on well especially with the Chief Inspector of Schools in Southwark, and had regular meetings. Southwark funded us in kind by giving us a base at the library used by all Southwark schools. The O+I artist

'Stop and Search' drama project.

team were paid from ILEA remainder funds for which we were indebted to an inspirational ILEA member who had initiated *The ILEA Cultural Review* to examine the place of culture in education.

　　　　We recruited a team of artists: Robena Rose, a filmmaker; Carlyle Reedy, an artist poet and performance artist; Rita Keegan using photocopying techniques as visuals; Dave Carr did the camerawork for our video interviews, and John and I conducted the interviews. The teachers' responses ranged from being so completely swamped with their work that they were unable to cope and just wanted us to help them, to being resentful of us as we apparently had some freedom, which could interrupt their schedules. One school jumped onto the artist poet Carlyle Reedy and wanted far more than she was able to give in the time frame. With 12 schools and the inspectorate to deal with, we found we had taken on a great deal more than we could handle in paid time. I was adamant that artists would be paid at a commensurate rate to other professionals (this was one of the premises of O+I) but we could only do so much time on those rates. The Borough paid in kind by providing us with 'The Base' to work at. At the end we showed a series of films of our interviews at Southwark town hall using monitors provided by Granada TV and held a series of discussions. The presentation used the same format and approach as our 1970 Hayward Gallery show *INNO70* which was our first use of 'The Sculpture', a mock-up boardroom where artists met and discussed with industrialists and government ministers.

Latham: What this project allowed was something as much for the benefit of the teachers as it was for the children. The benefit for the teachers was to think up to date I suppose. I think they probably felt that there was something different and were pleased. I never met one who was grumpy except the one who didn't like my asking questions of each child in front of the others about what they'd done. The teachers tended to be very modest about what they'd done and couldn't talk about it. It was embarrassing because they didn't have great control of language. I thought our project would switch the teachers onto the need to encourage the children to say what they thought they were doing, to encourage them in conversation about it.

Harding: So what do you think about the government now trying to encourage young people to be more creative? What do you think that's all about?

Latham: I'm seriously concerned about what they think creativity is about. It's just another kind of mysticism which they've been taught to feel is a good thing, and then they find the boredom, of the same, the same, the same coming over the media. If it's the same you don't have attention. Attention doesn't go to repetition. Attention is always drawn to what's different. A kind of life force comes back.

Harding: Do you think the children in the schools went away recognising they had learned something special from this experience?

Latham: I think they would remember it. The ones who got something special from the making event would remember it either as something crazy that they would never do in real life, or some of them may have decided that that was the only thing they could think of to do, that they might set themselves up as artists.

The following excerpt is a sample of the research carried out for the Southwark Educational Research Project.

Video Interview With the Headteacher of Pilgrims Way Primary School, Southwark, May 1990.

Headteacher: We feel that many teachers are frightened of art, they don't see the breadth of art. Many teachers interpret it as just painting and drawing, we can help them bring out their ideas and work with them, to give many more children a chance. Kids don't have to be super intelligent for art. It can be multi-cultural, work across social divides. Few lower and working class children have the chance to handle materials. With the expertise of an artist and enthusiasm of a teacher we can give each child a chance to express themselves with different forms. Many children gather enormous kudos from being good with their hands, good at clay models. With the National Curriculum constraints, art is not looked upon favourably as it can't be measured.

We put energy in because we feel Southwark children deserve a better deal than they are getting from society in general. The area is unstimulating, parents are too busy, children are not taken out or stimulated. If we can put in stimulus, even if one child goes through and is totally stimulated, then it's a worthwhile exercise.

Latham: Do you recognise a crisis in education? Do you have anything to say about it?

Education has always been a political hot potato. The feeling for how important it is changes with each political party. It is not currently considered important. This will come to the front line with the next election. I worked for ILEA for many years. It was unwieldy, it needed restructuring, but not killing by political whim. Now things are worse, split into Boroughs which are too small, responsibilities have been given to people with no experience of it, it's almost half of the Borough's budget, and they are thinking, perhaps we can use the money for other things?

Children's lives are important. Money needs to be directed where it's needed. We're not a business with an end result you can market and sell. The rate of change has been too fast. Local management of schools means funding will be cut, children will suffer – these are political decisions. The last thing considered are children. Those with enough money buy private education. I was lucky I had the chance to go to a school with some well-off children in it. That would be ideal. That's what comprehensive education was about. Private means creaming off the fortunate children to Bakers and Haberdashers' Askes (selective schools in this area) at the expense of the state system.

Can you see a worldwide crisis of which this is a reflection?

Many countries don't value education highly enough. Britain is at the bottom of the pile in Europe. In Japan they extend education into the workplace. We must train people in order to have a better society.

Is there a possibility of a shift in terms of reference?

Political parties are getting much closer to each other now and all seem to realise that market forces govern our country. Even the Communist Party realise money and the market runs the world.

Photo collage by
Rita Keegan.

De- and Re-territorialising the classroom and art: wochenklausur in school, vienna, 1995-1996

Gerald Raunig

The Viennese group WochenKlausur has carried out interventions in the social
space on invitation from art and cultural institutions since 1993, when Europe's
boom in interventionist and participatory art practices began with projects
like Park Fiction, Minimal Club, Clegg & Guttmann, BüroBert, Ressler/Krenn,
Wohlfahrtsausschüsse, FrischmacherInnen and many more.[1] Abstractly formulated,
WochenKlausur's goal is to develop sustainable means for the improvement of
existing structures. The choice of themes arises from the topical issues of each
location without the influence of inviting institutions – and is, in principle, not
subject to restrictions (and not prescribed by themes from the art field). For a
time span of several weeks, six to eight artists usually with experience in other
professional fields as well (for example science, social and cultural work, economy,
political activism), meet in an intense "Klausur" (conference) and dedicate
themselves exclusively to site-specific and theme-related issues and the intervention
in specific structures. The "concrete interventions" – the group's own name for
their projects – have engaged with an extremely wide range of issues, such as
medical care for the homeless at Vienna's Karlsplatz, the interwoven issues of sex
work and drug use in Zurich, the social status of the elderly in Civitella d'Agliano,
Italy, the conditions at deportation centres in Salzburg, the situation of the
unemployed in Berlin, the limitations of voting rights in Stockholm, and raising
public awareness of subcultures in Helsingborg, Sweden. They have been invited
to make these projects by contemporary art institutions including the Vienna
Secession, the Shedhalle in Zurich, the Austrian Pavilion of the Venice Biennial,
the Steirische Herbst festival in Graz, Austria, NGBK Gallery in Berlin and the
Dunkers Kulturhus in Helsingborg.

In close collaboration with specialists in these issues, WochenKlausur
attempts to develop concepts for structurally effective measures, and to secure
financing to ensure sustainability of the solutions that they come up with. With

criteria such as efficiency, flexibility, multi-disciplinarity and project work, the group treads a line dangerously close to the central concepts of neo-liberal ideology, such as self-government and the pressure to succeed, confounding the distinction between social projects in general and social projects in art in particular. WochenKlausur's successful interventions achieve sustainable changes in organisational forms. Whereas in less precisely defined social projects, the mix of 'humanity' and 'flexibility' often cause any political effects to deflate into improvements for only a few individuals, here the principles of efficiency and temporary project structure are used to produce precise political (that is, structural and sustainable) effects. Of prime importance here is that structures are changed and models created for an improvement in production apparatus. In keeping with Walter Benjamin's idea, explained in his famous essay "The Author as Producer", that there is no political art production that uses the production apparatus without changing it, the work of WochenKlausur is about changing structures and apparatuses.[2]

In three exemplary projects WochenKlausur adapted this specific method to the system of the school. Later school interventions in Macedonia, 1999, and Japan, 2000, differ fundamentally in their interventional character mainly because those who acted intervened in structures with which they were largely unfamiliar, whereby the methods assumed a necessarily precarious and experimental character.[3] In contrast to these, the project described below took place in Vienna, on terrain that was very familiar to the WochenKlausur members.[4]

In close collaboration with students at the Viennese gymnasium (secondary school), Stubenbastei and on invitation of the Academy of Applied Arts, WochenKlausur redesigned the classrooms of a second and a seventh year class from November 1995 to March 1996. They did this according to the principle that the inclusion of the end users of a public space leads to significantly more satisfactory solutions in terms of functional and aesthetic design, than would exclusive delegation to specialists. WochenKlausur did not assume the position of experts in school furnishing, but instead sought the most pragmatic means to improve the situation structurally. This does not require a distanced expert knowledge nor the use of an abstract and universal 'common sense', but rather the collective work of bringing together the specific experience and knowledge of all people involved.

After some collective debates with students and WochenKlausur members, a decisive pivotal point was found, promising structural transformation rather than mere superficial treatment: students have no say when it comes to the design of the space in which they spend many years of their lives. And, even more so, in the spatial layout of the classroom and other school spaces they are confronted with a structure that they must grasp as a rigid prerequisite of their everyday life and as something unchangeable, untouchable, which was not even discussed as a topic. They sit on chairs which perhaps conform to standards, but are not ergonomic, and at tables that are built for top-down teaching. Wall decoration follows the path of least resistance and is entirely absent, apart from a crucifix and the picture of the federal president that watch over the students' learning process. Whereas teaching methods may have been gradually discussed and improved over the past 30 years, the territory of the classroom in Austria is still precisely arranged, apportioned and never questioned. For WochenKlausur, the issue that arises is composing a collective debate about this taboo, creating a rupture line, an opening: a de-territorialisation of the classroom space as an act that simultaneously reorganises the space and also the social organisation of the class.

In contrast to professional interior designers, WochenKlausur wanted to simply ignore the prescribed norms of interior design for secondary schools. Instead they asked students for their ideas and for what they required in terms of the arrangement of the room. The fact that regulations prescribe that the light must necessarily come from the left not only discriminates against left-handed persons, but also leads to a top-down teaching situation. Similarly absurd is that students of all different sizes sit on chairs that are all the same height.

The pupils sat in closely spaced rows facing a large green chalkboard. The lighting was harsh, the walls dirty. The coat racks in the back of the room were positioned so that the pupils in the last row often had to sit with wet coats and jackets at their backs in winter. Against this backdrop, the artist group initiated an open process for wish production for the classroom, concentrating on the seating arrangement and group work. With patience and long debates, particularly with the 12-year-olds in the second class, they sifted out the less feasible wishes such as bringing pets, concealed televisions, and jungle plants. Getting down to the less fantastic desires took some time and necessitated the use of indirect questioning. WochenKlausur invited the class to visit them at the University. They had hung up large photos of school classes around the world – from spontaneously organised African classes sitting outdoors to strict Japanese classrooms, which all look the same and are not heated in winter. Together they discussed the advantages and disadvantages of the various teaching situations; the kids rated each one and chose their top ten. Small groups were then formed to compare and contrast these with their existing classroom situation.

As improvements, the group built quarter-circle tables in four rows, arranged concentrically. This radial arrangement of the seats was more communicative and enabled a better view of the blackboard. In addition, the cloakroom was moved to the hallway and the space gained was transformed into a padded seating area according to the students' wishes. The lighting system was also improved to accommodate the new situation.

Classroom 1, model.

Classroom 2, model.

WochenKlausur collaborated even more intensely with 17-year-olds from the seventh-year class. This class, too, had a shortage of space. 18 practically fully grown adults had to make do with a mere 23 square meters. However, it was possible to make optimal use of this space with two round, concentric tables. The class's laborious process of deciding how to decorate the wall ultimately resulted in a painting in comic/graffiti style.

While the former 12- and 17-year-olds have long since graduated, their successors feel just as comfortable in the non-standard classrooms. Beyond the micro-political improvement of the school space, however, what shapes the work of WochenKlausur are meta-interventions in the art field. The group's projects evoke controversial discussion in a variety of possible contexts (project presentations in art institutions, reviews in art magazines, reflections in books, public debates about the conceptual change of art practices), generally in terms of the debate about the expansion of the concept of art, shaped by Constructivist considerations.[5] Even more concrete is the meta-intervention in the artists' concept of efficiency. Whereas the common cliché is that the realm of art is the last bastion of non-effectiveness, WochenKlausur overtly affirms the concept of neo-liberal efficiency, which assumes that in art practices, too, such as those of WochenKlausur, certain goals can be concealed, achieved, and examined: for those who create and love conventional art, this is a provocation of unparalleled proportions. The stream of de- and re-territorialisation in the WochenKlausur projects concerns not only the classroom, students, and social organisation of a class, but also the expansion of the borders of the art field, and thus the constant and offensive treatment of the question of what art is, and what it will be.

1 For a general introduction, see the group's website: http://www.wochenklausur.at/projekte/menu_en.htm, and also Gerald Raunig, *Charon. An Aesthetics of the Grenzüberschreitung*, Vienna: Passagen, 1999.

2 Raunig, Gerald, "The Author as Traitor", http://www.republicart.net/disc/aap/raunig07_en.htm.

3 See www.wochenklausur.at/projekte/11p_kurz_en.htm and http://www.wochenklausur.at/projekte/10p_kurz_en.htm.

4 See http://www.wochenklausur.at/projekte/05p_kurz_en.htm. Participating in this project were: Carmen Brucic, Simone Höller, Dominik Hruza, Pascale Jeannée, Felix Muhrhofer, Susanna Niedermayr, Stefania Pitscheider, Erich Steurer, and Wolfgang Zinggl.

5 See http://www.wochenklausur.at/texte/kunst_en.html.

Jef Geys school Projects
1960-2005

Jef Geys worked from 1960 to 1989 in his local school in the small town of Balen, Belgium, a school for eight- to 16-year-olds. His title was teacher of Positive Aesthetics, a term invented by Geys to describe what he proposed to contribute to the school. This was an entirely a unique position, set up with the support of an enlightened headteacher. Geys was given his own classroom and took the position on the understanding that he was under no obligation to attend school meetings. Instead he arranged for an assistant to prepare a monthly report accounting for his activity. Geys was interested in using his art practice to heighten young people's awareness of the world around them, presenting them with concepts and information through artworks normally considered only for adults. He engaged with the young people as intelligent individuals, democratising access to what he considered important current debates and artworks. His activity included borrowing the best of contemporary art from fellow artists and neighbouring museums to show in the classroom, including works by Lucio Fontana, Gilbert and George, Jan Vercruysse and many other well known artists of the day, which were installed around the room. He added a large wall frieze to the classroom in the mid 1960s which explained the difference between a Happening and an Environment – essential terminology which he felt was just as important for young people as it was to the rest of the art world. Geys collaborated with teachers of history and Dutch language to turn the playground into a large map of the world, an artwork that had clear educational benefits. This was against the express views of the geography teacher who felt that these small town children had no need to know about the wider world. Geys added some small and large footprints to the map, to enable children to gain a sense of scale and distance as they moved around the world. A notice board was set up beside the map for the display of current news cuttings, so that children could connect current news events with places on the map, to better understand their position in the world. They were all encouraged

to bring in news stories and then locate the events. In the classroom Geys put a large sheet of brown paper on which he regularly added questions collected from newspapers and magazines, collected on trips to the library. This series he called *women's questions*, to encourage viewers to consider whether there are questions that are only asked of women, in order to reflect on our own acceptance of stereotyping. Geys' determination to bring real world issues into the school agenda was an extended conceptual art project engaging with young people, teachers and the whole school community. Bringing real life into the school in this bold and exciting way made school life more lively and interesting to children, raising their interest in school and seeing the relevance of learning, which may arguably have helped their engagement in standard lessons across the school. One project designed in 1966-1967 but not then put to use was the *Feelings Play Box* (*Gevoelsspeeldoos*). Ten of these boxes were made, each containing a collection of colourful blocks, cylinders and rods, and cubes made of different materials (wood, cardboard, stone, feather, fur, etc.). The boxes were designed for use in schools, where children should be free to interact with them. Only in 2005 was the project finally put into use in the school system of Eindhoven in the build-up to a major exhibition of Geys' work at the Van Abbemuseum.[1] Geys' intention was that the boxes be used across the whole spectrum of the education system, with all ages from nursery to technical college, including special schools, all religious denominations as well as non-denominational schools, Montessori and Jena plan Schools. He was interested to see how the boxes would be used differently in the varying educational contexts. He carefully prepared a letter with the museum which was sent to a random cross-section of schools, explaining that the museum wished to be more involved in the city and inviting schools to introduce the box into their classes and to document its use. This was remarkably the first time that the education department of the Van Abbemusem had ventured out of its own building into schools, and also the first time that the museum's curator and head of education had worked together on a project, as normally the formal labour divisions of the institution kept them apart. It seemed amazing that this museum, world renowned for its conceptual art projects, had along with a group of similarly prestigious contemporary art museums across Europe until now avoided closer involvement with local schools; one can only assume that neither the institution nor the other exhibiting artists had been interested in this engagement. It seems no coincidence that this re-invitation of Geys by the Van Abbemuseum coincides with a newly found desire amongst institutions to appear accessible. The one-off museum project going into schools prompted by Geys and the collaboration between museum departments may be indicative of a new era for such art institutions. What was not stated in the communications with schools, which may seem rather problematic, was that the museum intended to present their documentation (video and photographs of the box in action) later in Geys' exhibition. Geys and the museum were interested to learn from how the schools and children use the kits, and were keen to avoid documentation being carefully stage-managed in the knowledge that it would be displayed in a prestigious museum. They wanted to maintain focus on the process of engagement, the acting out of the proposition made by the boxes. An arm's length approach was maintained to be less intrusive than visits to schools by artist, education department or curator, carefully letting the art function on its own merits as a conceptual artwork, where the set of instructions and how they are carried out is of interest. The box indicated that children can be entirely open to the propositions of conceptual artworks, more so than adults, who can have all sorts of preoccupations about whether something is art or not. Children will readily get on with exploring a concept or proposition if it is interesting and can be very inventive with it. This is what interests the artist, to see the ideas being played with, which is essential to the completion of the work, which a static museum display would not allow.

On my visit to a Year 4 class (aged eight to nine) at a Roman Catholic primary school in Eindhoven, a group of boys played with the box in a corner of the classroom while the rest of the class sat reading books at their tables. This calm and well-behaved class of approximately 22 children made good use of the box kit, which was allocated by lottery to a different group of children each day, who would get half an hour to play with it. On this particular day there were only boys working with the box, on a very co-operative building or design project, sharing advice, suggesting solutions to each other and problem-solving as a group. They showed me the way in to their space, which involved tunneling under a desk into their own world. Geys was interested in how different types of schools and group dynamics might deal with the box in a variety of ways. The impressive mutual co-operation which I witnessed, could be due to a rather homogeneous community or to the relaxed and productive atmosphere set up by an experienced teacher. The teacher said that he would be very pleased to keep using the box, which was in its second month of a three month stay. The children referred to the kit as the *Feel Box*, which is their adaptation of the original *Feelings Play Box*.

With today's renewed interest in the democratising of art practices, several of Geys' works have been revisited. His playground map was remade for a school playground in Bruges in 2002. *Colouring Books for Adults (Kleurbook voor Volwassenen)*, originally developed between 1963 and 1965, was reactivated for the exhibition *Performative Installation 3, Spaces of Communication* at the Museum für Gegenwartkunst in Siegen, Germany in 2003-2004. The colouring books feature seven motifs, such as car, maps, house, soldier, a woman's and a man's body, which emphasise the standardisation of visual culture. For the exhibition, reprinted colouring books were distributed to 99 children and teenagers in the schools of Siegen, who were each given two books to colour. One set they signed to be exhibited at the museum, the other was signed by Geys and then returned to the students to keep. Geys viewed this exchange of signatures as proof that they are equal authors, acknowledging that artists are invariably indebted to or inspired by other people's images. The children are experiencing highly conceptual propositions about intellectual property, authorship and collaboration and their participation is fully part of this conceptual work, not an add-on workshop after the show is installed. The colouring books were exhibited together with the original version of the books and large panels painted by the artist from the 1960s using the same motifs. Geys' work has remained underexposed internationally perhaps due to his preference for social, very local contexts and his insistence on working in Flemish language rather than the art world global language. His self-contextualising publications, such as the Kempens series of broadsheet magazines, produced on the occasion of each major project, often further problematise and complicate, rather than demystify the work. He remains an uncompromising conceptual artist who considers children fully conversant with his conceptual propositions.

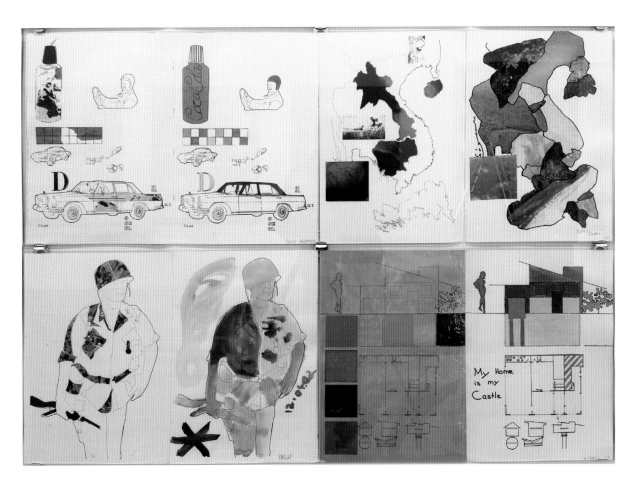

Jef Geys, *Colouring Book for Adults*, 1964, re-presented in *Performative Installation 3*, Siegen, Germany, 2003.

1 A previous scheduled show at the museum in 1971 was
  cancelled due to sensitivity of content. Rather than use
  the word pornography the city declared that the museum
  was not the place to do sociological work.

Artists and schools: interventions in Education systems

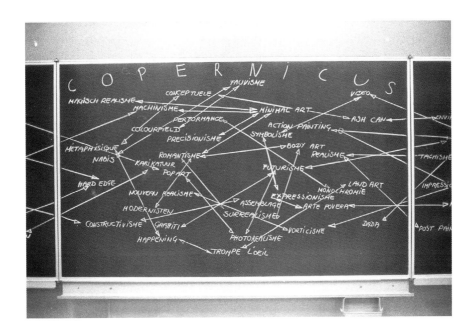

Artists and schools: interventions in Education systems

three

Aim Higher

out of and Beyond school

Working with young people who have largely opted out of conventional education, artists David Harding and Tim Rollins have acted as personal mentors to raise aspirations and in their accounts take great pride in the young people's subsequent achievements. They both speak from years of first-hand experience in impassioned accounts. Rollins' text is based on a public lecture given at a conference where he was speaking to an audience of fellow arts educators, while Harding's considered text reflects on lessons learned across a whole career and passes on invaluable advice to young artists embarking in this area for the first time. Kristin Lucas is a video artist whose interest in young women and technology as subject matter led to a collaboration with FACT in Liverpool in which a selection of girl bands were given the opportunity to develop song writing and performance skills which are featured in Lucas' new video work. Lucas' project is one of a series of fruitful community collaborations that have been developed by FACT to raise the aspirations of communities in Merseyside. A contrasting approach is presented by Tate Liverpool's collaboration with corporate sponsor, Rolls-Royce: their sponsorship and education departments worked together to devise a project based on the resources of the Tate, in which engineering apprentices training at Rolls-Royce were encouraged to develop a creative edge through the new skills acquired in working together to make and exhibit artworks. The Rolls-Royce apprentices were described before this project as stuck in conventional thinking due to schooling which resulted in a reluctance to stand out or speak out. In contrast, two image sections represent projects by Johan van der Keuken from 1957 and Christian Dorley-Brown from 1994-2004 give dignity to the emerging maturity of young people. These two artists capture a self-confidence and stature that artists have recognised in these young adults.

work as if you live in the
early days of a better society!
David Harding

Harding's socially engaged artwork in Scotland since the 1960s offers an exemplary practice for artists engaging in social inclusion today. With social inclusion in the arts high on the political agenda, his insights and experiences can assist contemporary artists who have similar ideals and convictions as artists of the 1960s and 70s. Harding argues that while new strategies are always being developed and practices evolving and becoming more sophisticated, there is no need to re-invent the wheel. He also looks for evidence of what good these projects did.

In the three decades after the Second World War many people believed that working for a better society would help to bring it about. As the years passed this did seem to be the case; things did get better. Now it seems that as each year passes things get worse. In place of that idealism, I find a cynical acceptance that, despite the great efforts of many groups and individuals, society will continue to fragment; the rich get richer and the poor get poorer and more marginalised. In his book, *Deschooling Society*, Ivan Illich pointed out that the major losers in education come largely from the less well off majority whose taxes actually pay for our educational systems.[1]

Imbued with that post war idealism, many artists directed their creative energies towards marginalised communities. They saw involvement in art as liberating and transformative and often best experienced outside the strictures and structures of formal education. In the early 1980s, when I taught on the Art and Social Contexts course at Dartington College of Arts, my advice to students going on placement was, "Don't set up a placement in a school!" This advice sounds perverse – schools were at least places where art was taught. But in my experience they often held very fixed presumptions about what art was and often students would be expected to carry out those presumptions. The aims for the placement were much broader than that. I further advised that, "If you want to work with

David Harding with Hugh McNulty at the Molindinar gable end mural, Blackhill, Glasgow, 1987, photograph by John Mackay.

teenagers, don't go into schools but engage with them on their own territory." For those young people for whom school was an alien, adversarial setting it would be better to engage with them out of the school environment and not on the limited terms offered by schools. I am not however claiming that it is fruitless for artists to work with and in schools. I, and many other artists, have worked on very successful projects in schools. However working with young people out of school on their territory could often realise projects that would be impossible in a school setting.

Another piece of advice I would give to my students was, "Offer a gift to the host setting." A gift in kind like doing a poster for a club sets up a two-way exchange. Anthropologists say, "the gift is not free" and often a gift will open up opportunities for more ambitious projects.

There is something special about artists working in public. It's an acknowledged fact attested by numerous artists that, when their work demands

work as if you live in the early days of a better society!

that they do it in a public, unregulated space, it begets a special experience. This has something to do with display and with the spectacle of performing one's skills in public. It becomes an event. It catches the gaze and interest of the casual passers-by. It has something to do with the resulting interaction with those passers-by and the frisson of excitement that derives from that engagement. It has something to do with making a visual contribution to and making a mark on a place adding to a stronger sense of that place. Often those places are either blighted by decay or by a numbing uniformity, the kinds of places where one never goes for a stroll just to enjoy and get to know them.

If these experiences mean something special to artists, then for young people working in similar settings, in unregulated public places, there is an equivalent if not enhanced experience of performance, identity, contribution, engagement and exchange. For this reason it has always seemed to me that contributing 'legitimate' marks to the surfaces and spaces of the public and built environment and, even more specifically, to one's own neighbourhood, taps into some of the things that prompt the often (though not always) alienated impulses for making graffiti or carrying out acts of vandalism. Working with artists in this way offers otherwise alienated young people the opportunity for performative display, attracting attention both to themselves and to their work. For some it can also be a transformative experience. This is different to graffiti in one major respect. Graffiti is done anonymously and often the only audience for the action are friends as collaborators or onlookers.

In the 1970s and 80s, the most common vehicle for these kinds of art projects was the large mural. Many of the street murals of this period are much maligned and sometimes for good reason. Too many contain all the old clichés and are badly done. They often seem to have been done without imagination or conviction and simply to occupy the young people who have been told, "do anything you like", in a failed attempt at free expression. I learned that young people respond to planning, organisation and the aspiration to achieve something special. Because of its size the mural is ideal for collaboration. And by collaboration I do mean a shared responsibility among a group of people for the development of the ideas, the design and the execution of the work.

I have done numerous art projects with young people since I began working as an artist in the 1960s, some of which carried that very special experience of somehow having "stepped out of the box", of having offered something special to a group of young people, something they had not experienced before. I witnessed in them a serious and intense commitment and a display of skills which I had not seen before. I have no idea how it came about but I seem always to have had an instinctual belief that involving young people in art projects was a good and rewarding thing. This belief is of course not unusual. However, I learned that they carried with them the same frisson of excitement and sense of achievement from which I also benefited. By young people I do mean all kinds of young people. But on the occasions when they were alienated or excluded young people, and/or from poor backgrounds, then those experiences were heightened. Simply, it seemed that the rewards were greater on both sides.

I taught art in a remote rural part of Nigeria for four years in the 1960s. Here I adopted a policy of not exposing my students to European art forms or history. I did not teach general lessons on proportion, perspective, colour or composition. Instead I insisted that ideas should be drawn from the students' own lived experience. My bible at the time was, as may be deduced, Herbert Read's *Education Through Art*. 320 kilometres away, not far by Nigerian distances, was the nearest university. I made a visit to the Fine Art sculpture department and was surprised to see that all the students making replica sculptures of the Italian Modern, figurative sculptor, Marino Marini. This I regarded as cultural colonialism and it could not have been further from my aims for my students.

When, in 1968, I was appointed artist to the new town of Glenrothes in Fife, it was not part of my contract to do anything other than "my own work". This was defined in my contract as: to contribute to the external built environment of the town. I rented a council house in the town in order to experience new town living as most other people experienced it. A common criticism of architects at the time was that, while they were quite happy to design council houses for others, they would never themselves live in one. I chose to set up my studio in the corporation workshops among the plumbers, joiners, bricklayers, etc.. Later I was to become a member of UCATT, the building workers' union. All of these things were connected to the notion I had of identifying with the people of the town and the notion that the artist was not necessarily a special person. This role was the artist as artisan. The bricklayers were skilled in one way and I was skilled in other ways.

As an artist, making public art, I had already developed what could be described as a 'contextual' practice. I certainly wanted to contribute to the developing built environment of the town but also wanted to create opportunities for other townspeople to do so as well. The early new towns, of which Glenrothes was one, were mostly built on greenfield sites, and the citizenry imported. Thus new communities were struggling to form, with little shared history and tradition, and often with broken extended family relationships. It seemed to me that one of the areas in which an artist could operate was in creating memorable landmarks within the fairly uniform housing areas and the incorporation of 'marks', however small, by local people. I made contact with a number of primary schools each of which were located in specific identifiable neighbourhoods. I organised whole classes (the staff wanted to select those pupils deemed good at art to work with me) of primary school children in modelling their own individual ceramic tiles and signing them on the front. When fired they were cemented by each child onto walls adjacent to their local play areas. I felt in this small way that each child might achieve a certain identification with the place where they lived. (On a recent visit to the town this was confirmed to me).

Throughout my ten years in Glenrothes numerous participatory works with different groups were carried out by myself and other artists who came to work with me – a group of graffiti 'vandals', met and engaged with on the street, youth clubs and school groups. One secondary school group was described by the headteacher of the school as "unteachable". I had them out of school for two weeks to design and paint a mural in a pedestrian underpass. They were involved from the beginning of the project in developing the ideas and the form of the design. They worked on the project with enthusiasm and commitment. Some time later I happened to meet the headteacher at some function. He said to me that the pupils had returned to the school transformed. They had organised other mural projects in the school and had engaged positively with their studies in ways that would have seemed impossible before the project in the underpass. "What on earth did you do with them?", he asked.

work as if you live in the early days of a better society!

David Harding assisting children in cementing their ceramic tiles to a wall adjacent to their play area, Glenrothes, 1970.

What could have brought about this transformation? Firstly they were given respect, which is easier to do with 'problem pupils' when it is a two week project out of school, compared to having to deal with them week in week out in a school environment. But then this is one of the things that justifies art projects such as this. It is out of school and so the pupils do feel liberated and, in that mood of liberation, transformative things can happen. They shared with the artists the responsibility of developing the ideas, the form and the colour of the mural. They worked in a very public place making images about things that interested them. It was a performance under constant public scrutiny and often enquiry. I'm not talking about great art here, but a well-executed decorative rendering of a dull, blighted, concrete pedestrian underpass which itself was transformed. It was a simple design; there were no figures and, very importantly, no rainbows!

Augusto Boal, the Brazilian theatre director and founder of the Theatre of the Oppressed, gave this contentious advice to artists: "Never go into a community until it has articulated its need for you." If this seems extreme and idealistic then so be it. It's good advice, if only to say to artists "be cautious and be respectful". In the late 1980s just such an articulation was made to me as head of a new department in the School of Fine Art at Glasgow School of Art. A tenants' association approached me through their local housing officer asking if my students and I would paint a gable-end mural for them. They had a site and they had the money. Blackhill was a small housing estate and, as its name could be taken to infer, had a bad name for poverty, unemployment and crime. In fact it was often described as one of the worst areas of deprivation in Glasgow. (How often we have heard that description applied all over the country?). It was special too because 90 metres from the gable end was the home of the most notorious family in Glasgow. The house, an extended, over-elaborate, ostentatious fake of a place, was known as "The Ponderosa". But for all that, I found Blackhill to be a community of good people well served by the activities and concerns of, among others, the local minister and priest.

I've always regarded what we did in Blackhill as one of the most rigorous and productive examples of socially engaged art practice. Working closely with the tenants' group, public meetings and workshops were held and many ideas were discussed. The students, Nathan Coley, Alan Dunn and Meg McLucas, drew on these prepared proposals and presented them for discussion. Slowly the concepts and the design were refined and then approved at a public meeting. The gable-end was about 12 metres high, facing a large stretch of waste ground. Though the winter was on us and despite the cold, the wind and the rain, quite a few local people, and even the housing officer, took time to assist in the painting. Young people joined in at weekends. There were, however, two brothers aged 13 and 14, Hugh and James McNulty, who worked with us more or less continuously throughout the four weeks it took to complete the mural. Asked why they were not at school they simply replied that they preferred to work on the mural. They were serious about it and worked hard. One day James brought a comic strip he had created and drawn with a ballpoint pen in a school exercise book. He made several copies on the school photocopier and distributed them around the area. Two or three other issues of the comic were done. This achievement impressed us and we visited the brothers at their home nearby.

It would be difficult to exaggerate the poverty in which they lived. In the experience of working on the mural the two of them seemed to have found something that they felt good about and something with which they strongly identified. When the mural was complete they featured in the television and newspaper reports of the project. Locally, they were recognised as major contributors to the mural. It gave them status and pride. This seemed to me to be as important as the actual mural itself. The 'dedication' of the mural (always a crucial element in helping to embed the work into the local community) took place as part of the annual Christmas procession around the streets of the area. Later, unknown to me, the city council fixed top lighting to the mural wired to the street lighting. Thus at dusk the mural burst into light. It remained virtually free of vandalism and in excellent condition until the general demolition of the area 16 years later. (Recently a police inspector, whose work often took him to Blackhill, told me that the 'godfather' of the gangster family ordered that the mural was to be protected.)

Of the three students who worked on this project, Alan Dunn has carried out billboard projects in Glasgow, Newcastle and Liverpool among others. He co-founded *tenantspin*, an interactive internet and TV project with a group of pensioners in a Liverpool tower block which is now part of FACT, a media art project in the city. Nathan Coley exhibits works such as *Urban Sanctuary*. He proposed the idea of, and succeeded in becoming, the artist-in-residence at the trial, in The Netherlands, of the man accused of the Lockerbie bombing.

Around the same time I organised a mural project for my students in the Douglas Inch Centre in Glasgow, a school for excluded secondary school pupils. It seemed to go very well and, at the party arranged for the dedication of the mural, this was repeatedly endorsed. However, it was not until I had received a letter from the centre that the full implication of what had been achieved became clear to me.

work as if you live in the early days of a better society!

GREATER GLASGOW HEALTH BOARD

MENTAL HEALTH UNIT

THE DOUGLAS INCH CENTRE
2 WOODSIDE TERRACE
GLASGOW G3 7UY

18th Dec 1987

Mr David Harding
School of Art
Glasgow

Dear David,

Just a note to express, once again, our gratitude for all the help and co-operation we have received from you and the boys over the past month or so

There is absolutely no doubt about how worthwhile the project was. It was a huge success. Exactly how much each of the pupils got out of it is for each of them to say. All we know, is that never once, did any of them complain about having to go across to work with the boys. Neither did we hear any of them say that they were not enjoying the work, and, believe me, they would have been very quick to comment had this been the case

As for Joe, Euan and John, we really could not say enough in praise. Their management of the pupils (and us!) was superb, their sense of humour (and firmness when it was needed) invaluable. To have chronic truants, delinquents volunteering to come in on their day off was nothing short of a miracle

For us the "End of Mural" party on Thursday will remain one of the highlights of our teaching career.

Again, Love, many thanks. Have a lovely Christmas ~ New Year ~ Mary ~ Fiona

---

I often hear of 'magic moments' experienced by other artists working in social settings.

A friend, Rosie Gibson, writes from Edinburgh:

In 1977, as Arts Centre Co-ordinator for Craigmillar Festival Society, a peripheral housing scheme in Edinburgh, we set up an art project for local primary schools on the theme of monsters using construction and performance. The children were aged about seven and, over six weekly sessions, they built their constructions and then paraded them through the streets of the local neighbourhood. Most teachers left the children with us and disappeared, but one, Miss Knowles, from St Francis School, sat through every minute of every session to my chagrin. For six weeks I imagined how she was seeing what was going on – chaos, noise, lack of discipline, etc. etc.. At the end of the project, she asked if she could have a word with me. I expected the worst. But instead, she said she wanted to thank us. We had given her the opportunity to see another side of her class. Children who struggled in the classroom situation had flourished during the project and some children who shone in the classroom found the arts centre project difficult. She said it had been a privilege to be given this insight and she would take it back into the school situation with her. I felt surprised, pleased, relieved and humbled in waves.

Another friend, Chrissie Orr, writes from Santa Fe:

> Recently I was at a party and this tall young man dressed in black leather sporting piercings and tattoos kept staring at me. Eventually he came over to where I was standing and asked me if I remembered him. At first I did not but when he told me his name and I imagined him three feet smaller, then it all came back. Jason had worked with me on a mural project eight years ago. He had been struggling at school and life in general – an outsider to his peers as he dressed and acted differently. He had been through a lot of trouble. He worked hard with me and I challenged his creative spirit.
> He told me that he hoped that one day he would run into me again so he could tell me that I had changed his life. He was now touring the world in a rock band and being honoured for his style and creativity.
> He returned to his friends and left me staring into my glass of wine. When I looked up there was a woman of about my age standing next to me. She was Jason's mother, and she too wanted to tell me how being involved in the mural project had changed her son's life. She took my hands and thanked me in such a truthful way that I had a hard time keeping the tears back. I did not know what to say. I remained silent.
> Later I realised that I had been given the truest honour. What more could one want as an artist.

Social inclusion in the arts is not new. In fact it was the very essence of what many artists were up to in the 1960s and 70s. It went under the name of community arts. Disaffected youths, socially and culturally excluded, were a major focus for the activities of many of these artists.

Did it do any good? Difficult to say. One never really knows fully the results of what happens to young people when they've been exposed to a genuine experience of art. For the artists, the idealism and conviction about the role that art can play as a dramatic, transformative tool in changing the lives of people was sufficient for them to do it. It was sufficient for them because it was a morally and politically good thing to do. Certainly most of them could describe examples of how individuals they had worked with had changed perceptibly for the better.

Today, with social inclusion in the arts being high on the political agenda, it is timely to revisit the work of that period. In describing in some detail a number of projects in which I, and others, were involved, it may serve to assist artists today who have similar ideals and convictions as those artists of the 60s and 70s. While new strategies are always being developed and practices evolving and becoming more sophisticated, often using new technologies, there is no need to go back to the beginning to re-invent the wheel.

1 Illich, Ivan, *Deschooling Society*, London: Calder and
  Boyars, 1971.

work as if you live in the early days of a better society!

we are 17
ɟohan van der ᴋeuken

We are 17 is the title of a book of photographs by 17-year-old Johan van der Keuken
in Amsterdam in 1957, who also took it upon himself to design and publish the
book. Depicting his friends in self-consciously pensive, perhaps bohemian poses,
the group come across as self-aware existentialists, artfully composed. Today the
apparent maturity captured in their expressions and poses (sipping glasses of wine,
smoking pipes, reading poetry or contemplative introspection) and the serious,
accomplished tone of van der Keuken's photography of the friends around him is
striking. Van der Keuken persuaded a friend of his father, an educational publisher,
to publish the book and another friend's father, a well-known popular writer,
to contribute an introductory essay. The book caused outrage at the time of
publication amongst the Dutch Catholic moral majority and a Catholic youth
group in Nijmwegen in the South of Holland published a counter-book called *We
are Also 17*, depicting smiling, healthy youths, playing sports and ballroom
dancing. Van der Keuken's *We are 17* was re-published in 2005 in its original
format and the images presented here are taken from that series.

Aim Higher Out of and Beyond School

Aim Higher Out of and Beyond School

shape of ideas: Rolls-Royce apprenticeship training scheme with Tate Liverpool

Gillian Brent

In September 2003 Tate Liverpool and Rolls-Royce in Derby initiated a unique new corporate partnership that aimed to develop team-based approaches to creative thinking and learning for young apprentices. The programme was designed to complement and extend current practice in apprenticeship training, re-defining the parameters of entry-level engineering training. Within a business context, the *Shape of Ideas* project set out to create a new model of training that integrates the acquisition of technical and team-based skills with personal, critical and creative thinking skills, through the trainees' engagement with the work of artists. In a tightly organised schematic between two corporations, what does the artist contribute to and gain from the process and how do the trainers and apprentices benefit?

Rolls-Royce has been a long-standing supporter of Tate. They are a founding corporate partner of Tate Modern, and for the first three years that the building was open Rolls-Royce was one of its key supporters. This project came out of the idea that Rolls-Royce wanted to be more than a passive sponsor of the arts, to become more of an active partner. The project was conceived around a table with all parties present, all listening to one another, looking at what Rolls-Royce wanted to get out of it and what Tate Liverpool wanted to get out of it. Tate wanted to look at the question of how the arts can influence creative thinking and learning in the workplace, and how they can influence team-based working, bonding skills and better relationships. It has enabled Tate to look at how the arts can affect the core of what a business is trying to achieve for the future.

The project was very much a two-way learning process. As Jayne Hobin Wright, Tate Liverpool Development Manager said in a speech at the opening of the Rolls-Royce Derby exhibition: "We have learned as much from working with you as you have from us... We could use this model to work with other exhibitions and other businesses in future. Thanks to Rolls-Royce for having the foresight to do something that no other business has tried out."

Olafur Eliasson, *The Weather Project*, October 2003-March 2004, Tate Modern, London.

The project was conceived through discussion with staff from Rolls-Royce and Tate Liverpool as a way of exploring how art can have a longer term impact on a business through training. Funding from Rolls-Royce was then matched by an investment from Arts and Business New Partners, a national initiative by the government-funded organisation, formerly called ABSA, who have held a key role in encouraging business sponsorship of the arts. Both Rolls-Royce and Tate were interested in looking at change within organisations, and at creativity in management. The approach taken in this project is one used by Tate Education team since the opening of Tate Liverpool in 1988: that of making connections with people's existing knowledge and experience, in this case drawing on processes that participants were already familiar with, and using this as a starting point to develop their conceptual understanding.

The project built on Tate's student-centred approach to teaching and learning and the Rolls-Royce model of team-based working. The emphasis of the partnership focused on the development of creative thinking skills and how these can be transferred to the workplace, through critically engaging with the work of modern and contemporary artists, and through experiencing and making art. The starting point for the project was Tate Liverpool's exhibition, *The Shape of Ideas: models and small sculptures from the Tate Collection*, 13 December 2003-31 May 2004. Focusing upon artists' maquettes (the prototypes from which larger sculptures are made), the exhibition gave an insight into the creative and technical processes involved in taking an idea from concept to realisation.

Following introductory sessions for all 55 engineering apprentices and 18 training officers, a core group of 18 trainees and two training officers took part in the project. In January 2004 during the *Exploration* phase, the group spent two days in Liverpool working with sculptor Gillian Brent investigating *The Shape of Ideas* exhibition, developing their critical and creative thinking skills. They then investigated the ideas behind artists' work through gallery and studio-based drawing tasks. Following a presentation and a discussion about how artists have used found objects in modern sculpture, the trainees then made three-dimensional constructions in wire and card, based on objects set up in 'still life' compositions.

In the second phase, *Experimentation*, the apprentices increased their understanding of modern and contemporary sculpture through hands-on sessions at the Engineering Workshop at the Rolls-Royce Learning and Career Development Centre in Derby. Practical workshops were designed to develop trainees' 'creativity' and 'innovation', requiring them to work in teams, and they were taken on a number of visits to broaden their experience of looking at art in other settings such as Tate Modern, Tate Britain, Yorkshire Sculpture Park and Yorkshire ArtSpace in Sheffield, where the artist Gillian Brent has her studio.

In the last phase of the project, *Chemistry*, the trainees made models and larger scale sculptures for three exhibitions, connected to the theme of transformation, both literal and metaphorical, for exhibition. The trainees chose the exhibition's title, *Chemistry*, to link their final sculptures, to reflect the processes materials undergo during manufacturing, as well as the learning processes that they experienced through the project. They also felt that the title echoed the changing relationships between all those involved – personal, professional and corporate – as the project developed. Three exhibitions were eventually organised, each curated by a project team of six trainees, supported by staff.[1]

Six final sculptures were developed by teams of three apprentices, all unconventional in terms of art production, but enabling them to develop crucial team-working skills, which was a key focus for Rolls-Royce. A lot of the emphasis was on problem-solving skills around issues of making, important for their engineering skills, although generating their own themes and concepts and working with these was also important. The transition from non-art specialists to presenting a highly polished exhibition of fabricated works six months later gave all the trainees a great sense of achievement, giving a message that engineers also have the potential to be creative. However, to think that it is this easy to realise a museum exhibition may have been a little misleading to these budding artists.

The trainees worked with sculptor Gillian Brent, along with Rolls-Royce and Tate Liverpool staff led by Naomi Horlock, Education Curator, Young People. Gillian was selected for the project after all the schematics of the sessions had already been decided, a conventional approach to working with artists which perhaps rather limited her scope to contribute creatively to her full potential. She works with steel and large-scale structures, which was important in her selection, having in common with the apprentices a familiarity with materials and technical processes. She had also worked previously with youth groups.

Gillian Brent, the artist: The apprentices are already makers. As a creative person you have an idea and see it from start to finish. It's about reaction, thinking process and consequences. As an artist you are exposed to lots of different things, whereas in industry you can be one small cog in a big wheel. We are in a new era of lean engineering, so Rolls-Royce want the workforce to feel if you have an idea then you have something to contribute.

My role was to get the trainees to play, through thinking up practical activities. We looked at formal things such as how materials behave, also critical skills, such as "What constitutes a work of art?" A central aspect of the project, which may seem anathema to conventional fine art practice, was team-building. The strengths of art school teaching are probably around team-building, with the emphasis on seminars which are about peer critique, challenging people's ideas and getting them to justify their choices and decisions.

I found the team-building aspect quite difficult to justify to the trainees, especially as I generally don't collaborate when making my own work. It brings up interesting issues around roles and responsibilities, peer-led mentoring, supporting from within. The value of the project to me as a creative person is that trying to explain to others clarifies for yourself what you do. It does change your practice in terms of clarity. It's an interesting opportunity for me to work in an industrial environment. Also I haven't worked with galleries in this way before. It's the first project where my knowledge of other artists has been important. Whereas usually it's hands-on, doing stuff, here it's more opening people's eyes to art, not just about making something, but imparting ideas, its about widening audiences and consumers for art. I was trying to find a way of switching their thinking from "I can't do that" to "let's find a way of doing it". It's about seeing things from a different point of view.

At Rolls-Royce you expect a smoothly oiled machine, it's at a high level, there's so much at stake, there's a lot of pride in the company, yet people have the same human foibles everywhere.

I am familiar with working in a male environment as I work with steel, ordering materials or getting things made. I work from the principle that people think you're mad. Being a woman is part of that too. This gives you a freedom.

At first it was awkward having people who were not part of the Tate project around at the Rolls-Royce workshops. We didn't have our own space and I felt awkward going into the office, but I took to asking advice of the other trainers and they seemed to appreciate that. Instructors not involved in the project were suspicious, they kept saying that the apprentices who had been on the Tate project were raising health and safety risks because they were doing unorthodox things. Dave, Manager Engineering Skills, said to them "Rolls-Royce has signed up for this, it's all our project, not just the Tate's." It was good in the end that we all worked together in the same space because something must have rubbed off.

At Rolls-Royce we were in a workshop set up for making machine components, not larger objects. Space is a big issue for three-dimensional practical work. When we worked with willow in the workshops it was difficult.

I was wary that the trainees would criticise my skills – that was quite intimidating. But then I realised I could do things that they couldn't, which gave me confidence. Like any teaching, it's a good way to assess what you think. I have taught them to justify what they are doing, to be prepared to stand up for themselves, to answer back, to take criticism. They enjoyed it. They are very proud of their work.

Dave Hazelwood, Manager Engineering Skills, trainer: At the start I said "We're going to run with it, we don't know what will come out of it but let's see."

Now we have to figure out how we can repeat, sustain and build on the good things. A fundamental is that each youngster should have the opportunity to express ideas, to work an idea through, to implement them, to stand up and tell others. Communications and teamwork are already part of the Production Engineering NVQ (National Vocational Qualification). But this really gives freedom of expression. What we need is to get back to practical making – perhaps ditch all paperwork. Things have got so stilted. There is a big push on process excellence: how well do we do what we say we can. Compliance with requirements is something we are good at, but how do we improve on what we do? How do we teach this if we are still saying "do as you're told"? You need courage to express ideas. It's about giving credibility to someone else's idea, about listening, selecting which idea to work on. There's a phrase in industry: "not invented here", that if an idea is not from here we won't do it. Instead we are now encouraging: "hear it, see what it's good for", learn to listen to each other's opinions, to work as a team.

Lee, trainer: This has been my first year of training people myself, although I have been working for the department for nine years. It has been a great way of shortening my learning curve. It's just been a brilliant project.

Anna Harding: What is transferable that you might use in your training in future?

Lee: Being more flexible with the trainees, giving them the opportunity to take some control of what they are doing, even if it means they make some mistakes along the way.

Rather than standing over them and giving them every single instruction to the letter, it's about giving them some leeway, giving them the opportunity to be creative.

It has helped me develop my role as facilitator rather than always training. I'm a far better facilitator now than I was at the beginning of the project. When we started I wasn't surprised at the trainees' lack of interest in art because there are very few 16- to 19-year-olds who are interested in modern art. They wouldn't have an opinion on art. You would get comments like "To be honest I don't know a lot about it." A year ago the speeches they made today would have taken ten times as long because of the nerves. On the stage they represented themselves brilliantly.

The trainers working on this project I think were chosen for our age, rather than our opinion on art. What we volunteered for originally was just to drive the bus to Liverpool. I was already interested in art. Whenever I go to London I make a point of going to Tate Modern, or if I am in Cornwall I go to Tate St Ives. It's turned into quite a commitment, one that has been really worthwhile.

All the other trainers have been involved on Friday afternoons helping with the projects. Right at the start there were some questions about how this would help the apprentices. People who had been in training for many years may be somewhat set in their ways. Apart from anything else, we had a guided tour of Tate Modern, which was fantastic, with someone knowledgeable, who can answer questions. We've also been to a private view at Tate Liverpool of Mike Kelley's exhibition *The Uncanny*. It was different! You definitely have to go in with an open mind.

It used to be when you came on an apprenticeship you did your skills, your trade, then you learned to be creative. You followed instructions, processes exactly for the first three or four years, then at the end of it you had earned the respect from others to finally be creative. These days we like to start with creative people and give them the skills to use that creativity. That's what our aim is as Rolls-Royce training officers, to create creative people for Rolls-Royce. They are going to take that creativity into the company. The more creative people, the better the company will perform. This idea has been building up for five to ten years. This is definitely the biggest step I've seen in workshop training.

We have all the Rolls-Royce business values and behaviours, the key ethics of Rolls-Royce up here (points to banners hanging from ceiling). We are slowly working towards them. It started out with staff team-based working. We now run team-based working with apprentices, there's some competition between the teams, they are self-managed and take on more responsibility. We as trainers are becoming far more facilitators than trainers.

The trainees' organisational skills are far better than they were, as you would expect after their first year in industry. But compared to the apprentices we had last year, since the Tate project there's a far different approach to the way they work, the way they organise themselves. It's not just the ones who have been on the Tate project. The ones who took part have taught the others to organise themselves better because they have been more confident. Tom wouldn't have any problems explaining to his peers how to fill in their log-book.

It has influenced some of my contemporaries. I've had to make room for this on top of my other training. They're all now working a lot better.

The trainees [From a speech by the group at the exhibition opening at Rolls-Royce, Derby]: When we started we imagined we would make some models, do some trips. We didn't think about what we would get out of the project. The project broadened our minds. Previously we thought logically, didn't think outside the box, now we use our imagination a lot more. We have got better communication skills. Before we found it really hard to communicate with instructors or anyone outside of Rolls-Royce. We have better organisational skills: sometimes before we forgot to relate to each other, sometimes we worked as individuals not as a group. Now we allocate roles, sit down, have meetings setting out objectives of what has to be done. We were quite reserved, we didn't challenge what we were told, we just got on with our work. Now we have more confidence to ask questions, which will benefit us not just in our work but in life in general.

Simon: It was about having an idea with no boundaries to it. Previously we would look at how something was made, now we think about why it was made, we follow the ideas.

Daniel: We had to come up with the ideas, the structure. Usually we have a plan to follow. Here you go round problems in different ways rather than just the logical route

Dan: I used to be scared to pick up the phone if we had to order materials or something. I've learned confidence working in a group. Usually we are working within a tolerance of quarter of a millimetre. It was weird having to loosen up. It definitely gave me more confidence.

Tom: Basically, we were quite narrow-minded before Tate. We learned to use our imagination, think outside the box.

Nathan: We've learned a lot, that you just can't think logically all the time.

I'm employed by SEMTA, a government scheme, I'm not actually employed by Rolls-Royce. I will go on to work in a small company. This project has brought me and the Rolls-Royce trainees together. Before we would sit in our own small group. Now it's given me more confidence with them.

When I went to college I was stuck between the choice of Art and Engineering. I thought Engineering would be a better career option, but I studied art for GCSE – it's one of my hobbies – now I think about art in a lot more depth, what the artist is trying to say through his work. You see more than just what you are seeing. I've been here for a year and am meant to have a job by now.

I think it is essential for apprentices to do something like this. It makes them realise there are more options. I really enjoyed drawing, sketching, now I realise there are a lot more similarities between art and engineering than just practical drawing.

Tom: Due to this project I will have the courage to speak up with more extreme solutions, think more openly.

In conclusion, this project could be viewed as a success for all parties involved, although for many artists it may be galling to realise that Rolls-Royce apprentices are taken seriously as artists and given exhibitions in major museums due to their corporate links and the innovative nature of the corporate collaboration, rather than the innovative nature of the artworks themselves. The apprentices may also have received a false impression about the ease with which an artist moves from production to exhibition. However, despite reservations presented by these rather unrealistic circumstances, the idea that creative processes in industry or business can benefit from programmes devised jointly by education and fund-raising departments or arts organisations is a growing area of activity.

1 The three exhibitions were: *Chemistry I: creativity and innovation* at Rolls-Royce Learning and Career Development Centre, Derby, 13 July 2004; *Chemistry II: creative process and collaboration* at Derby Museum and Art Gallery, 17 July-22 August 2004; and *Chemistry III: shaping ideas* at Tate Liverpool Studio, 11-19 September 2004.

Aim Higher Out Of and Beyond School

15 seconds
christian Dorley-Brown

15 Seconds by Christian Dorley-Brown consists of side-by-side video clips of young people, the first filmed at age ten in 1994, the second a decade later. Participants were instructed to communicate to the camera only via facial expression. "This project is an eye-opening social documentary and an elegiac meditation on the passage of time and the loss of childhood innocence" stated Sandra Kemp, curator of the exhibition *Future Face* at the Science Museum, London featuring this work. The differences in each pair of images are startling and hugely revealing. The ten-year-olds move a lot, make faces, engage in play, giggle, and are quite animated. The 20-year-olds are almost entirely still, holding their expressions for long periods, smiling in stony fashion, and, most heartbreaking of all, their eyes are filled with sadness. Laura Sullivan reviewing the exhibition stated: "Never have I seen a silent video piece expose so much about how social dynamics wear down young people, stomping out all their spirit, emotionality, and hope. I stared at the compelling pairs of clips for ages." (*Mute Online*, February 2005). The videos with ten-year-olds were made with schools in Essex. The work will be on permanent display at the Wellcome Gallery, London.

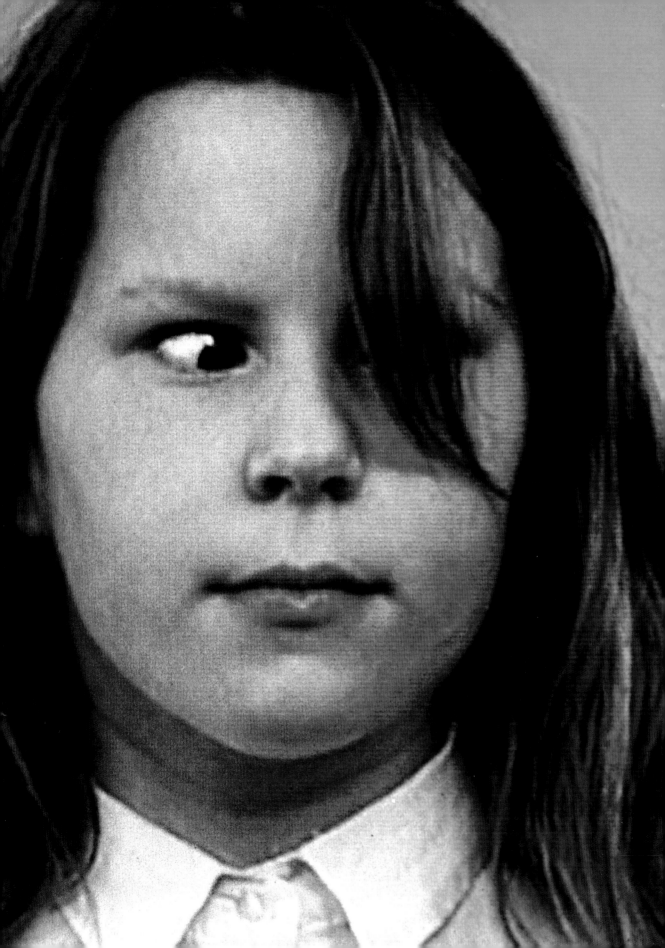

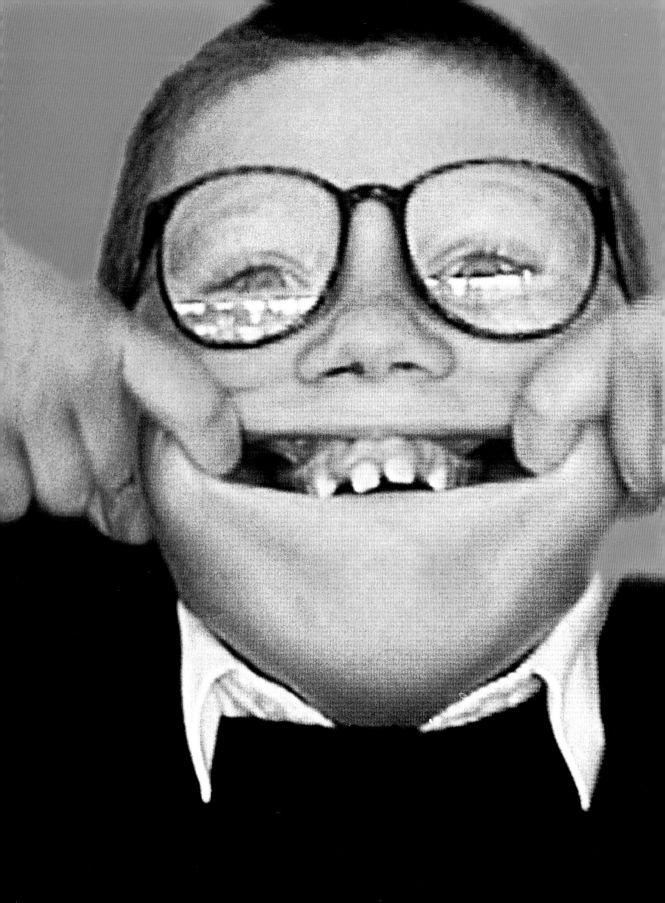

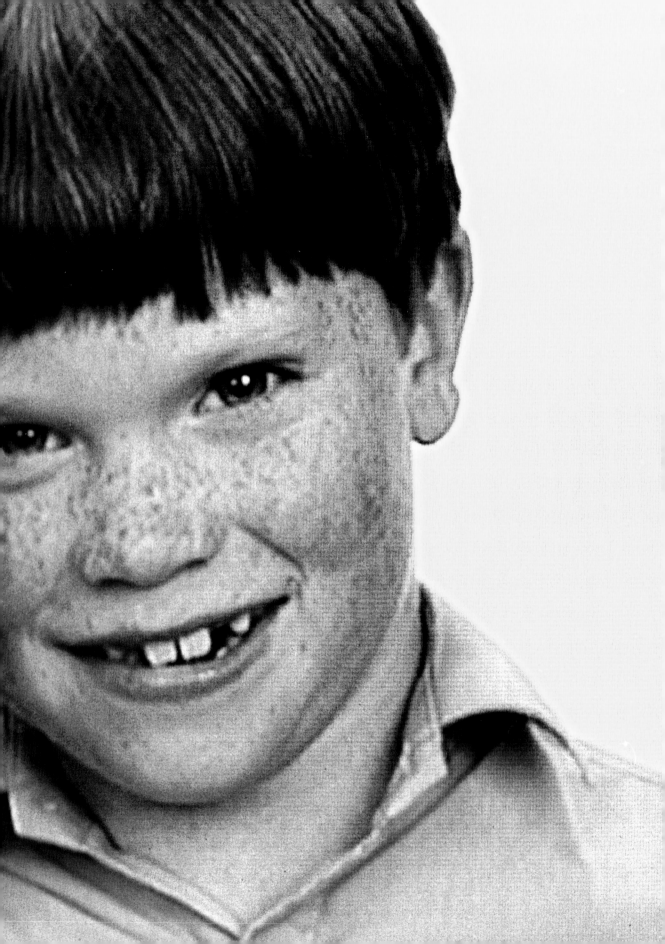

celebrations for breaking routine with flamingo 50, venus and exit 3

Anna Harding, Kristin Lucas and Marie-Anne McQuay

This collaborative video commission was created by artist Kristin Lucas, local girl bands and the FACT Centre in Liverpool, where it was exhibited in 2003. The project shows how the different needs of artists, participants and an art institution were all met by one project.

American artist Kristin Lucas is recognised as one of a new generation of women artists dealing with contemporary anxiety of young women in a technology- and media-driven age. She works with video, installation, performance and interactive Web projects. Other contemporaries working with video include Sadie Benning and Miranda July. The backdrop to Lucas' work is the empty world of day-time television, cable shopping channels and shopping malls. She is interested in the fears and desires surrounding new developments in technology and how they affect our daily lives. Her work resonates with a sense of social isolation and alienation reinforced by computer, television and electronic media which she feels that many young women experience, who are at best seen as passive consumers of the latest commercial products. Her work often references outmoded signifiers of the future such as satellite dishes and silver space outfits that entered public consciousness through science fiction fantasy.

She acknowledges that many young girls play video games and are inseparable from their computers, but then why do we have Gameboys but no Gamegirls? This interest does not filter through into the predominantly male-dominated games and technology industries. Lucas remembers hanging out for long hours at the local arcade as a teenager. She also babysat for a seven-year-old girl who controlled the video game joystick with her feet, hands-free! She didn't own a personal computer until age 26 (an Amiga 2000), although she took computer programming in high school.

At the time I experienced an impenetrable bubble around the community as a young woman, even at high school level. My sister was encouraged to go into engineering, not because she was a computer programming prodigy, but because affirmative action in the United States meant that young women suddenly had the rare opportunity of being placed in high paying technical jobs within a male-dominated field.

There are very few women in positions to influence the direction of emergent technologies. The industry continues to be male-dominated and market-driven. Women of all ages are taken seriously as consumers – a sacred market group – but women in the technology-related work force are commonly employed as assembly line workers whose bodies are surveyed and controlled. Many technologies and procedures are marketed to a target group of teenage girls and young women, yet this group seems to have little voice in the direction of evolving technologies. Technology continues to be synonymous with progress despite the consequences of our so-called achievements (for example the industrialisation of death, a trade governed by corporate interest, keeping AIDS and HIV medications out of economic reach of the world's masses). The gap is widening between those with the knowledge to design, modify, and influence, and those on the other side – consumers and labourers. These themes are all picked up in Lucas' work.

Celebrations for Breaking Routine (*C4BR*) was commissioned originally by FACT (Foundation for Art and Creative Technology), the UK's leading organisation for the development, support and exhibition of film, video and new and emerging media.

Based in Liverpool, the organisation is central to the regeneration underway in the city centre; its new building, the £10 million ($17,700,000) FACT Centre, opened in 2002 – the first dedicated arts venue to be built in Liverpool since the Philharmonic Hall was completed in 1939. With a reputation as a regenerating city that is only now recovering from the decline of the UK's dock industry, with not much work on offer apart from the cultural industries, Liverpool is attempting transition into a cultural centre and was selected as European City of Culture 2008, which was announced during Kristin's exhibition. FACT's Collaboration Programme, a key commissioning strand that brings together high profile international artists with communities to create new works of art, joined forces with FACT's Exhibition Programme to produce this ambitious project which became the second major exhibition in the FACT Centre's main gallery following Isaac Julien's opening show, and exemplifies the status that FACT gave to collaborative commissions within its artistic programme.[1]

Kristin worked through 2001-2003 with three Liverpool girl bands to produce original compositions around their 'visions of the future', to encourage unique and less heard voices on this subject. Her project acknowledges Liverpool as a city in transition from industrial working class to international city of culture, and takes occasion to empower under-recognised voices within the greater Liverpool community while highlighting its thriving, diverse, historic and resilient music scene. The resulting songs – "Like a Lady", "Right to Speak", and "Science and Nature", reflect concerns with the young women's environment and global politics as well as personal dreams and aspirations. Each band's recording session was videotaped. Lucas recorded additional footage around the city's neighbourhoods, landmarks and places of transition. The edited videos lie between documentary and pop video, giving visual shape to each band's vision

Kristin Lucas,
exhibition
installation
at FACT.

of the future. In a memorable image, members of the band Venus wore personalised strap-on satellite dishes for a shoot in a Liverpool cafe, an image carrying a tone of seriousness as well as humour with the lyrics: "How can I be myself and get what I want from the future? It's already set out for me!"

In the development of *C4BR* Lucas considered the fanfare and optimism around World Fairs, optimism about new technologies, the future, and utopia. Considering the art world too infected with fashionable fanfare around its huge international biennales and museum openings, she piggybacked on the existing buzz about the new FACT Centre and built a World Fair-inspired cardboard dome. The music videos of the girl bands' songs were presented inside the dome, referencing optimism about the future around the time of Fuller's invention while also considering Fuller's geodesic designs as energy efficient. The structure felt like a huge playhouse, a make-believe structure. Audience members could enter the dome and sing along to the music videos using a microphone and teleprompter, almost karaoke. They could choose to be passive and read the teleprompter, or internalise the lyrics without having to vocalise them. Most chose to watch the videos from the benches.

The content of the show was created through a two-year relationship between FACT, the artist, local bands and other participants. Initial research and development to source girl bands started in 2001, a time when the Spice Girls had peaked in popularity and Atomic Kitten were about to take over as top girl band. A less overtly glamorous and manufactured style of girl band was sought out to take part in Lucas' project through the rich underground Liverpool music scene and FACT's own community contacts. Majorettes and a brass band were involved at a later stage of the project and played a key role in the videos that accompanied the songs.

FACT rented a flat for Lucas' visits to Liverpool – trips ranging from one week to five weeks at a time.

> It seemed every minute of every trip, even the longer trips, was filled with meetings (bands, majorettes, composer and Exit 3 mentor, production team, visiting bands, designer/seamstress, FACT Collaboration Programme, Exhibition and Installation teams, site visits… to name a few!)…. During these trips FACT set me up with a laptop (eventually three, considering long render times for animations), an external hard drive, cameras, anything I needed so that I could work on logging and editing footage at the flat. I shot additional footage independently. I took the drive back to New York and finished the video editing there on my home computer, returned in April 2003 to master the videos and install the exhibition.

Lucas was genuinely engaged with the collaboration, which was central to the success of the commission, and ideas flowed freely between the artist and the participants. Lucas asked the young women to write a song about the future but did not seek to influence style or content. Workshops on songwriting were as productive for the creation of content as casual cups of tea with the artists when people swapped CDs and recommendations of music. She worked with them whenever she was in the UK and remained in touch by email in between. FACT's project manager kept in contact with the groups and helped to co-ordinate their sessions. Kristin's videos were a response to the songs and used the influence of the bands – the songs were a gift to her and the videos were a gift in return to the bands.

Exit 3 was formed from a youth group called VENUS based in north Liverpool. This is an area dislocated from the cultural regeneration of the city centre. VENUS offer support for young women within this area, providing advice, child care and a drop-in centre and also creative projects. They have worked on one other major collaborative commission with FACT since *Celebrations* took place. Exit 3 comprised two young women aged 16 and 17 who had not previously felt confident enough to take part in creative projects in a major way and a young woman (aged 18) who had shown great promise as a song-writer and worked with them as a mentor. FACT also enlisted a composer to work with the group and they met regularly to work on the song writing process.

The second band, called Venus (purely a coincidence in terms of name), were a school band comprised of five schoolgirls (aged 17) from Widnes. They had only ever performed covers but had come to the attention of a local record producer. FACT enlisted his support and the group began writing their first original composition.

The third band, Flamingo 50, performed regularly and had had some radio play on late night Radio 1 via Steve Lamacq and the late John Peel. They were recent graduates (aged 21) who had stayed on in Liverpool and the most accomplished in terms of writing their own songs and defining their own style. They had a male drummer but he was allowed into the project as a girl band exception! They also had a distinctive girl punk sound in contrast to a classic pop girl band.

Lucas' first visit to Liverpool to plan the project was in October 2001. She met the girl-led bands and the majorettes in February 2002. In mid June 2002, she returned to work with groups prior to recording at Parr Street

Studios. The three tracks were recorded and one was chosen by Kristin to be translated into a brass band tune by a local composer and recorded on location by Rainford Silver Band.

In October 2002, Lucas returned to create individual videos with all three bands and a video for the brass band version of the punk track. Filming took place in the centre of Liverpool, at the Albert Dock and Bootle Strand. Some of the young women were involved in additional audio recording for the exhibition at NOVA film production studios. The videos were presented in the gallery-based installation at FACT from May to June 2003.

The songs produced were of a staggeringly high quality and incredibly diverse in style (Exit 3's "Right to speak" (R&B); Venus's "Like a Lady" (rock/pop); and Flamingo 50's "Science and Nature" (punk). The brass band recording of a punk track worked well – the song had such a tight structure than when transposed for brass it still held together as a song. Brass bands and majorette

dancers was a motif that linked the United States to England's north west; Lucas had grown up playing in college bands that were led by cheerleaders and in the north west brass bands are a tradition remaining from mining culture and many majorette troupes perform, partly influenced also by Irish traditional dancing. The brass band, composer of the track and majorettes all became part of the collaboration and part of the artwork through their involvement.

In terms of personal outcomes for the individual members of the bands, the two younger participants of Exit 3 were both inspired to follow creative paths further; both went on to attend Liverpool Community College studying dance and drama. After the end of Kristin's project they joined further projects at FACT. The third participant, a talented dancer and singer who had already shown great promise before this project, has undertaken work for both VENUS and other voluntary organisations as a junior youth worker and gone back to college to complete A Levels in dance and music, and has successfully retaken GSCE maths.

She used the work made with Exit 3 as part of her portfolio for these A Levels and gained a place at London Contemporary Dance School (FACT acted as one of her referees). Venus felt a great sense of achievement in creating their first song and whilst they couldn't continue the group after A Levels due to university commitments, the lead singer has since been signed by a local record label. Flamingo 50 were so pleased with the song that they included it in their debut album and continue to play it live. They have since toured to France and played in New York.

Lucas said of the exhibition:

> What I did not expect was that Exit 3, who formed from VENUS Resource Centre, would be so empowered by their experience that they would take the stage for an impromptu performance of their song during the opening. They really made the project their own. That was the best feeling, that I had struck a balance between directing the form and flow of the project, leaving it open enough in the collaboration that something unimaginable could happen.

The project presents an alternative to corporate music videos that mass-market young female musicians, and it continued to grow after Liverpool as Lucas went on to involve new girl bands and make new videos. She continued to travel to cities internationally recognised for their music scenes and invite young girl-led bands to write songs about the future, working with bands zero2nine and Dew in Basel with the support of the digital arts outfit [Plug In]. These community-based collaborations have resulted in alternative visions of female empowerment and identity in a media-driven culture. A comprehensive album of all recorded *C4BR* music is being released through Kristin's further collaborations with Jennifer Blauvelt and Artists Alliance in New York and the video is available from Electronic Arts Intermix, a non-profit resource for video art and interactive media based in New York.

1 Collaboration Programme projects have been exhibited in the public realm since the early 1990s and have featured in FACT's own Video Positive Festival, 1991-2000, and Liverpool Biennial 2004, as well a variety of off-site, non-gallery contexts.

kids of survival

Tim Rollins

It was 1980. I was straight out of art and grad school in New York City. I was 23 years old, from the hillbilly hills of rural Maine called the Central Highlands. Even after four years in the big city, I was still as green as a field, picking pine needles out of my hair. And still I thought I was all that and a bag of crisps. I was going to be The Lifesaver… I was Sydney Poitier in *Sir with Love*. I was Anne Sullivan in the *Miracle Worker*. I was Sean Connery in *Finding Forrester*. I believed I could teach anybody, anything, anywhere, anytime and anyhow.

Around this time after my university studies, in 1981, a very dynamic Puerto Rican American principal named George Gallego recruited me. George had seen me in action while training non-artist teachers how to incorporate the arts in their curricula. He said he wanted to get this intense, naive white guy into his own school, the infamous Intermediate School 52 on Kelly Street in the middle of the South Bronx. IS52 had two well-known distinctions. First, it was the *alma mater* of General Colin Powell; I am sure he learned some of his strategic techniques there. Second, this was the school in all of New York City with the highest number of violent incidents against the teachers. When Gallego offered me a job I said, "You think I am going to teach here? You are out of your mind!"

Much of the South Bronx neighbourhood was literally on fire at the time. You would walk out of the subway – ironically located on a street named Prospect Avenue – and it stank like downtown Manhattan after 9/11; this awful, sickening, acrid air that smelled like rubber tyres burning. The entire area surrounding the school was almost completely decimated. You couldn't imagine people living there, let alone being able to truly study. George was persistent and so I figured out a compromise. I was going to come up for two weeks, help the school get a structured art programme together, and then I was out of there. You know how some of us liberal white guys are? "Oh, I'm going to the ghetto and I'll help poor children of colour for two whole weeks, and then I'll pat myself on the back and congratulate myself for the rest of my life at cocktail parties and art openings."

When I got there, I was just amazed at the chaos of the place. Leading me to the third floor of the school where they had located a makeshift art room for me, I remember six metre ceilings covered with graffiti in charcoal. "George, I have to ask you something. How did the kids get up there to tag? How did they do it?" Gallego was blasé. "Oh, they took these long broom handles that they use to open these big windows and taped the charcoal to the ends – then they drew on the ceilings while their art teacher looked on helpless." "Like late Matisse", I thought. In my art room, all the windows were knocked out and replaced with crude sheets of plywood also covered in even cruder graffiti done in black marker pens. There was a sink that leaked into a white plastic bucket underneath to catch the drips. And they thought this was really a great art room! In my mind I repeated over and over: "Only two weeks, only two weeks."

Soon after this introduction to my new unreal reality, a long siren-like bell went off and here they were: my first class. The students were excited to meet me... only because nothing was more exciting than a new victim. I immediately went militant on them and after providing paper and pencils presented them with their first assignment. "In the next hour I want each and every one of you to make the best drawing you have ever made in your life. No pressure!" The entire group went silent... and then some giggled softly, nervously. And then they went to work, drawing furiously while I blasted what was then old school hip hop music in the background. Watching all this passionate mark-making going on, I was amazed. These kids were incredible – like drawing machines – and what they were creating on their own was very, very good. Interesting, because the kids were all classified as 'Special Education' students. They had been diagnosed as 'at-risk', 'learning disabled', 'emotionally handicapped', 'academically challenged'. My favourite label was a new category called ADD or 'Attention Deficit Disorder'. Here were kids who can play video games for seven hours straight without even blinking an eye or going to the toilet and they have Attention Deficit Disorder? I don't think so. I think they had Teacher Deficit Disorder. True, maybe some of these pupils couldn't read or write well at the age of 12 or 13, and they couldn't even approach math, but my God, what they could do in art! There was something powerful and immediately evident going on here. One hour into teaching, and these young artists were blowing my mind.

At the end of the workshop, I'm looking at the results. One of the kids, egged on by the others, looked me straight in the eye and said "We're good ain't we?" Now I was trying to have that mean teacher face you learn to have on your first day, especially in places like the Bronx. "You're OK." "No", he came right back at me, "We're REAL good and you know it too because it is written all over your face! Now let me ask you another question. Are you gonna to stay and be our art teacher or are you gonna leave like all the others?" I was embarrassed. "I'm only supposed to be here two weeks." Again, he's right back at me. "Would you stay?" "Let me think about it, all right?" What was going on here? What had I got myself into?

I immediately ran down to Gallego's office. He was grinning. "They are pretty good, aren't they?" I said, "George, I know I don't have that much experience, but they are the best and most promising young artists I've ever encountered." He popped the question that would completely change my life:

"So why don't you stay? This is going to work. I can feel it." So I took on the job of being the Special Ed art teacher at IS52. Announcing my decision to my class the next day I made it clear. "I'm not here because I'm thrilled to be here. And I'm not here because I'm a missionary type. And I'm not here because I'm such a nice guy. I'm here because there is something deep inside of me, something I can feel that is telling me this one true fact: we are going to make art in here, but we are also going to make history." The kids were silent and looking at me like I was crazy. They loved this.

I stayed at IS52 for seven years before establishing our own after-school studio programme three blocks away. In 1982, a group of about twelve of my most dedicated and devoted young art students, aged 11 to 17, called themselves KOS (for "Kids of Survival"). In 1984, together we got our own studio called "The Art and Knowledge Workshop" in a nearby community centre. In 1987 I was able to leave the public school system and devote myself full-time to Kids of Survival. We are now celebrating 23 years in the South Bronx community, and I continue to live and work in that very neighbourhood that once filled me with trepidation.

But I did not stay out of this goody-goodiness that I see so often in missionary types that go into distressed neighbourhoods, stay for a year, and then leave. We stayed and we continue working with youth not only in our local South Bronx and New York City communities but also with kids from distressed communities across the USA and throughout the world. I do not do this out of altruism. I do this because I'm angry. As a teenager, my hero growing up was the Reverend Dr Martin Luther King Jr. In one of his great sermons King reminds us that the Norse root for the word 'anger' means 'to grieve'. I don't have rage; I am all about the power of joy. But I am angry. And I grieve. I grieve for the fact that an impossible number of our kids have been used and written off as unreachable, useless, a threat. Things are better in the Bronx, but in the bad old days it was like witnessing the intellectual genocide of children. It was generally assumed that they were not going to make it, so why even bother? People were just going through the motions. And I am angered that this talent, these amazing gifts that these kids had, were not discerned, appreciated, disciplined, developed, demonstrated and promoted by the educational system at the time.

I have been a witness to art as a great power capable of transforming the artistic, physical, spiritual, economic and educational cultures of a neighbourhood. In spite of the material poverty, ours is an art-loving community and that passion has had a lot to do with the South Bronx renaissance and the influence of its culture internationally.

To my kids, books were the enemy. To read was to have your daily situation made obvious and contradicted. If you were well read you were "acting white". If you walked around the Bronx with books under your arm you might get the crap beaten out of you. The attitude was "Who do you think you are? You want to rise above us?"... a classic underclass attitude. Very DH Lawrence. And I thought, this is ridiculous. This was a time when the system was paying hundreds of thousands of dollars to so-called experts to tell us what our kids could not do. They would say that our kids couldn't read, that they were dyslexic with low attention spans, and so on. But aside from their obvious creativity and artistic talent, I had always been amazed how many of the students could memorise just about anything they could hear. The most talented artist in our group was 12 years old and severely dyslexic, but he knew every single word, phrase, sound and beat of a rap song and could repeat it on command without one flaw. So I came up with a very simple but highly effective solution. Using a cheap tape recorder and reading to myself in the evenings, I made my own books on tape. Our first book we listened to was *1984* by George Orwell. Remember, all we had in those beginning days was photocopy paper and pencils. I explained to the group an idea coming from the wonderful nineteenth century Symbolist Odilon Redon. When an artist is inspired by a text he can go into a reverie, a trance, and make what we could call a 'visual correspondence' with that literature. This is what I asked the kids to do. Don't illustrate the novel you are hearing. Make a visual correspondence. What does this book that I am reading to you remind you of in your everyday life and can you show this to us in your drawings? While listening to my recorded reading of the book, the kids drew and drew and drew, producing literally hundreds of small drawings, visual free associations inspired by the writing. After several weeks of listening and drawing, we would all then sit down together and decide which images seemed the most true, the most sincere, the most powerful, the most impressive. Then, using these little permanent black ink markers, we would trace these images on sheets of transparent acetate. Using an overhead projector on a rolling cart, we would then project these enlarged drawings onto a field of book pages taken from the novel and carefully glued in a perfect grid onto large sheets of paper or canvas.

Our next project involved the horror stories *Frankenstein* by Mary Shelley and Bram Stoker's *Dracula*. At that time in the early 1980s, we were all very much influenced by Marvel Comics and graffiti but eventually we had more to say in a whole new way. We had to move on. We had to transcend that stuff. As an educator I believe it is very important not to patronise and to challenge your kids, to challenge yourself. I've been accused of being an elitist teacher. True. I believe in an elite experience, but I want that elite experience opened to *everyone*. Instead of subscribing to the current practice of teaching to the lowest common denominator, I seek to educate to the *highest* common denominator. That is how enduring art, knowledge and culture are created. The kids began questioning the macabre and lurid look of our work. The argument went like this: "You know what, these are violent, crazy paintings. Aren't we just representing what the outside world thinks of us living in the Bronx? It's not all bad here. Can we make something beautiful? When you get right down to it, only beauty can change things." The horror-story art had to go.

Where we went next was a surprise. By accident I came upon Franz Kafka's first and unfinished comic novel called *Amerika*, especially its surreal and visionary last chapter, "The Nature Theatre of Oklahoma". The protagonist is a very young man named Karl who leaves his dreary, dead-end existence in eastern Europe for the USA, pursuing the American Dream and seeking fame, fortune and, hopefully, true love. Immediately upon arriving, he gets caught up in a series of misadventures and ends up totally disappointed. He is about to return home in shame and dejection when he encounters, is recruited and is adopted by a utopian, Salvation Army-like commune called "The Nature Theatre of Oklahoma". This new and radical organisation is based on two essential principles: "Everyone is welcome!" and "Everyone an artist!" Well, this resembled the ethos of KOS, leading me to ask the kids, if they could portray their voice, their spirit, their own personal song in the form of a golden horn, what would that instrument look like? After months of experimenting, they were competing as to who could come up with the most eccentric and original forms. Once dozens of these horns were created they were then were accumulated together and painted in golden watercolour or acrylic on large four and a half metre canvases surfaced with book pages taken from copies of *Amerika*.

Enthusiasm for this new series of work was immediate, leading to several exhibitions, in New York, Philadelphia and Chicago, leading in turn to acquisitions by The Museum of Modern Art, the Philadelphia Museum of Modern Art and the Tate in London for their permanent collections. Indeed it had happened. KOS and I were not only making art, but also making history – and we started making money. It was wonderful to be fully independent and free of any state, federal or city funding.

The Scarlet Letter by Nathaniel Hawthorne inspired our next paintings. The main character, a woman named Hester, is living in puritanical Boston. She has a baby out of wedlock and refuses to reveal the identity of the father. As punishment she is condemned to wear the letter 'A' on the breast of her clothing, clearly visible as the mark of her shame. KOS and I thought the great thing about Hester was that she was an artist, a master of embroidery. She actually embroidered the vestments of those very governors in power who were condemning her. So, instead of wearing a rag-tag looking A, she designed an A that was resplendent in scarlet and gold. That was our cue. And I asked the kids if they could be like Hester and transform a stigma of shame into an emblem of transcendent and triumphant pride, if they could portray their humanity in a form of a scarlet letter A. We then enlarged and accumulated these letterforms and painted them of the pages of the American classic.

In our works based on Stephen Crane's classic of the American Civil War *The Red Badge of Courage*, the members of KOS created their own personal interpretation of wounds... physical wounds, psychological wounds, spiritual wounds. While the first attempts were very literal, obvious and gory, it wasn't long before what they were painting evolved into more ephemeral, jewel and planet-like forms that suggest an alternative cosmos when arranged all together on the text. The works especially are about the beauty of survival.

In the collection of both the Museum of Modern Art and The Studio Museum in Harlem the paintings from our series inspired by *The Autobiography of Malcolm X* features an abstract, team-designed logo that aims to visualise the radical volition and hope of Malcolm. While we were having our work acquired by museums and private collections throughout the world, this design has also been produced as prints, drawings, posters and even T-shirts. As Malcolm X says, "I was seeking for the truth and I was trying to weigh objectively everything on its own merit. What I was against was straitjacketed thinking and straitjacketed society." This is precisely why art is often feared and considered dangerous. Art that matters is an enemy of straitjacketed thinking.

KOS and I study the history of world art in order to find ways to make our own work, engaging with a tradition with the aim of adding to and advancing that tradition. For works based on George Orwell's *Animal Farm*, we drew upon the rich art history of zoomorphic caricature, especially the political graphic work of artists like Honore Daumier, JJ Grandville and Charles Philippon. Then after researching the appearance and demeanour of world leaders through magazines, videos and televised news reports, we turned Margaret Thatcher into a pompous goose, Ronald Reagan into a wizened turtle and extraordinary right-wing

Republican Jesse Helms into a barnyard dog. In 1992 another *Animal Farm* painting, a very large work at three by 14 metres, depicted 120 world leaders as barnyard animals and was shown at the Hirshhorn Museum in Washington, DC just before George Bush was defeated in the presidential election. The show was cancelled twice – this was during all the censorship and culture wars controversy – but the museum finally allowed us to exhibit the painting if we promised not to depict animals having sex! The only problem we had was at the opening of the exhibition. An official from Peru came up to us livid. We'd shown his president as a little fly, the size of a little fly on a huge painting. The ambassador was furious: "He shouldn't be a fly! Our President is more than a fly! You could have made him a horse or a beautiful bird, but he is not a fly!"

The early 1990s were great years for us. The Dia Center for the Arts in New York and the Museum of Contemporary Art in LA organised a major exhibition of all 13 of our *Amerika* paintings. We also had major solo shows in Switzerland, Germany, Mexico and the UK, and showed in the Venice Biennale, Documenta, the Carnegie International and the Whitney Biennial. Our work was on the cover of *Artforum* and we were awarded the Joseph Beuys Prize. KOS and I travelled everywhere, wearing Versace and Armani. All the kids were in school and doing well. It was during this incredible time we became obsessed with the strange book, *The Temptation of St Antony* by Gustave Flaubert. The insufferably pious St Antony is having a long and deeply challenging philosophical dialogue with the Devil. The saint intones, "Where am I going? I have just glimpsed the shape of the Evil One." The Evil One? Isn't it ironic that at the height of our good fortune, we were all furiously attracted to the idea of what Evil might look like? Soon, using syringes and other medical instruments we started making these horrific spills, splatters and messes on single pages of the text in animal blood and alcohol. It was during the making of these *Temptation* works that we truly discovered what Evil looked like – in real life. In 1993, things fell apart and the centre did not hold.

It was St Valentine's Day in 1993. I was in London, at an elegant Chinese restaurant, planning a group show for the Hayward Gallery. I was meeting a couple that had just flown in from New York. Knowing I worked in the South Bronx, they were anxious to tell me. "It was awful, did you hear about the horrible St Valentine's Day Massacre?" I asked, "What are you talking about?" "Oh, it happened somewhere in the South Bronx just before we got on the plane. Six people all shot in one apartment." I became defensive – "Well, you know what? If six people were all killed in one apartment, they probably were involved with drug dealing and they deserved it." I actually said that.

Upon returning to my hotel I received an urgent message from home, from the studio. I called. One of my favourite, youngest, most promising kids, Christopher Hernandez, had turned 14 a few days earlier. He was now dead – just murdered – one of the six victims in the South Bronx apartment we were speaking of in the restaurant. An innocent bystander, he was about to enter his tower block when four gunmen grabbed him, forcing themselves into the building. They were after a young drug dealer who lived on the top floor. They used Christopher as a decoy to enter the dealer's apartment where he lived with his mother and sisters. Chris and the entire household were laid on the floor and shot execution-style.

Taking an emergency flight back to the Bronx, I arrived to find KOS all waiting and grieving together in the studio. There were dozens of news reporters waiting as well. The kids were stoic and trying to keep it together. Not me. I told the reporters "I want your asses out of here right now!" They protested. "No, you can't do this! This is a story, a great story." I was shouting. "No! This was my kid! He is not a story; he's a human being. And guess what? He was a lot more interesting when he was alive, making all this beautiful work, than he is now. The media is only interested in our kids when they are killing, dying or dead. If it bleeds, it leads. I want you out of here."

And when they left, there was a silence, a long, sustained sadness. No matter all the success and victories of our project, I had lost so many kids, kids that I had given my life to. And now this. One of the most dedicated KOS members decided to quit. He put it this way: "Fuck this art crap, man. Art makes a way out of no way? Art will change your life? We are not going to survive. Look at Chris; he was the most innocent one of us all. I am not planning to go out the way Chris did, but if I do, then I am going out on the other end of the gun!"

Six months later, it seemed we lost everything. The art market crashed, including ours. I could hardly get up in the morning, drinking myself to sleep every night to avoid the tragedy, the horror. The remaining KOS members – now genuine survivors – tried to work but everything was erratic. No ideas would come, just memories of Christopher and our earlier days. We were finally evicted from our beautiful studio. We didn't even have the money to move. We could only take the things that we could fit in our arms. As we were going through stuff trying to decide what to take, Jorge, Christopher's classmate and best friend, found a portfolio labelled 'CH' in large painted letters on its cover. It was filled with these delicate yet boisterous drawings of cartoon frog-like forms. Frogs. *The Frogs?* In the months before Chris was taken, KOS were talking about working with the ancient comedy by Aristophanes and getting nowhere fast. Jorge said "You know what? Chris must have been making these drawings in secret so he could spring them on us at the right time. He was always doing that. With these drawings we can get Chris back." I said, "What are you talking about?" "Just touch the marks on the paper, Tim. He's there." And so he was. We got our joy back.

In *The Frogs* the last of the great dramatists, Euripides, has died and has been transported to Hades. The city of Athens is in great distress and is suffering war, disease and civil turmoil. Dionysus has to travel to the netherworld to bring Euripides back believing that "only a poet can save the city. Only the artist can save the city" – I believe that's true to this day. Dionysus must row his boat across the burning lake of Hell. All around the Lake of Hell are thousands of singing, dancing, partying frogs. Their song: "*Brekekek koax, koax! Brekekek koax, koax!* We are the swamp children, green and tiny. Lifting our voices all the time, we *Brekekek koax, koax!*" Dionysus is incredulous. "How can you be so happy? You're living in Hell! You should be suffering! You should be miserable!" And the frogs reply, "If we do not sing we shall swell up and die! *Brekekek koax, koax!*" Many folk outside our situation in the South Bronx are like Dionysus, wondering why we continue in the neighbourhood, how can we keep making art under such difficult and tragic circumstances, how we can we go on in the poorest Congressional District in the United States. They don't understand that art means *to make*. It doesn't mean to take, and it doesn't mean to fake. Art is unspeakable joy made visible. Like those irrational frogs, we don't make art to become rich and famous (although that was great while it lasted!). KOS and I continue to make this work because *we must*. If we don't, we'll swell up and die, *brekakek, koax, koax!*

On a kitchen table, KOS and I started making watercolours based on *The Frogs* and Christopher's original drawings. Once again, our work was about joy. Our team pulled itself together, found a much smaller affordable studio still in the neighbourhood, found new members and began working again.

In Harriet Jacobs' 1863 autobiography *Incidents in the Life of a Slave Girl* she describes her hiding in an attic space two by three by one metre for seven years. One of the things that get her through and help her survive are simply seeing, through a crack in boards of her prison, the brightly coloured costumes of the Johnkonnen – young slave men allowed to have carnival in the streets at Christmas time. I wondered and asked my kids, "What's the colour of your joy?" I thought KOS would laugh me out of the studio. Instead we spent months creating these personal palettes, self-portraits in the form of a single colour. We eventually invaded the Garment Centre in the middle of Manhattan, searching for satin ribbons matching the colours we had invented. Then we stretched these bands across Harriet Jacobs' historic text, allowing the glistening colours to pour off the canvas and flow onto the gallery floor.

This led to our next body of work, *I See the Promised Land*, inspired by the final sermon of the Rev Dr Martin Luther King Jr, on the eve of his assassination in 1968. All throughout his thought and preaching, King would repeatedly remind us that "Life at its best is a great triangle" and that a whole and complete personality must be three-dimensional, with height, breadth and depth. From the top of this triangle, this mountaintop, one can see the promised land of a beloved and loving community.

In the form of giant paintings, prints, posters and public installations, KOS and I created unique colours representing our Hope, painted in the form of triangles over King's world-changing sermon.

In the St Paul's community of Bristol, England, KOS and I collaborated with the area's youth to create several collaged paintings on *A Midsummer Night's Dream* by Shakespeare. Imitating that prototypical artist, Puck, the participants created their own magic flowers, the petals of which contain a juice that once trickled on the eyelids of sleeping people makes them fall in love with the first living thing they see upon waking. In this play is perhaps the greatest definition of art in the English language. Shakespeare writes:

> And as imagination bodies forth
> The forms of things unknown,
> The poet's pen turns them to shapes,
> And gives to airy nothing
> A local habitation and a name.

The last painting that Christopher Hernandez worked on before his murder was made in 1992 and based on Jules Verne's science fiction classic *From the Earth to the Moon*. Our team had all been struggling with this theme for years and nothing was working. Then one day Chris proudly marched into the studio. He had had a dream. He had dreamed of taking all the broken glass that was always on the streets and sidewalks of the South Bronx and turning these fragments into stars across the cosmos, creating an alternative universe. And that is just what we did; making a colossal painting in blue black and gluing broken glass in carefully ordered compositions to invent our own, endless, night sky. This painting was acquired by the Hirshhorn Museum – our national museum of modern art – for its permanent collection immediately after its exhibition in a gallery in New York.

Several years after the loss of Christopher, we received a call from the Hirshhorn. "We are going to be showing *From the Earth to the Moon*. We thought you might like to come down to the museum and see it." I said, "Let me think about this for a minute." And then Jorge said, "I am going whether you go or not." Then Robert said, "I'm going too." Soon everyone wanted to go, even those new members who had not known Chris. I said I'd go with them. So we took the train down to Washington; took taxis to the museum. I walked in with my kids and met the curator at the door. "Where is it?" She pointed. "It's downstairs. And Tim... it's beautiful." We took the escalator down and here is a huge painting by Anselm Kiefer, another amazing painting by Philip Guston and straight ahead a fluorescent light wall sculpture, *Monument to Tatlin* by Dan Flavin. And there it was, with its broken mirror pieces reflected in the light and shimmering like stars in a winter sky, *From the Earth to the Moon*. There was a large bench nearby. I sat down. We all sat down, even some of the kids who never knew Christopher, and we wept. It wasn't because we missed Chris, although we really do. The emotion was not sadness. What really hit me was that, before this experience, I thought I knew what art was all about. Gazing upon the painting, a revelation. Christopher was there, fully present. It was like to losing a child to the worst sort of violence, and then one day there's an unexpected knock at the door and they are there. He was so powerfully present in there. Maybe this is why those reporters wanted to concentrate on Christopher's story. He made something, something that will remain and endure for the ages.

Now it was clear. We make art to survive, to be affirmed as human voice, to make hope material, and vision manifest. I'm a witness, the work is a witness, and I want to encourage you too to be a witness.

four

young people challenging museums and galleries

Young people can bring their own style and language to art museums and galleries, presenting challenging and refreshing alternatives to the interpretation of collections and exhibitions generally perpetuated by museum professionals. Museums and galleries have employed artists to refresh their collections by providing reinstallations or commentaries that form a critique of their institutions and displays. This activity can carry stature and kudos with a well-known artist's name and authorship attached, as shown here in a project by Michael Asher with LACMALab at the Los Angeles County Museum of Art; but here Asher hands the job of reinstalling a permanent collection gallery to a group of teenagers from a local school as a conceptual gesture. A very different approach is described by educator and gallery educator Herne and McLaren: young people's perceptions of the exhibition *Live in Your Head* at the Whitechapel Art Gallery, London were developed into interpretational video commentaries which were displayed during the exhibition. In another project, also at the Whitechapel Art Gallery, Carmen Moersch presents a proposal for a creative response for artists employed in gallery education programmes: to respond creatively to these situations and the exploitative documentation which such projects generate. Lars Bang Larsen and Deborah Schwartz describe artist installations devised for children in museums; the first is an anarchic gesture of empowerment at the Moderna Museet in Sweden in the 1960s, the second a New York phenomenon where even pre-schoolers have been engaged in the thought processes behind art-making, with interactive displays by artists William Wegman, Elizabeth Murray, and Fred Wilson designed to animate their art-making processes.

While Michael Asher involved young people in reinstalling a permanent collection gallery, Danish activist Palle Neilsen turned the Moderna Museet Stockholm into a children's adventure playground, a museum-wide installation with children as collective agents in an act of revolution-by-proxy, as described in Lars Bang Larsen's article.

Student Reinstallation
of a Permanent Collection Gallery,
Los Angeles County Museum of Art,
June 2003-March 2004
Michael Asher

one: Anna Harding and
Robert L Sain, Director of LACMALab

Michael Asher, born in Los Angeles in 1943, is a seminal figure in the conceptual art scene. Since the late 1960s he has been creating projects that reveal how museums and galleries display art and how institutional practices shape our understanding of the art exhibited in those settings. Asher's work arises from the belief that no individual art object has a universal meaning, independent of its institutional context. Asher, along with other prominent conceptual artists who emerged in the 1970s, believes that the spaces and practices of the museum or gallery – its methods of interpreting, publicising, and displaying works of art – condition how we perceive and comprehend art. Throughout his career, he has dramatised this view by adopting the museum or institution as his "medium". His installations have been exhibited in numerous museums and galleries in the United States and internationally, but this is the first time he has made a project involving teenagers. *Student Reinstallation* is a radical project in the context of an institution with a rigid departmental structure and hierarchy. The use of critical art practices by institutions, which rely on the prerogative and privileged voice of the artist to declare their openness to new audiences and new ways of seeing their collections, rarely goes beyond a form of temporary questioning of the status quo. Generally speaking, once a temporary project finishes, it can always be washed over and forgotten, with collecting policies, staffing policies and other aspects of the institution's culture remaining intact.

Asher's commission for LACMALab got at the heart of museum practice and museum culture, the culture of the institution. It asked young people to examine how museums make ideas happen – a question which they are rarely encouraged to consider. The project was a sophisticated proposition about museum permission, the museum construct. Museums are conservative boxes sometimes containing risky contents. The general attitude toward a museum and its functions is, more often than not, very conservative. That's why Asher's work has been difficult for some institutions. An earlier project at MOMA New York involved researching the archive of their permanent collection and producing a catalogue of every work they had ever de-accessioned, which Asher had given out for free through the bookstore. To make this information public, including details of de-accessioning works by major artists such as Picasso, was unsettling and potentially damaging for the institution. The project disturbed the very core of the institution's decision-making authority, which tends to conceal such acts as it courts new donations, to be held in perpetuity.

LACMALab, the experimental research and development unit of the Los Angeles County Museum of Art, was set up to investigate new models for presenting art and engaging audiences at the premier visual arts museum in the Western United States, whose holdings include more than 150,000 works spanning the history of art from ancient times to the present day. The hallmark of LACMALab is the participation of commissioned artists to create new works for all ages through a collaborative process. Often their role involves articulating critiques of the institution, a method by which some art institutions have become adept at showing themselves as self-reflexive and open-minded. A famous example of this practice of institutional critique was Fred Wilson's *Mining the Museum* at the Baltimore Historical Society, 1992, in an extremely conservative institution whose exhibitions ordinarily made no reference to the role played in the city's history by Baltimore's sizeable African American community. Combing through the Historical Society's storage rooms, to which he was given free access, Wilson found slave shackles, a whipping post and a Ku Klux Klan hood among other never-exhibited objects and integrated them in the galleries with more conventional exhibits. In *Give & Take*, an exhibition over two sites at the Victoria and Albert Museum (V&A) and Serpentine Gallery in London, 2001, German conceptual artist Hans Haacke selected over 200 items from the V&A's collections to create *Mixed Messages*, a thought-provoking installation of objects from many different cultures, historical periods and a great variety of media, presented in at the contemporary Serpentine Gallery. Concurrently at the V&A 15 contemporary artists, selected by the Serpentine Gallery, exhibited across the Museum, setting up new dialogues with the collection.

For LACMALab's inaugural exhibition, *Made in California: NOW* Asher, one of 11 artists in the show, was invited to create a project that would engage young people and adults alike. Immediately intrigued by this proposition, as he had never worked with young people in such a way before, he proposed for students to re-install one of LACMA's Permanent Collection galleries. The museum had previously conducted a programme called *Kids Curate*, where the museum's typical audience of middle class families sign up their children to learn how to be like a curator. Asher's project was quite the opposite. The project was not about teaching kids, but considered what museums can find out what's in young people's heads about how to install a gallery and display art, and to contrast and compare this with the canon presented by the professionals.

Part of the original brief was that the project had to go through the standard Exhibition Committee of senior staff, which included the head of operations, head preparator (technician), head of exhibitions and budgets, head of conservation, and heads of Modern and contemporary curatorial departments.

The students would have to submit to the usual curatorial process of keeping to budgets and time-lines, and LACMALab would support students to work with real institutional resources. The students had to work within a budget of $5,000 (£2,700), the Museum's standard for a rotation of the permanent collection, which normally covers paint, labels, etc.. They had to take into account, for instance, that taking frames off paintings takes time and money. The task was about exhibition design, reinstalling the same objects in their own installation. They also wrote labels and wall texts.

LACMALab approached a high school within walking distance from the Museum. This is a school that resembles life in twenty-first century America. Fairfax High School, with 2000 plus students, is wildly diverse, with 116 languages spoken and kids from every corner of the planet. With a 1999 break down of: 12.58 per cent Asian, 2.34 per cent Filipino, 0.19 per cent Pacific Islander, 17.86 per cent Black, Non-Hispanic, 52.78 per cent Hispanic, 14.26 per cent White, Non-Hispanic (including Russian, European, Israeli), it also hosts a magnet school for visual arts, has an innovative, one-of-a-kind programme for gay and lesbian students, and one of the largest Special Education programs in the city that includes programmes for deaf and hard of hearing students and kids with autism.

The school's guidance counselor for 16- to 17-year-olds picked a group of 12 (it was agreed beforehand that a smaller group would be more feasible as well as more beneficial to the learning experience of the students), of whom about seven stayed with the project. A second group was selected to do a further gallery rotation the following year. Of the first group none of the students were art specialists. They spoke Spanish, Korean or Russian among themselves, and only English when staff walked in. For the first rotation, a facilitator was employed who was a freelance education consultant from another museum. After an extensive interviewing process, the facilitator for the first rotation was selected based on her experience working as an educator in one of the local museums. It was thought that with this experience, she would be able to guide the students through the rigorous museum installation process as well as provide detailed information on the historical context of the works they would be dealing with. It was decided early on to not use the same facilitator for both rotations. For the second rotation a local artist was selected who had experience in museum installation as well as teaching in one of the local art schools. This was someone they believed would be better able to provide direction while not biasing any of the students' decisions.

Asher was very careful to avoid telling the young people what to do. He met them, they experienced his other projects, what he is about. He was always available, he was totally engaged in what they were doing but most of the time he was not with the group. His role is about permission, an understanding of the artist as revealing issues of power. Perhaps the students' proposals were more conservative than Michael would have hoped, but he couldn't say that.

The role of facilitator was critical. LACMALab was involved more politically than hands-on, helping out when there was a problem or when the young people were ready to make proposals. They were dealing with two worlds – the art world and the business world. The hope was that the project was life transforming, as they started talking about applying to college to do work like this. Dealing with the bureaucracy at LACMA, which is not unlike many large institutions, would give you the confidence to deal with brick walls anywhere in life.

This project stood up simultaneously in multiple worlds: as a new mentoring programme, a new commission for Michael, a new activation for the permanent collection, and it might well have been a management consultancy to encourage senior staff to deal with new ideas, new questions which they may find difficult. In a quiet way it achieved all of these ends. Students met with senior staff to try to understand the roles, and carried out research in the library to understand the context. The museum convention is to tell you that "we are the professionals, this is the right way to do things", with a tacit implication that you are lucky to be there. For anyone outside the culture of that institution, it is hard to appreciate how alternative or radical it was, having an infiltration of the system through kids.

The group had to present their proposals to the Exhibitions Committee in a formal boardroom meeting, with 15 senior staff to whom they presented their case. This is an example of how they had to adopt what was considered normal professional behaviour in terms of presentation, format and style. At the presentation a kid said "Let me ask you a question: when was the first time you actually went to a museum?" The senior staff member answered "When I was about 30." This brilliant moment disarmed them, as they realised they weren't the only ones who had not grown up with this experience. The kids continued: "One of our goals is to remove barriers between public and art, therefore we would like to remove all the frames from the paintings." All those present said no. Then they realised that those who said no did not have the authority to say no – they needed the painting conservator who was not there, so they would defer the question to him. Joe the conservator later took the students into the gallery, took a painting by Corot off the wall and showed them how taking off the frame risks damaging the painting. This they understood. They were about to accept their disappointment when he said "but there are five paintings we could do it with". They would have to negotiate with the curators, but finally it was agreed that one painting by Sir Edwin Landseer could be unframed.

The museum staff didn't know what to do with the proposed project. Initially, some staff were exhilarated, others exasperated. The staff became worried and expressed their concerns that the students' reinstallation must be safe for the art, safe for the visitor and respect what they deemed the integrity of the art. One particularly odd anxiety from the Committee was: "What if they want to make frames out of marijuana?" Another concern was that it was not to be just designed for themselves and their peers (perhaps the museum staff were worried that they wouldn't understand it). Interestingly, guards and cleaners, not curators, are often the ones who enforce the most protective and conservative views about the collection. While the Contemporary curators totally supported the project, it was more difficult for non-contemporary staff to relate to a conceptual project and to commissioning new work. They wanted to know in advance what it would look like, and queried what exactly the artist Michael Asher was doing for his fee if he was not making the work himself.

The installation of the European Painting and Sculpture Gallery included a table on which you were encouraged to write what you think, decorated by real taggers in their own graffiti designs. The museum staff expressed concerns that it gave the wrong message by encouraging people to write on the table. A compromise which was agreed was that all people must be able to read it. The introduction of coloured lighting was a great moment for the technician who has quietly done the lighting for 20 years, who was really fired up by the project.

The Modern and Contemporary Gallery, which included Rene Magritte's painting *The Treason of Images* (*Ceci ne'st pas une pipe*), c.1928-1929, was normally painted in "LACMA beige". The young people decided to turn it into a street scene, with John Coltrane's saxophone sounds wafting through, mirrored walls and a cityscape design on dark blue paintwork. A new narrative was revealed by exposing the backs of paintings, which often shows their entire provenance (details of previous owners, loans to exhibitions, repairs, etc.). The museum designer was particularly enthused by the exercise of showing this previously invisible history.

This was a commissioned Michael Asher artwork, which is quite distinct from standard museum education projects. The artist owns the idea, the Museum would not do the project again without him. A legal contract with the artist regarding ownership of the work does not name the students, although they were credited in the gallery. Visitors to the galleries and the young people involved may have little conception of Michael Asher's authorship, even though this was explained in didactics (text panels) in the gallery.

two: Michael Asher,
Excerpts from a Lecture, London, June 2003

Student Reinstallation employs an experimental method in order to uncover questions I have about the practice of institutional museum critique and Arts Education at the Los Angeles County Museum of Art – questions such as: Could there be a way of involving young people that would be better than museum-controlled and museum-mediated programs that now exist at LACMA? And could there be a way of advancing display systems that reveal the shortcomings of existing museum conventions?

The aspect of experimentation most important to my work is not unpredictability generated by a finite structure, as much as it is a radical shift in dealing with a problem. More specifically, this work proposes an alternative approach to arts education at LACMA that abandons the top-down model whose primary function

is to legitimise the museum and its collection in favour of an approach that utilises museum resources as tools for advancing schooling while urging students to seek their untapped potential.

This work proposes that it might be possible to reconsider aspects of display systems by observing the language of non-professionals.

It is one thing for the staff to benefit from the students' idealism, but it is much harder for the museum to realise that it might profit by becoming a lab for many different types of experiments.

Besides operating experimentally, this artwork also functioned as a critical tool. On one level, it gives young people access to historical objects, and requests that they make judgements which will have a real-world effect upon reception. On another, it gives museum educators insight into the signs and beliefs of a few young people whose learning is a product entirely of their own motivation. Still another tool stems from the students. Not having an investment in affirming the status of the museum, nor participating in a critical art practice, they begin to touch on assumptions of each. They do this with an authenticity which is hard to overlook. This artwork is meant to generate many other types of experiments in arts education and museum critique.

three: conversation between Anna Harding and Michael Asher, December 2004-March 2005

Anna Harding: What was your aim in sharing authorship with young people?

Michael Asher: Let me give you a short background and then answer your question. In 1999 LACMALab at the Los Angeles County Museum of Art invited me to participate in the exhibition *Made in California: NOW*, which took place the following year. My proposal was geared toward youth involvement (in my case high school students) as were all other works in this part of *Made In*

California: NOW. Rather than animating a set of formal conditions, I requested that a group of 11th grade students (aged 16 to 17) fulfil a routine museum task. The one I chose was to reinstall the collection in one of the galleries housing the permanent collection. The students had to use all of the already existing art objects that the curator had arranged, which represented a version of history the museum wanted to convey to the public. I requested that the students reinstall the artwork so as to express the story they thought would be the most ideal and compelling for public reception. (This was to assume they might want to change it; otherwise they could keep it the same.) The mechanics of gallery presentation would be similar to those followed by the curators.

LACMALab and the students' facilitator were the most crucial in making sure the students were able to implement their project based on their own terms. LACMALab made sure that the museum bureaucracy understood what was needed for the students and attempted to ameliorate internal fears. The facilitator was an individual from the community who was an artist, had museum experience, and was knowledgeable in art history. This individual maintained a space where the students could ask the questions they needed and also find their own answers.

The concept, along with each alteration, was to be the students' alone, and not shaped due to the input of others. Therefore, if they happened to receive suggestions, they were under no obligation to follow them. Part of my proposal was dedicated to preserving the students' autonomy. Another part of the proposal was designed to enable them to make informed decisions about the artwork and the museum. This way, their results could not simply be written off as unknowing.

The group began by meeting with the staff of each separate department in order to understand their function. Simultaneously, they were to research on their own the history of the artwork in the gallery. The rest of the time was spent developing ideas. Once they had their final concept and all of its details, the students mocked it up with a scale model. As was expected of curators, the students also had to present their model to the Exhibition Committee. The Exhibition Committee included staff representatives from Conservation,

Design-Graphics, Security, Education, Curatorial and preparators (technicians). The Committee figured out the logistics. This included getting approvals, determining the feasibility of the proposal, deciding which staff would work on each part, setting dates for closing of the gallery and reopening, and anything else that was found to be necessary. The students met with the Committee a second time so final plans could be approved. Once the work on the reinstallation began, the students were expected to be in the gallery to answer any last-minute questions and, if possible, to help the staff.

My own participation was limited to designing the proposal and attending the students' second meeting for the purpose of discussing my proposal as well as my work. I also attended the Exhibition Committee meetings and was available if the students wanted to show me their progress. The only say that the Museum had was limited to accepting changes if the work of art was placed in a dangerous manner, if the viewer's safety was jeopardised, or if the texts meant for reading (such as wall labels) were not legible. The only other restriction on the students was their budget.

Hopefully, this description of how my work operated begins to give you a sense that not only did we not share authorship, we performed very different roles in the project. I did not share in their decisions and they didn't in mine. Sharing authorship would have eliminated the well-differentiated ways they chose to animate meaning, which seems to be defined not only through the way the students chose to understand their new situation, but also what was important to their collective experience. Perhaps just as important as taking on this new problem was that each group became responsible for both positive and negative dimensions of their learning rather than the Museum institution or an individual collaborator with greater authority making these judgements for them. If there is only an upside to this model of self-directed understanding of problems, which is suggested by these first two rotations, then why isn't it more prevalent in our museums, which often have resources to support it?

What could students achieve which you couldn't?

The students entered a situation which required them to organise their own ideas. They began with a list, which identified their own individual interests and at the same time found a way to represent them within a collective of other ideas. Quite fortunately and rather immediately, they were mining an area which was familiar to them and perhaps to sectors of their generation. Each rotation came up with solutions which were quite different from one another as well as quite different from what we see in the professional sphere.

If the students had been guided to become consumers of culture, then they would have brought forward solutions we recognise or otherwise might be able to achieve. But by having the reinstallation rooted in the students' experiences rather than mediated by the institution's or mine, the questions turned around how meaning was put together and the way the students wanted us to read the collection. This was most clear in the second rotation, particularly in the careful way the students grouped together very different works of art which shared one formal/visual sign or the way they put together very complicated spatial systems of display which were based upon their experiences of the city street, with its signs and billboards.

Why were you excited by this project, and what did you get out of it?

There was a real pleasure in developing a structure for young people to have a real world effect upon the public reception of art. But I had a particular interest in how the students became motivated to teach themselves and ultimately the impact that this new-found ability had on their schooling.

This project seemed to bring the best out of everyone involved at the Museum, which was a great plus. In the end I was able to see quite a large potential in an age group who simply had few outlets to express their thoughtful discoveries.

Does being an artist give you licence to break rules which others are not allowed to break? Is this relevant to the project?

I don't know if this question is relevant. The ultimate power resides with the museum. They have the ultimate licence to shape cultural thought. If they discover that working with an artist is helpful in this respect, then they will do so. My proposal was an attempt to maintain the museum's framework for reinstallation while using all the pre-existing works in the gallery, thereby employing that which was important to them. Similarly, my work refers to the Museum's mission statement in the area of education. One can see that the proposal agrees with the Museum's structure and philosophy but shifts the responsibility of installing the collection to young people. As a result, their work ends up casting doubt on the conventions of museum display. Ultimately, this work is meant to be a part of a much larger discussion of how well the Museum serves its public.

What do you feel the young people got from the project, and what evidence could you give of this?

You can understand from my proposal I hesitate in becoming an intermediary for the students. Their counsellor wrote to LACMALab explaining some of the changes that he noticed after the reinstallation. It's not just what the students got out of it, the urge is to focus on the students, yet it was a win-win situation for everyone involved, even if one or two resisted it.

How important was it that the young people considered themselves as working on your project versus working on a museum education project?

I believe it was clear that the young people were working for themselves. I have reason to believe from some of what they spoke about that I was associated with the implications of this line of inquiry. I don't know if it would be different or not if they believed themselves to be working on an education department project.

What about documentation?

This was originally a low priority. It was to avoid the self-consciousness that comes along with recording apparatus. Also, there was so much to take care of just to make this happen that documentation became difficult. The few times we tried documenting something it didn't work out. Suffice to say, most of the documentation is of the reinstallation.

four: letter to kelly carney, LACMALab programme co-ordinator

Dear Kelly,   April 3, 2001
I just wanted to take a few minutes to thank you for all that you have done to assist our students with the Michael Asher Reinstallation Project. The opportunity to work with you and the other people at the Los Angeles County Museum of Art has been a life-changing event for the five students involved.

   In November, you met with a group of quiet, shy students and told them about this project. Now, you can see the confidence in these students, and hear it in their voices. Last week, one of the counsellors at school commented on how much friendlier Monica Zentano has been lately. She's not friendlier, she's always been friendly. She's just more confident and willing to express herself. Hyo Jin Shin has always been quietly confident, but this project provided her with the chance to demonstrate her talent and her leadership skills. All five of the students involved in this project are better students and better people today than they were five months ago, and they have you and the people at LACMA to thank for that.

   Please extend my gratitude to Flora Ito, the project facilitator, Robert Sain, the director of LACMALab, Lynn Zelevansky, curator, and Michael Asher, artist, for all their time, patience, and energy. And thanks to all the people at LACMA who made this project possible.

   When I first spoke to you, I told you that we have great kids at Fairfax, and you've given five of them an experience that they will never forget. I hope that when another opportunity arises, you will think of Fairfax again. Again, thank you for everything.

Sincerely, Denis Myles Furlong
Fairfax High School Counsellor

Art Inside Out at the children's museum of manhattan
Deborah F schwartz

Art Inside Out is an exhibition that resulted from an ongoing commitment at
the Children's Museum of Manhattan to engage their visitors in authentic art
experiences through a variety of programmes and exhibitions. The Museum
regularly mounts exhibitions of original works by well-known children's book
illustrators, and offers daily art-making workshops. But a major exhibition
featuring original artworks by prominent fine artists, enveloped inside an
interactive environment is something else entirely. Originally discussed in 2000
as an exhibition that would feature one great historical work of art, conversation
turned fairly quickly to an exhibit that could introduce families to the work of
contemporary artists. The planning team saw the potential for something far more
innovative, that would be dynamic and that held the promise of taking the museum
into a new relationship to the world of art and artists. Response from various
constituents, ranging from artists to the Museum's trustees was wildly enthusiastic.

Two months into the process, three extraordinary artists – Elizabeth
Murray, William Wegman and Fred Wilson – had agreed to work with us on
the exhibition, to lend us original work, to talk with children about their work,
and to help develop interactive components of the exhibition. One of our first
preparatory tasks was to put together teams of eight- and nine-year-old children
to meet with the artists and talk with them about their work. Each team of
children was different. Some of the children knew very little about art, others
knew a good deal, some were from public schools and others from private
schools. The conversations with Murray and Wegman took place in their studios
where they could show the children how they worked, and since Fred Wilson
makes very conceptual art, the conversation took place at his gallery, where the
children could actually look at some of his work made from found objects. Each
conversation was distinct and specific to the particular work that the children
saw. Discussion was not in the least generic, and the children had an

extraordinary ability to see qualities in the work that were particular to the vision of the individual artist. These conversations were video taped, and became a central planning tool in thinking about what sorts of questions children had when they looked at these artists' work, and in determining what sorts of issues would be easiest or hardest to convey to children.

The challenges were very real: children's museums tend to serve a very complex mix of audiences, with pre-school children representing a very significant component of the audience. So, while the ideal audience for this exhibition was six- to twelve-year-olds, there was no question that the little ones would come and explore as well. That meant that at least some portion of the exhibition had to satisfy the physical and kinetic needs of very young children, even while it invited older children to think about how an artist conveys very complex intellectual ideas through visual imagery.

Together, the Museum's talented staff, myself, the guest curator, and the artists worked to invent a type of exhibition that was new to us all; an exhibition that brought important original works of art to a children's museum, and at the same time, an exhibition that had the playful, hands-on qualities that audiences have come to expect from a children's museum.

One of the ways in which we were able to succeed in melding these usually separate exhibition models, was by testing our ideas directly with children. Formative tests with children indicated what might work and what might not, when our interactive exhibitions actually conveyed the ideas that we wanted and when they did not. Designers, interns, and knowledgeable exhibition developers watched, as children of various ages and backgrounds looked at reproductions of work on the potential checklist, and tested mock-up interactive components. Revision after revision led to the final product.

What follows is an interview that was released to the press, just prior to the opening of the exhibition in October 2002.

An interview with Deborah Schwartz, Curator, Art Inside Out

You began working with the Children's Museum of Manhattan on *Art Inside Out* in the fall of 2000. How did you get started? What were your first thoughts?

When we started work, the in-house team and I agreed that we should immediately pull together a group of children, to speak with them about art and learn how they thought about it. We also agreed that we should use the work and voices of living artists in an active way. Those two ideas merged fairly quickly. Instead of having the children talk with just the Museum team, we arranged for groups of kids to meet some of the artists who might collaborate with us.

How did you decide on these three artists: Elizabeth Murray, William Wegman, and Fred Wilson?

In the beginning, we put together long lists of artists who might have been friendly to the idea of this exhibition. Most of those artists, though not all, had children of their own. But very soon, we saw that we had to consider other criteria as well. We wanted artists who work in very different ways, so the exhibition could begin to reveal to kids that art isn't only one thing. It isn't all painting; it isn't all sculpture. And, of course, we wanted some diversity of gender and ethnic background.

Out of those discussions came a much shorter list; and out of that list, we were lucky enough to get the participation of Elizabeth, Bill, and Fred.

How did you go about putting together the children with the artists?

We set up the sessions pretty quickly, once the artists agreed to do the show with us. We brought together small groups of children, ages eight to ten, with six or seven kids talking to each artist. For the most part, by design, we chose kids who did not know much about art. We got these children from schools, not from art classes or museums. Also by design, they were a real mix: mostly public school kids but some from private schools, with girls, boys, and every ethnic background we could get our hands on.

We videotaped the sessions, and out of that came all sorts of ideas for the show.

Where did these sessions take place – at the Museum?

No. One group met with Elizabeth in her studio. A second group met with Wegman in his photo studio with his dogs, where they did a photo session together. A third group met with Fred Wilson at the Metro Pictures gallery, since Fred doesn't really have a studio. His studio's in his head. So, each session happened in a different context, and a different group of kids participated each time.

We said to the artists, "Start talking about your art any way you want. We just want this to be a conversation." In each case, the kids were totally fascinated. And in each case, the nature of their questions was completely different. They had everything to do with what the artists were showing.

What were the conversations like?

With Elizabeth, the kids mostly wanted to do know how she paints: how she picks her colors, how she makes her choices. One of the key decisions about the exhibition came out of that conversation.

The kids were looking at a huge painting she'd just finished, *Plan 9*, and one of the youngest of them said to Elizabeth, "What I'd really like to do is jump into the picture." And another kid said, "Oh, yeah. Not just jump into it. Maybe we could take the painting and turn it into a set of rooms you could walk through. This could be a hallway." And he began to talk about how the painting could be changed into a structure.

The next thing we knew, our Museum team was thinking about how to convert this same painting into a space that kids could walk through and explore. We didn't know how Elizabeth would feel about that – but when we came back to her with it, she loved the idea. She was totally game, and I think it was because the suggestion really had come from the kids.

What happened when the kids got together with William Wegman?

William Wegman,
installation views.

With Bill, the kids wanted to know how he trains the dogs. So he talked a lot
about how he actually *doesn't* train them, about how they like to work and to
co-operate. He also spoke about the way the dogs inspire him, that his ideas
about a new work of art often come directly from looking at the dogs. Bill's
sense of humor is very dry, and he talks about art in very sophisticated ways
that I wasn't sure would be conducive to a conversation with kids. But he was
very comfortable demonstrating how he dresses up a dog, puts it on a stool,
and has someone stand behind to be the dog's arms. He actually did that with the
kids, and of course they got a tremendous kick out of it.

Through that experience, I think, the kids began to see that artists can
have all sorts of wacky tools. Elizabeth has her paints; Bill has the dogs. Of course,
the dogs are also a part of his life and his art, in a profound way. I'm not sure that
the children understood that. But they did start to get an idea that has become
key to the exhibition, this notion that artists can work with almost anything.

**Elizabeth Murray and William Wegman both make objects. Fred Wilson does
not. He takes objects out of museum collections and arranges them to create
installations. Could the children really get a handle on his work?**

When we initially proposed working with Fred, some of the adults involved in
the project asked, "How are children going to understand him?" In fact, during
his session with the kids, Fred described what he does, and one of the kids said,
"Now, let me get this straight. You take other people's art, and you make it into
your *own* art?" Fred said, "Yes, that's exactly what I do." And all the kids said,
"Oh. OK." Not a problem. It just wasn't a problem for them.

So now, when adults ask me, "How can you think that children will
understand Fred Wilson's work?" I just say, "Believe me, they do." Kids don't
yet have the boundaries that adults do. It turns out that they can understand
art on different levels, conceptual as well as formal – and that, too, is one of the
most important ideas we're incorporating into the exhibition.

William Wegman,
installation view.

As you moved beyond these sessions with the artists, what challenges did you encounter as you began to define the contents of the exhibition?

Doing an art exhibition at the Children's Museum is in some respects much harder and more complicated than doing it at an art museum. You're constantly moving back and forth between doing right by the works of art and making sure that children are engaged in ways that are appropriate for them. Fortunately, I was surrounded at the Children's Museum by people who have spent many years of their professional lives watching kids, testing things with them, making sure that activities don't just represent what adults think kids ought to be interested in but are genuinely meaningful for kids.

At first, when we wanted to explain why a particular work of art is important, or why it might have an emotional impact on us, I thought we could just write something. And everybody in the Children's Museum would say to me, "Actually, no, we can't. We have to figure out what children can do that will make that idea real for them." That's a very different process from the one I was used to.

Can you give us an example of how the staff would figure out an activity?

In the Fred Wilson section, we wanted to have a piece in which kids would use objects to put together their own 'installations', to express an idea they would like to convey. So, to test the piece, we gave some kids a little group of figurines that included characters from *The Wizard of Oz*. Well, when you use objects like that, you find they're already infused with meaning. If you ask kids to express

Fred Wilson,
installation view.

the idea of 'a bad day at school' and they've got a figurine of the Wicked Witch, the scenario is going to be pretty obvious.

So we tested this activity again, using a set of wooden blocks. We thought the kids might be able to express 'a bad day at school' with completely neutral objects. But blocks are blocks. The kids completely ignored the project we'd proposed for them and used the blocks to make buildings.

For the next test – and this is a testament to the Museum's incredibly talented staff – we came up with a set of egg-shaped blocks. They were no longer building blocks, because they were oval. By virtue of being oval they had the quality of a head or a body, but they were also abstract. Suddenly, kids were able to create scenarios out of them. That's the kind of back-and-forth we've had.

Have you tested anything that the children have absolutely hated?

We wanted to see how the kids would react to William Wegman's early videos. I wanted to show them in the exhibition, because they're hysterically funny but also odd and edgy. When we tested them, some of them made the kids say, "This is *horrible*. I *hate* this!" Others just puzzled the kids, and still others, mostly the ones with the dogs, they liked. In the end, we decided to leave in a few of the videos the kids thought were weird and one of the videos they really didn't like.

Why would you do that?

We did it because kids should know they don't have to like everything in an exhibition, nor should they expect to. Also, grown-ups shouldn't expect that every kid will react in the exact same way.

So we used the information from our test groups, but we didn't use it slavishly. And we were rewarded with some pleasant surprises. It turned out that the kids loved Bill's more abstract work, in which the dogs don't appear as dogs. For example, there's a gorgeous triptych, a seascape, where the back of the dogs are rocks along the beach. The kids thought that was the coolest thing they'd ever seen. Nobody expected that; they thought the kids would respond more to Bill's more illustrative photographs, like *Little Red Riding Hood* and *Cinderella*.

What do you hope kids will get out of this exhibition?

It seems very routine to me to say "Colour, line, and form are what children really understand in art, so we'll talk about those." I care less about whether kids focus on the formal qualities of art than whether they understand that art is about ideas, and that it helps us to see the world in different ways. Without using words – mostly – artists represent their thoughts and feelings about the world. And that's provocative. Art can shake the world up, make us see, feel, and think in creative ways. For me, that's the satisfaction of looking, and I think that's what kids like about it, too.

The point is, artists go through a process that's very much about problem-solving. Sometimes it's problem-solving in a very concrete way. Elizabeth will say, "I'm going to pose a problem for myself with these peculiar-shaped canvases and this set of colors. What can I do with these things?" The solution is the painting. Elizabeth says that when there's no problem to solve, the work doesn't interest her.

But there's also a kind of problem-solving that's about something being amiss in the world. Visual images help us explore our social and cultural world. Fred Wilson gets into historical, social, and political issues all the time. And so do kids, when they make drawings or tell stories. That's part of what's breathtaking about putting artists together with children – you see that there's a shared ground.

In your experience, are the artists excited about that shared ground?

Absolutely. They seem to be having enormous fun in this environment. I also feel that all of the adults involved in this exhibition have been willing to have conversations about art that are not constricted by art-world jargon, by preconceived expectations. Thanks to this setting, we're able to talk in very basic terms about the significance of art and the issues it can raise. And all of that has been translated into the final exhibition.

One final question. What has it meant to you, as an experienced museum educator, to participate in creating *Art Inside Out*?

For me, this is about breaking out of some of the confines of an art museum. It feels to me that some of the things that are most compelling to me as an art educator, trained as an art historian, have now been put into a new setting, where fundamental, important ideas about the nature of art can be laid out for children and their families.

These are basic ideas about the process of creativity, about artists being problem-solvers, about artists coming from all sorts of different backgrounds

Fred Wilson,
installation view.

and using different kinds of tools, about artists responding to the world around them. There's a certain level of risk to the way we're setting forth those ideas in *Art Inside Out*. But I'm sure the risk is worth it – because the people who visit this exhibition are going to be directly, actively engaged with the works of art.

A good museum is essentially a big invitation to participate in works of art. Whether you're relating to a painting or sculpture one-on-one or whether you're talking it over with a friend or a parent, that idea of you as an active participant is crucial. In *Art Inside Out*, we're expanding on that notion, thanks to the encouragement of these three artists and thanks to the special nature of the Children's Museum of Manhattan. I'm eager for our visitors to begin joining in.

Application: Proposal for a Youth Project Dealing with Forms of Youth Visibility in Galleries

Carmen Moersch

This proposal has been partly created as a reflection on gallery education and its dependency on documentation. Educational activities in the gallery are performative and temporal. Their participants take their presence away with them, embodied in personal memories and narrations of the events. Documentary images therefore form their only enduring visibility, the only proof that 'something happened'. They play a significant role in the economic reproduction and the legitimation of gallery education programmes, as they serve in funding applications as a proof of their social and educational effects. Until now, there has been little discourse about the universal and universalising narrations these images create.

Artists are professionally dedicated to take a critical approach towards the production of images. The fact that artists are involved in conceiving and conducting gallery education projects could be seen as an unrealised potential to use their expertise also for a critical approach towards forms of documentation of these activities. Secondly, the present paradigm of gallery education to engage people in the creation of their own representations could potentially lead to the idea that they should also be actively participating in the modes of documenting these activities. This underlying general proposal is developed using the observation of a specific situation as a starting point – the observation of a 'magic moment'.

Observation

A renowned public art gallery in London shows a retrospective of an architect who belongs to the canon of twentieth century, Western architectural history. The gallery borrowed the exhibition from a major New York museum. With the loan, a few of the gallery's rules change temporarily. For one, the room, which usually displays contemporary art, seems more museum-like than it normally does: an elaborate exhibition design picks up on and quotes the formal and stylistic elements of the architect, it divides the room, which is actually quite wide, into little cabinets.

Whereas normally there is no charge for entry, visitors have to pay for this exhibition. With the admission ticket, they receive a round sticker for their coat or jacket, which allows the attendants to confirm from a distance that the guests have paid. The variously coloured stickers, in clear contrast to the subdued winter clothing, can be seen everywhere. The attendants are instructed to pay particularly close attention to make sure that no one touches the exhibits – it is said that just one single little tree on the precise replicas of the master architect's models costs £100 ($175).

During this exhibition, a special audience is in the gallery. These are people who bring along the necessary financial resources and sufficient interest in the theme to pay the rather considerable entry fee – primarily architects and architecture students wanting to see the visionary models, whose influence on architecture's development right through to the present day is clearly legible. Through the audience's strict dress code, its whiteness and bourgeois bearing, it seems even more homogenous than usual in this institution, which, since the beginning of the twentieth century, has consistently endeavoured to facilitate "social inclusion" and the utilisation of art for educational purposes.

The gallery is situated in the East End of the city, in an area where diverse immigrant groups have lived since its development. Even 100 years ago, the founders of the gallery were interested in using their exhibition activities to mediate between the various ethnic groups in the sense of cultural diversity and social inclusion: on the one hand, to cultivate the 'locals'' respect for the 'foreigners' and on the other, to show that the latter are only temporarily foreign, because in the end they become familiar, and with time assimilate. Similar to the formal language of the architect on display, this discourse also continues into the present, and it too produces its specific visibility.

At first this is articulated in the exhibition space, through the seemingly constant presence of groups of mainly Asian and black British young people in school uniforms. Their presence can be attributed to the involvement of the gallery's Education Department, which works together with a majority of the schools in the locality to ensure that as many local school classes as possible visit at least one of the exhibitions and participate in a related workshop.

The starting point for my considerations is a visit to the exhibition by Year Eight pupils (aged 12 to 13) from a neighbouring girls' school. I was able to accompany the girls' visit in my function as a researcher studying artists who work in gallery education in England. For three months I accompanied parts of the education programme of the Whitechapel Gallery, interviewed artists who worked in projects there and undertook observations in their workshops. I introduced myself to the participants of the workshops as a German researcher who is trying to learn about good practice in gallery education in the UK, to bring it to institutions in my own country. That coincided nicely with the fact that an exhibition of an architect considered as being of German origin formed the stage for our interactions. It seemed that I was more easily accepted as I was offered by the pupils to take on the position of expert for the things on display.

To reconstruct the situation means telling a story, yet the aim is not to describe how it really was with "real facts". The narration rests on my perception and thus forms a constructed and deliberately condensed version of events.

collecting Data

The pupils have already met the artist leading this gallery visit. They had visited her studio the week before and grappled with her largely immaterial artistic practice, which at the time mainly comprised running networks, urban guerilla actions, and the kinds of educational activities for which we had gathered this morning in the gallery. In the subsequent weeks, she would come to the school on several occasions and do practical work with the students based on the architect's works. Additionally, in the next three months she would develop her own work, to take place in the context of the school. All of this is part of the project for which she was commissioned by the gallery's Education Department.

As I learned from a number of interviews with the artist, she understands the interplay of her various fields of activity as politically motivated artistic practice. She positions her work explicitly in an interstice between art and education. She has a critical relationship with both systems and analyses their mechanisms of inclusion, exclusion and disciplination (disciplinary action in the sense described by Michel Foucault).[1]

She is aware of the fact that the pupils with whom she will view the architect's models are far removed from most of what comprises this context. The houses in which they live are remote from the architecture on view, designed for wealthy property owners who are interested in purist stylistic forms. Their everyday lives are far removed from the territorial and economic relations that enable this type of architecture in the first place. The areas that the students come from also seem remote from the spatial structures and the socio-historical context embodied by the gallery in which the exhibition is taking place. They are presumably far away from their own personal interests – this is a school outing and what is happening here is instruction. The artist is also aware that, besides the teacher, she will be the only white person in the group and that this also perpetuates, at least visually, the Victorian and philanthropic tradition in which the phenomenon of education through art in the gallery is historically founded. And she is also aware of the function of the galleries and museums as a "civilising ritual".[2]

In the gallery's foyer, adjoining the exhibition space, the pupils are given their stickers. As a school class they are admitted free of charge to this exhibition, but the marker is important so that the attendants can identify them as legitimate gallery visitors. The pupils are warned to put their stickers in a visible place on their school uniforms. They stand out in bright yellow against the black and blue fabric.

The artist has carefully prepared for the students' visit. She has made up a worksheet on which there are questions that they are meant to answer as they wander through the gallery. "Use your own feelings as a guide to help you learn about architecture. Start with this room – the art gallery" is the header on the sheet of paper. The questions that follow function like a connecting thread, to make the work of the architect accessible, but also for the understanding of, and critical reflection on the gallery space. With questions such as: "How is the atmosphere in here achieved, what makes this the kind of room it is?", the pupils are challenged to produce a full description: they are meant to record the atmosphere of the gallery space, its architectural details, and their perception of the space. At the same time the artist gives them responsibility for a video camera, to record the architectural models and the spaces of the gallery from their own perspective. This is a particular privilege, as filming and photography is actually prohibited in the exhibition.

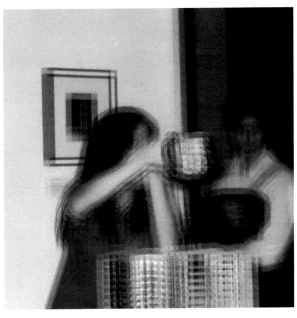

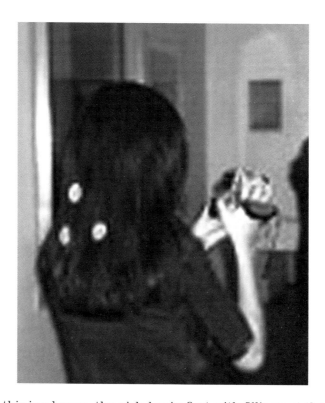

Since this is a lesson, the girls begin first with filling out the worksheets. However, the gesture of concentrated obedience does not last long. The written answers on the questionnaires become increasingly sparse. These pupils who, according to their teachers, already have a reputation for their "lack of discipline" mix among the other visitors to the exhibition, which is particularly well-attended on this day, and hang around, giggle about themselves and others, and for the most part seem to be waiting for the gallery visit to end. Five of them join with a small, select group from an international auction house, being led around the exhibition by an art historian, who is lecturing passionately about the architect's drawings. They imitate the enacted gestures of serious interest and set off a brief disturbance in the group.

Only one girl, who has the camera, is still busy with the task to which she was assigned. She seems to be fascinated by the details of the models extracted by the camera lens and, mainly, with the use of the equipment itself. After a while, the others recognise her immersion. One of them pulls the yellow sticker off of her jacket and sticks it into the hair of the girl with the camera. The girl doesn't notice it; her hair is quite thick and long. In her hair, the sticker looks like a precious jewel. The prank spreads quickly among the girls. One by one they all pull their stickers off of their clothes and secretly stick them in her hair. The control stickers progressively transform into confetti and gold coins and back again. The girl with the camera still doesn't notice anything, although in the meantime at least 20 yellow dots are stuck on her head. The others can hardly control themselves. At some point, the girl with the camera sees her laughing classmates before her eyes, mirrored in the glass of a picture frame. She registers that something has shifted in the situation and that for some reason or another she is the focus of this shift. In the mirrored reflection, she discovers the yellow dots in her hair. But instead of getting angry (as I expected), she begins to laugh and turns admiringly in front of the mirror. She takes her own yellow sticker off of her uniform and adds it to the others in her hair.

Along with me, a gallery attendant also witnesses the sticker transformation action. This man, who otherwise always looks quite grumpy, laughs so hard on this occasion that he ends up crying. It is the first time that I have ever even seen him laugh and the change in his appearance is impressive.

In the remaining half hour, all of the pupils walk around the gallery without their sticker. However, none are reprimanded by the attendants.

interpretation

In my view, the students' action simultaneously reveals and undermines the established manner of movement and behaviour in the gallery space. From this perspective, one can link it to the way of reading the gallery critically, as had been proposed to them in the artist's questions on the worksheet. They found a way to fulfil the artist's appeal for a deconstruction of the situation. Furthermore, they take an additional step by displacing the yellow badges – the visible signs of institutional legitimisation and control, to which their own attendance is subjected. They reinterpret them to suit their own interests: from entry stickers to a prank on a classmate, to a festive hair decoration, to confetti, for example – and what is most interesting – to oscillate between all of these at the same time.

It is empirically difficult to prove whether the artist's critical questions on the worksheet inspired the pupils to this action. What is certain is that it could not have taken place in a strictly structured setting clearly aiming at the reproduction of available knowledge. At the same time, the moment of involuntariness in the group's attendance has resulted in this form of self-articulation. It is no more and no less than a successful way to pass the time, a playful testing out of the rules and the borders of the situation with which they are expected to deal.

Documentation

At the time when this situation took place, I had begun to work regularly in the archives that are found in the gallery's basement, under the floor where the visitors walk around. Stored there is the gallery's entire preserved written, acoustic and visual documentation collected since its founding more than 100 years ago. On a large set of shelves, overloaded with notebooks and files, is documentation of the Education Department's activities since 1976 – when the first full-time Education Officer was hired by the gallery – until 2001.[3] According to my estimates, this section of the archive holds several thousand pictures. They all show situations from workshops, gallery talks, artist-in-school projects and community projects. At first glance, they almost all look alike, apart from a few significant fashion changes that have occurred over the past 25 years. They show people, mainly children and teenagers, who stand or sit at tables and do or produce things. Or people sitting or standing around artworks in the gallery. The photos seem to create an ornament, which at first glance doesn't have much meaning other than perhaps as a souvenir for the participating subjects.

And these thousands of pictures are merely from one gallery! Day after day, in almost all of the public art institutions in Great Britain, more of this documentation is produced; a never-ending conveyor belt of redundant visual production. Mainly, the pictures serve as proof of two things: first, they prove that projects have taken place and second, that it is impossible to photographically capture the truly important processes of these activities. For example, the various encounters of the subjects and the art through language, the jokes and struggles, the experiences and learning processes during the creation and during collective negotiations are not visible in the pictures. And just like my photos of the previously described situation, they do not relate anything about the little moments, the subversions and resistances which arise in the educational setting in which learning takes place (perhaps) which is, in any case, difficult to verify.

Perception changes when the pictures are placed in a context – for example in a number of artists' books, which arose as project documentation mainly in the 1980s, of which some can be found in the archives. In the better of these, rather than serving primarily as a means of evidence, the pictures present parallel visual narrations to a poetic and critical questioning of the described projects. According to the amount of effort put into them, they also refer implicitly to the different individual production conditions: were sufficient resources available to allow time for a well conceived documentation, how seriously did the institution take the participating artists and other subjects? It seems true that meanings stabilise through contextualisation. Their function changes according to the commentary, design, and addressee.

In the next stage, the next problem appears: the problem of instrumentalising visual representations of participants, mainly so-called marginalised persons – i.e., people with immigrant backgrounds or with disabilities – for interests that are beyond their reach, mainly for the financing of the art institution, something which has become a common and compulsory practice. Education Departments are confronted with the economically existential necessity of having to produce documentation in a language that can be understood by state and private sponsors and which functions as evidence of the projects' requisite socio-cultural effectiveness. The production of these images is usually completed without the participation or input of the depicted subjects. To put it somewhat cynically, it is problematic that at this moment, the project's propagated act of inclusion shifts away from interaction to the level of the picture. Suddenly there is the issue of the value in the fund-raising market of a photo that depicts several girls who are clearly marked by their clothing as belonging to the Muslim faith and are standing around discussing a model by a famous Western architect. This issue is central to the content that the artist-educator sought to work on in collaboration with the students. But as it is about the level of documentation and not the actual workshop content, it remains undiscussed.

As a researcher authorised by the gallery, I had permission to take photos of the situation I observed. Because I was fascinated by the action with the stickers described in this text, I attempted to record it with the camera. Since I was not allowed to use a flash when taking pictures in the gallery, the photos are blurred. In them, neither the people nor the works nor the location can be clearly identified. They are open for very different interpretations. In this essay they can be seen as more of an atmospheric illustration of that which has been told, rather than as pieces of evidence providing verification. Their imperfection makes them useless for economic purposes. Therefore I allowed myself to introduce them here, at a time when my concerns about the instrumentalisation of workshop images for funding means have made me reluctant to use images at all.

proposal

In light of the necessity of such structured project reports for the continuation of these projects, it is trite to criticise the existing practice. But how is it possible to give the interdependence between subjects and their instrumental role in fund-raising a productive visibility? How could the production and contextual framework for these pictures be designed differently? How could participants gain more control over the production of visual representations of their bodies and how could the documentation articulate that which they found to be important in the project? Is it possible to learn from the practices of contemporary artists, not only through gallery education workshops, but also through their documentation?

From the perspective of these questions, the many thousands of photos form not only an indifferent visual stream, but also an overwhelmingly eloquent, very specific body of visual culture. In order to develop a more reflexive approach to these phenomena, one that would more strongly empower the participants, my suggestion would be to first invite artists-in-residence throughout the country to galleries and to offer them the task of developing collaborative educational projects that refer to the galleries' previously created documentation photos, and to carry this out together with students and other participating communities (or perhaps, more accurately: interest groups). The residencies must last at least six to 12 months to guarantee an intense confrontation with the extensive material. The invited artists must have experience in gallery education and be interested in its critical reflection. In their work, they should deal with issues relating to the politics of visual representation.

Imagine the walls of the education rooms of a gallery covered for a time with all of the workshop photos that the archive has to offer! This type of installation could form the starting point for a critical discussion about this material – in collaboration with those who are visible in it – for the reworking of new, collective guidelines for making pictures with the greatest degree of transparency for the various interests interwoven in their production.

In any case, the education departments could follow the good practice of the girls of Central Foundation School in the exhibition of the famous architect. Placing an experimental, exploratory and reflexive approach to the production of annual reports at the centre of artistic-educative project work could, in the best case, mean a playful testing out of the rules and the borders of a situation that one is supposed to endure on a daily basis.

1 For mechanisms of the educational system see Michel Foucault, *Discipline and Punish: The Birth of the Prison*, London: Penguin, 1978. For a present approach see Henry Giroux et al, *Counter Narratives. Cultural Studies and Critical Pedagogies in Postmodern Spaces.* For mechanisms of the art system see Pierre Bourdieu, *Distinction. A social critique of the judgment of taste*, Cambridge, MA: Harvard University Press, 1987.

2 Duncan, Carol, *Civilising Rituals: inside public art museums*, London: Routledge, 1995. Duncan analyses the historical and present educational, 'civilising' effects of public museum buildings and collections by the way they are structured, selected and presented.

3 See Carmen Moersch, "From Oppositions to Interstices", *The Art of Encounter, Engage*, no. 15, Summer 2004.

Play and Nothingness
The Model for a Qualitative Society,
an Activist Project at the
Moderna Museet, Stockholm 1968
Lars Bang Larsen

During the 1970s, certain critical and pedagogical discourses framed childhood
as a form of being separate from society: 'Society' was seen as an adult supercoding
of representations and space that marginalised children. Moreover, childhood
was culturally transcendent. *Children are a People* was an anthropological
photo exhibition held at the Louisiana Museum in Copenhagen in 1978 about
the smallest members of the family of man. The more politically slanted texts
in the exhibition catalogue framed the child as a kind of outlaw, its identity
whittled down by the regimentation of institutions and urban space:

> When the children aren't at home or in school, they are drifting
> aimlessly around in society – on streets and roads. Society keeps
> them in cheap pubs – in shopping centres, where it is easier
> to steal than to be allowed to pay, in skating rinks and sports
> clubs, where they learn that the strongest one wins. What it is
> about is to win at any cost. This is society.[1]

Today the relation between child and society is rarely discussed in terms of
alienation. Apart from the fact that revolution – or cultural revolution, in the
words of the pedagogue Paulo Freire – is no longer a dominant horizon for
behaviour, one can speculate as to the reasons why: Is it simply because we
no longer fantasise about a pre-capitalist nature state?[2] Is it because the
commodification of society has rendered the classification of child- and adulthood
into interchangeable signs within the realm of consumer subjectivity?

Today, visual art is again engaged in social practices and political
investigations. This stems without doubt from a genuine desire in artists and
audiences for societal change; however, from the perspective of the 'engaged
art' of the 1960s and 70s some unresolved issues are: what are art's particular
properties for political agency? How does art avoid the risk of abandoning these
capacities to the always stronger, real political economies outside of the art

system? Is it necessarily self-explanatory to do 'social' or 'political' art? Also, it is interesting to take a closer look at the reasons why ideas of the social and the political have come to the fore again in a time when capitalism is no longer driven by industrial turnover, but has become directly operative in the sphere of social exchange through symbolic operations and the service industries.

In the following essay, I will discuss the representation of childhood in a major art activist project from 1968 called *The Model for a Qualitative Society*, conceived of by the Danish artist Palle Nielsen and organised together with a group of activists at the Moderna Museet in Stockholm. *The Model* was a protest-oriented version of what the theorist Brian O'Doherty has discussed as the artistic 'gesture' of the gallery space, namely the strategy or 'take' of incorporating the exhibition space itself into the artistic work. Such an artwork is characterised by the fact that "it isn't art, perhaps, but has a meta-life around and about art".[3] The artist does not accept the established framework of the art institution or the concept of art and, rather than making yet another piece to be circulated within the art system, sets to work on the framework itself and re-frames its symbolic economies, such as the logic of the art market, the politics of museum architecture, the ideology of the collection, etc.... However, the question is whether this notion of the 'gesture' is still valid when the White Cube is articulated by collective agency rather than by the flippancy of an author's gesture. If the furore around Marcel Duchamp's pissoir-turned-art object was an authored gesture, *The Model* (an adventure playground as readymade if you wish) had no less of a "meta-life in and about art", as it deconstructed conventional modes of spectatorship and display in the museum – but in activist terms rather than through exaltation of the artistic signature. *The Model* is a radical example of an inclusive use of the gallery space and an immodest political vision; with it, we can investigate the artistic representation of childhood as a political utopianism of late Modernism.

The Pre-school of the Revolution

The 1960s and the early 70s were the heydays of extra-parliamentarism and the era's struggles for liberation – feminism, anti-colonial wars, nuclear protest, squatting – resonated with the politics of the child, oppressed by the adult world. By early September 1968 there were clashes in Stockholm between police, teachers, guardians and child power militants, lead by 'intellectual children'. It is reported – with a revolutionary fervour whose factual validity is somewhat difficult to gauge – how children demonstrated for their rights to representation in the educational system and cultural politics. For example, a group of eight-year-olds occupied a Stockholm youth centre. The police were called in but mismanaged the situation and in a few days the uprising had "spread to schools and crèches all over the country".[4]

Palle Nielsen was then a 26-year-old dropout from the painting school at the Royal Academy of Fine Arts in Copenhagen who thought that painting was comparable to "masturbating on the wall" and instead found work with a municipal architect in the Copenhagen suburb Gladsaxe. He devoted himself to activism with students of architecture and students from Copenhagen University. As a form of constructive extra-parliamentarism they built children's playgrounds in the underprivileged boroughs of Copenhagen and its new satellite towns. Nielsen designed playgrounds to fit selected inner city courtyards without facilities for play and through unions and unemployment offices, activists would be mobilised for a raid. In one such action in March 1968, residents were woken up early one Saturday morning and told that their yard was due for an unauthorised slum clearance:

> From almost total chaos the action developed during the day to a veritable picnic. Everybody worked hard, but the atmosphere was very nice.... From having been scared and cautious, the activists relaxed when they saw the positive reactions of the residents (and that the police stayed away). From being the most boring to hell courtyard it had during 12 hours become the best and most beautiful children's playground in town.[5]

In June 1968 Nielsen was invited to Stockholm to participate in the organisation of *Aktion Samtal* (*Action Dialogue*), a series of courtyard interventions with the purpose of expanding children's liberty of action. Through friends Nielsen approached Pontus Hultén – director of the Moderna Museet, the city's most prominent institution for contemporary and Modern art – about the possibility of realising a children's playground on the Museum's premises as the conclusion to *Aktion Samtal*. Hultén agreed to let Nielsen and his activist network take over the Museum for a period of three weeks (provided he took the full organisational and financial responsibility). Initially Nielsen was criticised by his activist associates as it was believed that *The Model* was his own artistic project, rather than a collectivist one. However, having recently enrolled as a PhD student at the Copenhagen School of Architecture, he argued that his status as a researcher would facilitate fund-raising for the project – which was accepted by his critics.

The Moderna Museet's exhibition space at the time consisted of a single large hall with a masonite floor and new walls to paint on. Jungle gyms, a foam rubber basin, swings, climbing ropes and sliding ponds were installed. During the exhibition period, the gallery space would be gradually transformed by the children's interaction: materials to further creativity were at the visiting children's disposal: paint, tools, building materials and fabrics. There were even turntables connected to loudspeaker towers in every corner of the space for the children to play records from a selection of music, ranging from top ten hits to dance music from the Renaissance. Members of the public and The Royal Theatre in Stockholm donated costumes, and Nielsen acquired carnival masks to enhance the political aspects of role-playing: 100 masks of Mao, 100 of de Gaulle, and 100 of Lyndon B Johnson. Entrance was free for all children, and during its three weeks of existence almost 35,000 people visited the project, 20,000 of whom were children. After a week, admission to the playground had to be limited to 350-380 children per hour.[6] To ensure full accessibility, a playground was also erected outside the museum's entrance. Halfway through the exhibition period Stockholm's fire chief closed the exhibition allegedly due to the concentration of flammable foam rubber. The activists saw this as a political intervention, rebuilt *The Model* over a weekend and re-opened with red banners unfolding from the ceiling and revolutionary quotes painted large on the walls.

The project radicalised the open artwork of the 1960s, oriented towards space and audience participation, and took it in the direction of the social model: a creative utopia forged by counter culture in order to recuperate children's play and prevent them from replicating an impoverished adult reality.[7] It was "the pre-school of the revolution", as one journalist wrote.[8] Making children's playgrounds, however, was only a means to an end: "One doesn't need a children's playground. One needs changed attitudes, to change society into a socialist world where people can communicate."[9] The type of action that Nielsen and his comrades took was thus an alternative form to demonstrations, which were perceived to subsume the individual in an anonymous mass. Instead, Nielsen wanted to "attack the concrete issues" by working with specific political categories such as the individual and her relationship to her environment. In other words, a sort of macro-pedagogical endeavour where subjectivity was the ideological battleground on which capitalist indoctrination and behavioural patterns would be broken down from within.

The 'concrete issues' dealt with stemmed from urbanisation. In 1960s Scandinavia, the boom in urban expansion followed a pattern recognisable from the rest of the Western world, with the possible difference that the changes in the urban fabric took place even more rapidly. It was as late as 1963 that Denmark's industrial production superseded its agricultural output, which brought about a sudden increase in the urban population. Nielsen and his group of activists felt that the new living spaces had irremediably destabilised the working class. Parents and the middle-aged, isolated in flats somewhere in the suburbs, were politically and existentially speaking done for, lured into ideological traps of consumerism and the nuclear family. However, as an act of revolution-by-proxy, the adults could provide their children with a free space, unfettered by urbanism, in which the children could be empowered with the possibility of a freedom from which capitalist indoctrination had cut the adults off. In Marxist terms, the child's play was here perceived as a truly creative form of production. In the activism of children's playgrounds, the child was thus the harbinger of a proletarian sphere, the playground replaced the factory as the site of the fashioning of the real body of life.

Anti-Art, Non-Exhibition

The Model embodied a vision of a society where the subject came from within through play, the project's aim being to refine subjectivity in the direction of non-competitiveness and group relations. In a pamphlet accompanying the project – containing short pedagogical essays and quotations from children, Mao Tse Tung and Kierkegaard – Nielsen declared in the editorial:

> All these meanings carry their own signals.
> But they are also linked to "a model" at the Moderna Museet
> 30/9-20/10 1968.
> The idea is to create a frame for the children's own creative play.
> Children of all ages will continue to work on this frame.
> Indoors and outdoors – in all kinds of play – they shall be given
> the right to tell about their ability to express themselves.
> Their playing is the exhibition.
> The exhibition is the children's own work.
> There is no exhibition.
> It is only an exhibition because the children are playing in an
> art museum.
> It is only an exhibition for those who do not play.
> That is why we call it a model.
> Maybe it will be the model of a society that the children want.
> Maybe the children can tell us so much about their own world
> that it also becomes a model for us.
> We hope so.
> This is why we let the children present their model for those
> who work with or have the responsibility for the conditions that

the children are given outside – in the world of the adults.
We believe that children can articulate their own needs.
And that they want something else than what is expected of them.

The project's promise to communicate the undiscovered or repressed reality of the child was not only to give adults a better understanding of children's needs, but a model for a revolutionised society with comprehensively redistributed power relationships. The double-sided claim that "The exhibition is the children's own work.... There is no exhibition" is a puzzling dialectic, since Nielsen's motive for approaching the Moderna Museet in the first place was to realise and amplify a playground action under the aegis of a high cultural institution, for it to be used as a ram into the public sphere. *The Model* was anti-art in that it embodied anti-elitism and democracy. To the activists, the fact that "there is no exhibition" meant that museum preconditions did not apply to *The Model*: there were no artists and no art, and hence no immortal objects to be collected and archived. The annulment of the exhibition also consisted of changing the passive, subjective modes of looking at art into the collective interaction and corporeal styles of the children who are traditionally excluded from the museum while the adult audience – from a societal viewpoint, the only real subjects – had no authority in the gallery space; Nielsen's documentation shows parents standing pressed up against the walls, deterritorialised by hundreds of dressed-up children engaged in play, visitors to a new and alien territory they couldn't enter. The gallery space wasn't organised according to the visual enjoyment of individual beholder or by scientific classification, but was meant to stimulate the subject's sensory experience as part of a multitude.

Although seen as a truer form of art, the project's status was ultimately undefined. It was called neither art nor activism; it was a "model". However, inherent to the claim that the Museum offered an unfettered space for children to communicate "their own world", is the acceptance of the conventional Modernist ideology of the White Cube gallery space as autonomous and value-free. Nielsen employed the avant-garde strategy of using art's culturally acknowledged space of non-reality to produce new differences. Since *The Model* gravitated towards the Other space of a future reality, it was seen to transgress established classifications; any artistic or institutional representation was secondary to the future liberation imagined by the child and unimaginable to the adult. *The Model* mounted a social critique of the White Cube at the same time as accepting it as a space of non-reality; not just as a physically protected environment but as an ideologically uncontaminated space. Of course, the nothingness of the exhibition is the "everything" of the museum as a site. In Werner Hamcher's words,

Everything can be a museum, and the museum is the site of everything that can be said about the museum, the site of everything that can be said about this site – about this site as an ideal, or ideological site; as a commercial and social, political and topographical site. It is thus the site about which never enough can be said or the site of which never enough can be shown – the site of art that no artwork and no art of theory can possibly saturate.[10]

The notion that "there is no exhibition" articulates *The Model*'s compromise between urban space and White Cube, indoctrination and natural life, reason and play, present and future, writing and non-writing, abject adulthood and creative childhood. The absence of exhibition places itself between the roster of dichotomies that organises *The Model*'s space and that makes its logic of representation a dizzying dynamic between what is essentially present and ideally absent. It is a tug-of-war between activist ideology and utopian projection resonating with both Plato's *Republic* and Rousseau's notions of the pure world of the child. It can be argued that this play of absences lends *The Model* its imaginary power, it bypasses the art activist dialectics of action/reaction with surplus and affirmative energy.

In their statement the activists seem to imply that the format of art exhibitions is alienating, or at least insufficient: "It is only an exhibition for those who do not play." With a horizon evoked beyond art and any of its formats, Nielsen followed the constructive models of the historical avant-gardes who integrated art forms to counteract self-expression and subjective taste, aesthetic waste products of a defunct class. Distrusting the eye, 1920s Constructivists used *real* materials – paint was for forging illusions, whereas Constructivist art had the potential of innovating the production apparatus and large-scale communication. In the Bolshevik mass feast of the 1920s for example, appropriations of religious or aristocratic architecture and their conversion into propaganda, were hoped to anticipate and realise socialism's ideal. If trains could be used as mobile classrooms and exhibition spaces to educate the people of the Soviet provinces, as happened after the Russian revolution, then why not turn the museum into a playground? Within the Constructivist frame of reference, exhibitions and their conventional representational logic nullified the Real. Commenting on the tower envisioned by Tatlin which was planned to rise 400 metres above Moscow as a monument to the Communist International, Soviet curator Mel'nikov shrugged off the impotent aesthetic horizon of capitalist bourgeois culture, showing his contempt for an edifice built for an exposition "outside" of reality by use of italics: "The Eiffel tower is only 300 metres high, and it was built to adorn a world *fair*."[11] Paradoxically it is in the staging of absences – between children's play outside of representation and the capitalist bourgeois negativity and vacuity – that the Real appears in *The Model*'s ideology.

Free subjectivity and Lessons in Civics

The Model can be said to be an example of what the art historian Jean-Francois Chevrier, following Michel Foucault, calls the conquest of space in the visual art of the 1960s. This is not least considering that the central question of all political activity during May 1968 was that of the institution.[12] What can explain *The Model*'s absence in art history, then, is arguably its unorthodox use of institutional space, its mix of utopian anti-rationalism and material dialectics, and the way the project ran counter to established divisions between art and protest. Chevrier states, "The spectacle of the street had long since entered the museum. But it was in the street itself that the social protests and riots against segregation took place."[13] However, *The Model* as a revolutionary proposition inside the museum walls, is similar to how the art historian Troels Andersen described the way day-nurseries were organised in occupied buildings during the May revolt in Paris: freedom existed inside, whereas the street was "the terrain of the bourgeoisie".[14]

In late 1969, a year after *The Model* closed at the Moderna Museet, Nielsen wrote as a PhD scholar about the consequences of the aesthetic conquest of space:

Space was our [the architects'] task and is our task. Those, or these, human spaces have to contain human functions. A couple of statements: Space is the delimitation of activities. This implies that we cannot assess the space's form/aesthetics without making such an assessment in relation to the degree of activity. This also implies that form is no longer merely a static notion. Because it changes the perception of aesthetic problems from being visual to being also social.[15]

Nielsen's vision of an ecstatic society offered an architectural and artistic procedure for the psychic and social integration of an environment free of normalisation techniques. It aligns him with such contemporaries as the Swedish Öyvind Fahlström and his idea for "pleasure houses", an architecture of ecstasy for new sensory and mental input; or Helio Oiticica's work with the development of a social, three-dimensional painting, in dialogue with the ideas of fellow Brazilian Paulo Freire, arguing in favour of "informal education".[16]

 The Model accepted the basic premises of the modern exhibition and the museum space but radicalised them and made them operative to its own ends, employing the space of the museum as a technology of progress, aligned with the way twentieth century museums began to orient themselves towards the future, in Foucault's words as "utopias of ultimate development". It enlisted its primary audience, the children, as progressive subjects and thereby assigned them a place in an evolutionary process.[17] Let us take a closer look at how *The Model* conceived of subjectivity through the use of the museum.

 In an argument modifying Foucault's theory of the disciplinary society, the museum theorist Tony Bennett argues that "Museums, galleries, and more intermittently, exhibitions, played a pivotal role in the formation of the modern state and are fundamental to its conception as, among other things, a set of educative and civilizing agencies."[18] It may be that in Modernism, punishment and correctional discipline had been withdrawn from public gaze and transferred to the enclosed space of the penitentiary, as Foucault had it; this is just one aspect of a revision of lessons in civics that children and their parents were now invited to attend museums. Bennett uses the term 'exhibitionary complex' to define the scopic regime and knowledge transfers of the public museums and big fairs as organs of public instruction. The exhibitionary complex functioned not by coercion but instead by "placing itself on the side of the people by affording them a place within its workings; a power which placed the people behind it, inveigled into complicity with it rather than cowed into submission before it".[19] In this light *The Model* worked in continuation of the modern art space's function in state building and fostering of citizenship, and its serving as an instrument for differentiating populations.

 However, in *The Model*, the state and its citizens could only be glimpsed because in this case they were yet to mature, the differentiation of populations wasn't between working and middle class, but between children and adults. What is more, the chaotic children's playground disaffirmed the modern museum's authoritative visuality, where the audience could see itself seeing itself, and hence celebrate and regulate itself. In opposition to conventional museum pedagogics, *The Model* aimed at anti-disciplinary effects, *The Model* valorised childhood as otherness and made a spectacle of it. In so doing, *The Model* established a power hierarchy turned topsy-turvy.

But wasn't it indeed "a model for people who want to see people", as it says in the project leaflet? If *The Model* phased out a visual command of the exhibition space, it also changed Foucault's definition of the principle of the spectacle, from "rendering a small number of objects accessible to the inspection of a multitude of men", to the spectacle as a direct way of making crowds visible to themselves, and hence accessible to their own inspection.[20] For the adults who did, after all, make up more than one third of the audience, and for the media as well as for students of pedagogy and psychology, it was a kind of test site for the observation of children and their behaviour in a "free, generous environment". Even the Minister of Education, Olof Palme, was photographed jumping about in the foam rubber basin for a Stockholm daily newspaper.[21] "There is nothing new in this", a journalist writes after a week of playing at the Moderna Museet, bypassing the widespread media concern of the children's safety in the crowded playground:

> Generations of adults have in the same way passively observed the play of the children. It would be productive, on the other hand, if one could stimulate the parents to play, with each other, with their children, with the children of others, tumble about with no consideration for age.... To thus distance oneself from the adult world and hold the blue-eyed belief that a new generation must create a better world is pure illusionism.... Without support from the adult world the children are nothing. They find it downright difficult to make meaningful decisions. What is more, the children's world can often be very brutal and in some respects tougher as well as more vulgar than the world of the adults. She who claims that, "children know what they do" is utopian.[22]

My reason for quoting this is not to criticise the project along the lines of exploitation or instrumentalisation. Yes, *The Model* was a politicised environment and not as pedagogically innocent as Nielsen and the activists would have it, but the children were not exposed to political dogma and no artistic signature reaped surplus value from the children's presence. Nor is it to suggest that the project's artistic logic was compromised, which would be trivial. What matters to us today is whether *The Model* remains a project that can provoke reflections on our ideas of childhood and society, and on the limits and possibilities of visual art and its discourses on urbanism, artistic cognition and the politics of the gallery space. Rather, we need to work through equivocal moments in *The Model's* politics, where its irrational, un-scientific futurism connects unexpectedly to the revolutionary transformation of the museum as an instrument of collective instruction; something which reaches back, not only to the Russian Revolution but also to the way the French Revolution opened up private collections to the public as a way of propounding the democracy and utility of the Republic.

One aspect of the project was its success in communicating on a large scale, with which it undoubtedly helped to usher in an era of pedagogical reform. As the director Pontus Hultén wrote in the project pamphlet, "The present school form is a reactionary element in society, since in the future artistic criteria in all probability will play a crucial role when decisions are made."[23] Another aspect was its deterministic impulse to translate play and creativity into direct democracy. Here the project fissured ideologically between the harmonious unity of children's play and the social engineering of a new populace. The Constructivist artist Mazajev said of the Bolshevik mass feast that "its specific feature is play, self-realisation".[24] Play and self-realisation in the Soviet Union were undoubtedly less experimental processes than was the case with *The Model* and its more diffuse teleology, but Nielsen shared the utopian aim of creating a new man, the qualitative human being. The exhibition brochure quotes Mao Tse Tung, who states:

> We must concentrate our energy and time on those strata and groups about which we may assume that they listen and still are capable of thinking. Here a true work of education is possible. But not at random. The indoctrination has already gone too far for that.[25]

That the child's malleability makes it susceptible to a true work of education is echoed elsewhere in the publication by Anna-Clara Tjerneld, pedagogue and author of one of the catalogue essays, who states that children are "more open and flexible, more generally interested and active, less blocked than many adults."[26]

In *The Model*, Nielsen could be said to operate with a kind of behaviourism in reverse, seeming to work from the reasoning that if the stimulus is freed then the response will be revolutionary. We can speculate – taking our cue from the carnivalesque elements in *The Model*, for example – that the idea was to indefinitely postpone the closure of identity through play, facilitating continuous work with individuals' impulses and attitudes, bringing *The Model*'s identity politics close to the post-modern idea of identity as a fiction. However, by emphasising the corporal and the expressive, rather than language and its reiterative power, *The Model* suggested that there is a stable, coherent subject, a corporeal style of identity prior to entry into culture.

The Italian philosopher, Giorgio Agamben, perceives the concentration camp of the twentieth century totalitarian state to be the extreme, but thinkable, scenario of governmental sovereignty. Here the human subject is stripped of all rights and reduced to naked life. The child seen as a subject outside culture, and hence politics, is in a similar sense a non-citizen, with the difference that the child's nakedness here holds a liberating potential for the future. Nakedness was of course a major trope for the hippies and youth revolutionaries; authorities and Oedipal laws were challenged through a sexual or psychedelic liberation of the body. It was not only a symbolic deposition of norms and uniforms, but also an indication of physiology as a political element. The hippies identified the state's sovereign power to depoliticise the citizen by stripping her of her rights, and attempted to re-politicise the naked body through freaking out. Similarly, Nielsen declared the White Cube as a space of exception where laws and norms of adult society did not apply to the child, thereby eliminating differences in the social sphere and in fact limiting the project's political scope. In this perspective they failed to intervene in the logic of the sovereign power that had in the first place established the opposition between naked life and civic rights. The attempt to politicise the body by proposing naked life as originary remains insufficient: in order to collapse the dichotomy between natural life and political life, subjectivity cannot be separated from its cultured life forms.

Living Reality

Just as it was the ambition of May '68 to create 'one, two, many Vietnams', Nielsen and his fellow activists were out to create one, two, many children's playgrounds, a world revolution of child power. After the project had terminated at the Moderna Museet, Nielsen was involved in anti-commercial actions against the Teenage Fair,

a fair for a then new segment of consumers. Work also continued on *The Model*. After its three weeks of institutional life it was reconstructed in a residential area in the city of Västerås. During the winter and spring of 1968-1969 it resided here in a large, inflated tent, with seven people working full time to oversee the now completely public playground.

The departure from the museum space also spelt the end for the children's playground as an intervention into artistic discourse. One can imagine Nielsen asserting that he had as little need for museums as he ultimately had of playgrounds, and he made no effort towards conceptualising the Västerås version of the playground as an art project; instead he saw it as a positive intervention in a housing area. It is improbable, however, that Nielsen as an art student only thought of the propaganda value of working with a museum when he realised *The Model*, and not also the discussion it implied about a people's art; the art institution was, after all, envisioned to help kick off the qualitative society. Probably Nielsen also relied on the era's cultural synergy between the forms of arts and politics to account for the artistic potential of the playgrounds. Here the political performance of art was paramount, rather than discussions about its classificatory status.

The Modernist dichotomies that underpinned *The Model* are in a palpable way laid bare in the journey that it enacted between the inside and the outside of the museum, between the artistic space of illusion and the 'real world'. As a journalist wrote about the relocation of *The Model* to Västerås, "The anti-authoritarian exhibition moved into living reality." Leaving the museum's zone of visibility and possibility for archiving, *The Model* was thus annihilated as an art project. It withstood the possibility of being collected; now it can be narrated as the generous event that it was.

Today, the child's transition to knowledge and citizenship is a closely guarded process. In Europe, neo-liberal policy-makers otherwise concerned with privatisation and de-regulation leave nothing to coincidence when it comes to education; it must be saved from the fluffy ideologies and barefoot pedagogies of the 1970s *and* exposed to the benefits of the marketplace. They propose that the best thing we can do for our children is to provide them with the competitive edge in (and through) learning. The state has developed an acute awareness of the fact that the child is always already entered into society, and it wants to make sure to be the first to greet it. In this respect contemporary life is still characterised by 'public misery', as Kenneth Galbraith is quoted in *The Model*'s pamphlet. As for children's place in the museum, this has become a widespread service through outreach programs and children's project rooms, rather than a revolutionary proposal. But still, no public art gallery would today allow any activist to take it over for the purpose of uncontrolled social experimentation.

1 Strandgaard, Charlotte and Kim Foss Hansen, "Børn – samfundets fremtid?", in *Louisiana Revy 19*, no. 1, August 1978, p. 13.

2 Freire, Paulo, *Kulturaktion for Friheden*, Copenhagen: Christian Ejlers' Forlag, 1974.

3 O'Doherty, Brian, *Inside the White Cube, The Ideology of the Gallery Space*, London: University of California Press, 1986, p. 70. O'Doherty continues, "By definition, a gesture is made to "emphasize ideas, emotions, etc." and is "often… made only for effect." This deals with its immediate impact. For the gesture must snare attention or it will not preserve itself long enough to gather its content. But there is a hitch in a gesture's time which is its real medium. Its content, as revealed by time and circumstance, may be out of register with its presenting form. So there is both an immediate and a remote effect, the first containing the latter, but imperfectly… Gestures are thus the most instinctive of artworks in that they do not proceed from full knowledge of what provokes them. Indeed, they are born out of a desire for knowledge, which time may make available." pp. 105-106.

4 Rasmusson, Ludvig, *Modellen: En Modell för ett kvalitativt samhälle*, Stockholm: Moderna Museet, 1968, p. 17. Rasmusson clarifies the concept of 'Barn Power', child power, and repudiates those who hold the belief that this should mean the children's take-over of power in society. He continues: "Others believe that the children simply wish to isolate themselves from the adult and implement separate children's societies, where they can be allowed to loaf around as they desire and eat ice cream and sweets all day. However, only a very small and rather uninfluential minority of three- and four-year-olds holds this intention. It is easy to observe an increasing understanding for the adults the older the children themselves get. And since it is the strong twelve-year-olds who have the power in Barn Power, the separatist endeavours lack significance."

5 "Ekstra-parlamentarisk rapport. Rapport til venstresocialisternes 2. kongres, maj 1969", in *På vej mod ekstraparlamentarisme*, Copenhagen: Sorte Fane, 1970, p. 148. David Gurin of *The Village Voice* writes in a report from Copenhagen about a similar raid at the residential suburb Høje Gladsaxe in the spring of 1969: "The playground is a series of multi-levelled structures, all interconnected by wooden ladders, rope ladders and aluminum slides, with a safe jump to sand at the bottom. It was put together in parts over a period of several days, then assembled from 3 am to noon one day and guarded by residents so it wouldn't be destroyed by the authorities – the fate of a playground built on a slum site during Copenhagen week. The playground's popularity finally forced the Gladsaxe administrative bureaucracy to accept it." "Bursting the Gates of a Welfare Utopia", *The Village Voice*, November 27, New York, 1969.

6 *Dagens Nyheter*, 7 October, 1968. *Modellen* is only cursorily mentioned in Swedish anthologies and surveys of the 1960s, and has curiously enough never received any attention in Danish art historical research. See Leif Nylén, *Den öppna konsten, Sveriges allmänna konstförening*, 1998; Folke Edwards, "The 60s in Sweden. Euphory and Indignation", in *The Nordic Sixties*, Nordiskt Konstcentrum, 1991; and Lars Bang Larsen, "Sometimes I'm Up, Sometimes I'm Down, Sometimes I'm Underground", in *Like Virginity, Once Lost*, Birnbaum and Nilsson eds., *Propexus*, 1999.

7 The title *Modellen – en modell för ett kvalitativt samhälle* (*The Model – a Model for a Qualitative Society*) followed the work theorist André Gortz: "… in a developed society, the needs are not merely quantitative (the need for commodities for consumption), they are also qualitative: the need for a diverse and free development of human ability, the need for information, communication and human community, the need for liberation not just from exploitation, but also from coercion and isolation during work and in spare time." André Gortz, from the exhibition catalogue, p. 6 (my translation).

8 Nilsson, Macke, "Ni tror att dom bara lattjar! Men i själva verket bygger dom upp morgondagen samhälle", *Aftonbladet*, October 5, 1968.

9 "Attack the Concrete Issues", interview with Palle Nielsen, *Paletten*, no. 4, 1968, pp. 7-8.

10 Hamacher, Werner: "Expositions of the Mother A Quick Stroll through Various Museums", in *The End(s) of the Museum*, Barcelona: Fundació Antopni Tapiés, 1995, pp. 81-82.

11 Mel'nikov in conversation with the art critic R Broby-Johansen, in *Quod Felix, Akademisk Tidsskrift*, no. 10, February 15, 1926, pp. 134-135. Quoted from Vladimir Tatlin exhibition catalogue, Bergqvist Lindegren, Hultén, Feuk eds., Stockholm: Moderna Museet, 1968, p. 63. In the 1960s the Moderna Museet broke ground in presenting the work of the Russian Constructivists to a Western audience, introducing among others Malevich and Tatlin to a Western audience.

12 Cornelius Castoriadis puts forward the claim of the institutional focus of the youth revolt in the essay "The Movements of the Sixties". Elsewhere he writes, which can be taken to describe the institutional logic that the activists wanted to revolutionise: "The institution produces, in conformity with its norms, individuals that by construction are not only able to but bound to reproduce the institution. The 'law' produces the 'elements' in such a way that their very functioning embodies, reproduces, and perpetuates the 'law'." "The Imaginary", in *World in Fragments Writings on Politics, Society, Psychoanalysis, and the Imagination*, Stanford: Stanford University Press, 1997, p. 52 and p. 7.

13 Chevrier, Jean-Francois, *The Year 1967 From Art Objects to Public Things, Or Variations on the Conquest of Space*, Barcelona: Fundacio Antoni Tápies, 1997, p. 136.

14 Andersen, Troels, *Set er sket. Artikler, 1961-1970*, p. 76. Copenhagen: Borgen, 1972 (my translation).

15 *Arkitekten*, December 1969, p. 18. Interestingly, Nielsen's formulation about the non-static form implies the genealogy of political art that runs through kinetic art's elementary involvement with space and the spectator, and that *Modellen* can be seen as a part of.

16 "They [Fahlström and Oiticica] are modern but anti-rationalist geographers who conceive of space as a psychic and social territory, in the manner of Aldo van Eyck". Chevrier, p. 208. Á propos of planetary consciousness, it was the Swedish psychedelic (or underground) artist Sture Johannesson who produced the exhibition poster for *Modellen*; a high-quality print in Johannesson's trademark dense and elaborated, Constructivist psychedelic style where a tilted Swedish flag displays in its blue squares photographs of a concrete high-rise, placed symmetrically and ornamentally. The yellow cross is dynamised with a collage with images from a variety of sources – from the anti-authoritarian underground lore to photos of children playing. Neither Nielsen nor Johannesson are mentioned; rather, as a nod to *Modellen*'s collectivist spirit, there is in the poster's bottom left corner a photo of the team from Permild & Rosengreen's printing house in Copenhagen, where the poster was

produced. Nielsen used the poster under protest, as he considered its drug references irrelevant or harmful to *The Model*'s message. Another poster of Johannesson aptly sums up the politics of *The Model: Turn on the Insitutions*, 1967, where the royal castle in Stockholm has been endowed with a pink neon sign reading "The kingdom is within you".

17 Foucault, quoted in Tony Bennett, *The Birth of the Museum History, theory, politics*, London: Routledge, 1995, p. 213.

18 Bennett, *The Birth of the Museum History, theory, politics*, p. 66.

19 Bennett, *The Birth of the Museum History, theory, politics*, p. 67.

20 Even though surveillance cameras were installed in the playground, connected to TV screens in the cafeteria, in order to placate parents.

21 Bennett, *The Birth of the Museum History, theory, politics*, p. 86.

22 Evert René, Hans, "So Old-Fashioned!", *Expressen*, 9 October, 1968.

23 *The Model* exhibition pamphlet, p. 32, my translation.

24 *Poetry must be made by all! Transform the world!*, Stockholm: Moderna Museet, 1969, p. 47.

25 *The Model* exhibition pamphlet, p. 28 (my translation).

26 *The Model* exhibition pamphlet, p. 13 (my translation).

A Toe in the water:
Giving Young People a voice
at the whitechapel Art Gallery
steve Herne and Janice McLaren

The Whitechapel Art Gallery, located in the East End of London, has for over 100 years presented exhibitions of contemporary, Modern and, occasionally, pre-twentieth century art. From the mid 1980s to the late 1990s, under the Directorship of Catherine Lampert, the Whitechapel offered its audiences a balance of exhibitions by celebrated artists such as Lucien Freud and Cindy Sherman through to work by lesser-known figures such as the Jamdani Weavers of West Bengal and the Catalan painter and sculptor Miquel Barceló.

The gallery has a long and distinguished history of innovative education projects, including the *Artists in Schools* programme. Developed in the late 1970s and early 80s, this initiative became a national model for gallery and museum education. The following case study focuses on the gallery's introductory videos produced by and for young people and relates to the development of young people's critical awareness of art and culture. These introductory videos for the Whitechapel's exhibitions – made through collaborations between young people and a small support group of adults – fostered an exemplary, creative space for the students' experience and articulation.

The Whitechapel's work with young people and video began in 1999 as part of the Schools and Whitechapel Artists' Programme (SWAP). The type of encounter the participating young people had with original works of art, as well as with artists and gallery staff, was fundamental to the programme. Their enquiries and critical responses to the work were valued by gallery staff and, through anecdotal feedback, numerous gallery visitors for the unique and individual perspective they offered. Students were invited to explore and familiarise themselves with the work prior to articulating their ideas and views on video within the exhibition spaces. The recorded footage was then edited – by a freelance video artist and a member of the gallery's education team – to a professional standard and shown in the gallery during the run of each show.

The videos were also posted to local schools, and marketed as peer-led introductions to each exhibition, offering questions and ideas to other students and teachers prior to their gallery visit. This linked with the project's primary aim of promoting the relevance of the Whitechapel's exhibitions to the interests and education of school-aged young people.

video as a tool for communication

Short videos can communicate ideas rapidly as well as give a visual impression of exhibition spaces and particularly, artworks. To quote one teacher who made use of the Whitechapel's videos in school: "It's a medium they are used to. It's amazing how much you can get over in a short time." The approach used by the Whitechapel's video programme in soliciting different voices from the dominant voice of the gallery, endorsing the 'layperson's' own take on the art encountered, helped to balance out the implicit authority of the gallery's own in-house interpretation.

It is important to underscore the principle that access to original works of art cannot be replaced by second-hand sources. However, a five to ten minute video can act as an excellent introduction and contextualisation for a forthcoming visit, or perhaps, whet the appetite for an independent visit. There are also situations where access to the original artwork is difficult or impossible, and then the video takes its rightful place alongside books and the Internet as a source for study.

The Whitechapel has produced introductory videos with young people for the *Alighiero e Boetti* (15 September-7 November 1999), *Gary Hume* (26 November 1999-23 January 2000), *Live in Your Head* (4 February-2 April 2000), *Francisco Toledo* (14 April-7 June 2000), *Protest and Survive* (15 September-12 November 2000), *Temporary Accommodation* (12 January-4 March 2001) and *Whitechapel Centenary* (21 March-20 May 2001) exhibitions.

student involvement in filming

Each video took four to five days to complete, from planning to filming to arriving at a final edited version. Students were involved in the production stages for two full days (normally one school day and one day on the weekend), with the gallery taking responsibility for post-production. Students were asked to commit to both days with no late arrivals or early departures tolerated unless unavoidable. Together, they would provide the footage for what would be edited down to a ten minute video introduction to the exhibition.

Along with the students, the production team consisted of an artist facilitator who was responsible for discussing the exhibition with each student; a video artist – charged with recording both sound and image; and a member of the gallery's education team – accountable for the filming schedule, checking that each young person's presentation was clear and generally overseeing the production. Class teachers were also usually present, particularly on school days.

Day one of the production time was reserved for research and planning. During the introduction session on the first morning, it was reiterated to all involved that they had come together to form a professional production team with specific roles and responsibilities. Students were asked about their prior experience of video production either in front of or behind the camera. Time was made available for questions and comments before moving to the work at hand. The group then entered into the exhibition spaces with little or no introduction to the work. This was *their* time to look at and think about the art on show, either in small groups or individually. Their teacher and other members of the production team – including the artist facilitator, video artist and gallery staff member – were on-hand to discuss work as appropriate. The group would then meet back in a non-exhibition space to discuss their first impressions. Occasionally this discussion was audio recorded but not videotaped so that students felt relaxed about offering their initial comments and observations. After everyone had had a chance to look at and discuss the exhibition, exhibiting artists were invited to meet with the team to discuss their work. By the end of the first production day, a dynamic was set amongst the production team. Ideally, by this time, the team would have worked out a shooting schedule for students and artworks for day two.

Day two of the production involved a tight, but democratic, schedule of the young people speaking to camera. They could choose to speak – one at a time or in small groups of two or three – about particular works that interested them. Importantly, these sessions were supported by a video artist with extensive experience of working with young people and an ability to relax and encourage each student to speak their mind while reassuring them that retakes were always on offer. As each presentation was filmed, the artist facilitator – also someone with a respect and sensitivity for the young people's interests and ideas – would work with the rest of the group in another part of the exhibition space to ensure they each felt confident about what they wanted to talk about and why. The gallery's Community Education Officer worked to support all involved and provided an extra 'ear' to the filming process, listening out for continuity in what each presenter had to say and encouraging them if they became nervous or lost their train of thought. The presenters, having spent a previous full day looking at and discussing the exhibition, were now experts and were respected as such. The end of the day provided an opportunity to view all footage as a group, offer feedback and congratulate all involved. The next time students would see this footage, it would be the final edited version – with music, titles and credits – at their school or during any subsequent visit to the exhibition.

An Introduction to Live in Your Head: Concept and Experiment in Britain 1965-1975
Whitechapel Art Gallery, London, 4 February-2 April, 2000

This introductory video was made for 14- to 18-year-olds by a group of Year Nine students, aged 13 and 14, from Kingsland Secondary School, London Borough of Hackney. It was produced by the Whitechapel Art Gallery as part of the SWAP programme in collaboration with the students, their art teacher Ruth Mochrie, SWAP artist Mark Ingham, video artist Shona Illingworth and on-line editor Seth Hopewell. Both the production and outcome of this video were evaluated by Steve Herne, through observations and interviews with members of the production team, in order to reflect upon what had been achieved and offer the gallery a series of recommendations for future work of this nature.

The *Live in Your Head* exhibition featured work by over 60 artists – including Rasheed Araeen, Art & Language, Susan Hiller, Yoko Ono and Stephen Willats – an enormous array of approaches to art and art-making, as well as to the role of the artist, were represented in media as diverse as film, installation, performance (both documentation and live), photography, concrete poetry and instructional texts. Very little of the work included in the exhibition, if any, would be standard fare for secondary pupils' 'knowledge and understanding'.

It was clear that this experience included a chance for the young people involved to spend a good deal of time in the art gallery getting to know the exhibition. Art is compulsory in school at Year Nine level but it is usually only taken for about one hour per week. However, within the programme, students were able to look at specific works of art that attracted their interest, supported by knowledgeable adults. One work that provided the group with fuel for a debate was Michael Craig-Martin's *An Oak Tree*, 1973.[4] Two of the students had very different responses:

Roelof Louw, *Pyramid (Soul City)*, 1967. *Pyramid* consists of 6,000 oranges, built into a rough pyramid shape, which visitors are invited to help themselves to.

> I don't know why [the artist] thinks this glass of water is an oak tree... I just think it's a glass of water.

> Well, if I just make it live in my head, most likely I could say it's an oak tree.

The young people were involved in the process of video making with all the paraphernalia of takes, retakes, different viewpoints, zooming in and out, sound levels, etc.. Further, this gave an excellent opportunity for the students to collaboratively write commentary for film, developing thinking and speaking skills, self-presentation and self-confidence. Some of the work in the exhibition dealt with important issues, such as the impact of racism (Rasheed Araeen's *For Oluwale*, 1971-1973). This further extended the range of experiences available as well as the opportunity for personal response and critical appraisal.

Artists' group:
*Inventory A Short
Treatise on
Methomania*, 2000.
Park bench with
original texts by
the artists.

As part of the SWAP programme, an artist was paired with a school on an ongoing basis and therefore was already known to the pupils when they first attended the exhibition. For the *Live in Your Head* video, artist Mark Ingham had spent the first day with the group exploring the exhibition. Between them they had worked out a list of questions to ask each other about specific works of their choice. This provided a framework for their responses and was very useful on the second day in helping them to think of a variety of things to say while being recorded in front of the camera. The questions included: What is it called? Who made it? When was it made? Describe the work, what is it made from? The materials, size and content? What happens when you look at it? What is the artist trying to say? How does this work relate to life? (This was a question many of them found most challenging.) And finally: Is it art?

Video artist Shona Illingworth worked to create a safe, supportive atmosphere with each student or set of students she filmed on the second day of production. The main challenge for Shona, and Janice who worked with her, was to maintain a delicate balance between remaining sensitive to each presenter's level of self-assurance, listening carefully and ensuring sound and light levels would portray the student at their clear, confident best. Students who were less comfortable or interested in speaking individually about specific works, were invited to speak in pairs or small groups. Each presenter was asked to express their comment or observation in a concise way with requests for re-takes for anything that became too long or unclear.

The creative ethos of trust and support enabled students to engage, feel comfortable and find a voice, as the following quotations illustrate:

Rasheed Araeen,
For Oluwale,
1971-1973.

We went to the gallery for a whole day. We talked it through and
they told us about the artist's work. Then we had a look round
the exhibition to find a piece of work we liked. We went home
and had to write up a little bit about it, to make a speech, make
a presentation. I think it went well; I enjoyed it.

They were sympathetic – didn't make you feel embarrassed.
At first I was a bit scared but got used to it as the day went on.

They are approachable, I enjoyed it; it was fun. I felt quite at
home, they did things slowly, at our own pace.

While many students were initially camera-shy and found it hard to articulate
clearly, given time and encouragement and after re-takes, they were able to
overcome their reserve and use descriptive and evaluative language. There was
also the beginning of genuine aesthetic debate, particularly in response to the
question: Is it art? As one would expect, there were varying levels of ability,
breadth of experience, range of self-confidence, performance skills and vocabulary.

Filming began in the morning when the gallery was closed to the public.
Later, as visitors began to enter the exhibition spaces, the group became much
more of a professional team and continued to work, observed by the gallery-
going public. They began to enjoy playing with ideas as well as responding to the
concepts embodied in the work on show. The education team struck a subtle
balance between informing and developing the students' understanding. This
provided a platform for them to develop their own critical perspectives and
articulate these within the social context of a filmmaking production team.

The students were often surprised at how effectively they could appear as cultural commentators. Teachers also expressed great pleasure at how articulate their students could become through this process, particularly those who had been seen as of lower ability within a classroom context.

The Editing Process

During the editing process, the video artist and the gallery staff member were responsible for selecting excerpts from up to three hours of commentary footage, and a further hour of installation or detail footage to produce a ten minute video which represented the students and the exhibition in a fair, clear and sensitive way. The process was pressured, normally lasting two days. Editing decisions had to be made with respect to each student's level of articulacy and confidence. This meant that from time to time, only an excerpt of a person's image would be shown in favour of installation shots of the work, and only a passage of their oral commentary would be used. Contemporary, club music was used as a linking mechanism to hold the video together. Due to the tight schedule students did not feed into the editing process although in different circumstances participation would have extended the experience and ownership of process immeasurably.

Evaluation

A group of Art and Design PGCE (Postgraduate Certificate in Education) students from Goldsmiths College had the following to say after seeing the *Live in Your Head* introductory video:

> It really showed that you've got to teach children to be articulate. They explained themselves quite adequately but there's a whole range of language that they need to have introduced to them so that they can go into a gallery, look at the works and talk about them.

> They were quite young pupils and their vocabulary was very much their own; it was very good.

The PGCE students were impressed by the quality of the young people's interaction with the art. They felt acutely that this was an excellent model that would break down preconceived barriers about those pieces on walls in big galleries that you couldn't get near or touch. Seeing the video sparked a lively debate about the extent to which art is accepted in our culture. Distinctions were drawn between their own sub-culture as art students, the views of middle England, and the culture of the kids themselves.

One of the successes of the project had been the focus on language development and the value of the film making process in supporting children's articulation of personal and visual responses in the art gallery context. As the PGCE students commented:

> [The video] demonstrates these students interacting with the work and the gallery context – excellent. It gets students thinking about work in and out of the gallery – finding connections – searching for understanding. [It] demonstrates that an understanding of art is hard work, challenging airy-fairy responses.

> This film is brilliant. Children tend to look to their peers.
> The kids were investigating the work in their own terms and
> stimulating others to think about art in their own context.

One of the real rewards of working with school-age young people is the surprising and original responses they make, which are often far removed from those more familiar with the grand narratives of twentieth century art and the conventions of gallery display. A two-way learning process is clearly evident as is an underlying principle which values, respects and supports independent thinking and individual response. Watching the video playing in one classroom, it became clear that there was little gap between those in the video and their audience. In the words of one of the SWAP teachers: "They show more interest than they would normally. It definitely engages them, looking at kids of their own age."

The production of these videos provided a space that sustains plurality, celebrates difference and promotes the possibility of multiple readings and interpretations valuable to new audiences amongst the community, as well as to peer group audiences in schools. Further, they present a model process in which students can be supported to creatively develop their critical thinking and articulation as cultural commentators, in response to the direct experience of contemporary art.

1 See www.whitechapel.org for more information.
2 SWAP, 1998-2001, organised by the Whitechapel Art Gallery, consisted of a triangular relationship between secondary art departments, the gallery's education department and six professional artists. Additional aspects of the project included the publication of a newsletter, gallery visits, studio visits, foyer exhibitions and gallery and schools-based workshops. One of the main aims of SWAP was to invest in the visual literacy of a generation of young people from five secondary schools and a local college, as well as to develop their awareness of the role and importance of artists within contemporary society and to allow the young people to have first-hand experience of art in a public setting.
3 Nesbitt, Judith ed., *Live in Your Head: Concept and Experimentation in Britain 1965-1975*, London: Whitechapel Art Gallery, 2000.
4 *An Oak Tree* is made up of a glass shelf upon which sits a glass tumbler partly filled with water. Beneath the shelf, slightly to one side, is a printed text featuring a series of question and answers about what the work is and questioning, in part, whether the work may or may not be an oak tree.

five

artists collaborate with young people in their community

Joost Conijn and ISEP, captivated by the magical qualities, resourcefulness and inventiveness of children at play, make work that joins in the play. ISEP's activities are traced over 30 years and in their later work we witness spontaneity becoming formalised due to economic necessities and needs for dissemination or replication of successful ideas. This pattern of development is echoed in accounts of Loraine Leeson's VOLCO project and of Magic Me intergenerational arts group. In these accounts an encroachment of management concerns may imply selling out or compromise, or it may be seen as reflecting maturity and sophistication in work which of necessity has adopted professional terminology. The projects in this section demonstrate long-term engagement with communities. The projects seem to rely entirely on individual artists' sheer commitment and determination, running well beyond the scope of funding or other practicalities. When artists become organisations and employees are involved, this seems to present an inevitable changing point in the terms of engagement. Yet behind all these accounts lies a deeply personal commitment to fostering what artists see as the great talents lying in the uncelebrated lives around them.

siddiequa, Firdaus, abdallah, soeleyman, moestafa, Hawwa, Dzoel-kifi by Joost conijn

Joost Conijn's film *Siddiequa, Firdaus, Abdallah, Soeleyman, Moestafa, Hawwa, Dzoel-kifi* depicts the lifestyle of a group of children living on the edge of Dutch society. It is a non-judgemental project that has been embraced by Dutch education experts for use in teaching textbooks, national teacher training lectures and national TV programmes about working with young people. This video has shocked the sensibilities of many Dutch people who find it hard to cope with the idea that a family is bringing up children outside of the norms of formal education and conventional aspirations of a highly developed Western nation.

Conijn's video presents a childhood of freedom to roam the countryside without danger of traffic or strangers. Two boys wade through muddy ditches, one wearing a clown suit; a girl and boy of around three or four make faces cheekily to the camera; the clown suit boy tries to start the motor on a scooter; another boy with a shaved Mohican has a try. A small girl with a hosepipe waters a child's tricycle in a game of car wash, then an older boy comes along with his go-cart and wants to take over. The children are inventive and resourceful in entertaining themselves, engaging in real life problem-solving and imaginative play. The irony is that these children's lifestyle poses some kind of threat to the Dutch authorities; they are not in school, their family has chosen a lifestyle apart from the norms of Dutch society. They live, you could say, in a constant tension between paradise and nightmare. These young children fend for themselves. A young boy using his fingers fills a bread roll from the scrapings round a large pan from a meal which the small children have prepared for themselves. They collect surplus bread from a depot and carry it home strapped on their bikes, stopping to look at the new windmills on their way. They teach each other puncture repair and other bicycle mending skills and practice bike stunts over an improvised ramp. Along with the idyll of freedom come hazards, which Conijn's video witnesses in a non-judgemental way as part of the daily lives of the children. A small boy

of about three years old shouts "I've done it!" as he smashes an axe through the window of an old caravan, an act which some might consider vandalism but which gives him a great sense of achievement. An adult calls out "be careful!" as the children cook round a brazier. In response, the children invent a chant: "Be careful! Don't do it!" and then check "What did he say? What does he mean, be careful?" They are unfamiliar with warnings or adults monitoring risk or danger, and see this as amusing and novel. Eventually the children fall asleep in a collection of chairs round the fire. The next scene shows them waking up on mattresses laid out on the ground under the sun, where they cook a breakfast of eggs and tinned fish, eaten with fingers or any implement to hand. The children are highly capable of looking after themselves compared to others of their age, although in their camping lifestyle their different notions of hygiene might disturb others. They are inventive, resourceful and full of mischief. Creating a way of life for themselves outside of the norms of society, they educate each other through play and the basic chores of survival normally associated with adult life such as fetching food, cooking, shopping, shoplifting for sweets. Everything becomes a game – a game of survival as much as a game played for fun. They stamp on ice across a muddy field, build a fortress of caravan parts and old furniture, lighting a bonfire in the middle of their fortified encampment.

Conijn shares in the children's sense of adventure and discovery, a kindly neighbour with a camera who identifies affectionately with their inventiveness, whose video shares their optimism and shows things as they are, without judgement. One boy holds a large box of chocolate cereal and cola bottle and asks Conijn "Wannadrinkabite?" This invented phrase seems to precisely reflect his actions, a creative invention of contemporary language! Conijn is clearly on their side, working together with them, not an outside authority figure. He has spent many years as their neighbour building this relationship of mutual respect and confidence, which is clearly evident in this respectful work. His predicament now is that by presenting the video publicly he does not want the work to spoil their relationship or the prospects of the children.

The children learn through risk, mending bikes, engines, wielding axes and hose pipes, they learn negotiation skills through play, they use active imaginations to fend for themselves. Ingenuity gets them a long way. The artist is complicit in a bit of shoplifting, but as the shopkeeper says affectionately when they offer him a mound of small coins: "I gave up counting it!" In an age of anxious and over-protective parenting, viewers of the video depending on their background may well make assumptions that the children may soon have a terrible accident. Kitchen hygiene may seem lacking as they scrape fingers round saucepans and mix an egg with a knife. But this is a world of camping, where some of the rules can go out of the window, hair is left unwashed and bodies unshowered, where plates may be wiped rather than washed.

This Dutch family follow the Muslim faith, which is read here in the dress of the girls. Debate was raging in the Dutch media at the time of writing as to whether the children's father has a right to bring seven children up in his own

artists collaborate with young people in their community

way, outside of the conventions of Western society. There are claims that they may miss out on opportunities provided by a formal education and a wider social network. In the heart of civilised Holland, their lifestyle appears hard to tolerate. The video leaves us complete ambiguity about the parents; it is a children's world presented, an interesting context for conjecture where viewers may become aware of their subjective assumptions. Living just ten minutes from the international airport of Amsterdam, this is not the advertisement for Dutch childhood which authorities might want us to see, not what we might expect in a society which prides itself on its education system and social services, and which has for decades ascribed to a self-image of tolerance, an open people embracing all comers – something that has in recent years appeared more like a marketing myth than a reality. The current political context of insularity is a backdrop to this work.

Living on the margin of the normalised and socially acceptable, they live as part of an alternative squatter community, like Christiania in Copenhagen or Bethanien in Berlin, part of a tradition of self-governing communities opting out of regulated lifestyles around them. Such communities have thrived on notions of personal freedom, but the children who grew up there, often in open or extended families, with few boundaries, often express insecurities or face difficulty in later life in fitting in with the rest of the world. At the same time they express optimism and a sense that things are possible. Squatters and travelling communities have always had a bad press, being depicted as Other, not corresponding to social norms of cleanliness and order, while it seems quite acceptable and even quaint for artists to live in this way. Conijn does not make clear in the video that he lives in a neighbouring caravan, that this is a lifestyle of choice for many artists.

This video shows children engaged, creative and alert, arguably better off in many ways than children deprived by parents working long hours, obsessed with material goods rather than emotional well-being or preoccupied with alcohol, drugs or depression. This inspiring video suggests that children used to constant adult attention might arguably benefit from a little neglect, a little more space to develop their own creative imaginations and resourcefulness.

Experimentation and risk-taking interest Conijn, the living out of impossibly optimistic projects considered unfeasible by most people. Often fuelled by naive optimisim or childlike ambition, these projects take him on unexpected journeys. The video *Wood Car*, 2002, tells the story of the wooden car he built using wood as fuel instead of petrol. With this car he undertook a journey through several countries including the Czech Republic, Slovakia, Hungary, Romania, Moldavia, Ukraine, Bulgaria, Macedonia and Albania. As the car runs on wood, his journey took him via sawmills and forests. In the video *C'est une Hek (It's a Fence)*, 1997, he travelled with companion Bart Lodewijks to Africa in search of an emptiness which seems lost in over-regulated, bureaucratic Holland. In a small Peugeot car with a trailer full of coach parts they crossed Europe to Gibraltar, took a boat and then drove into the Moroccan desert. In the sand Conijn built a fence of the coach parts, with a gate that opens when cars approach and closes after they have driven through. *Airplane*, 2000, is the story of the construction of a plane. He sets off towing the plane to Morocco and after many setbacks we see the eventual flight in the desert – another act of naive optimism against the odds.

Artists collaborate with young people in their community

Conijn's work has been applauded by the Dutch education system, which has shown his videos in schools. He is proud that *Wood Car* is presented in education text books and that a national lecture for school teachers cites his work as a good example of how to work with children. Dutch TV will feature *Siddieqa, Firdaus, Abdallah, Soelayman, Moestafa, Hawwa, Dzoel-kifi* in its full 42 minutes in an evening devoted to the topic "What are we doing with our children?" Recently the 15-year-old daughter of the family was a little disappointed after spending five hours with a camera crew that only a few minutes were included on the children's TV show *Q*; she was hopeful that they would send her the full footage as promised. Conijn was clearly worried at the impact of his work bringing too much media attention to this family and whether this would put the children at real risk from authorities with prescribed notions of how children should live their lives and what they consider best for them. Are these children losing out or are they living a contemporary *Swallows and Amazons* childhood that others would envy? As a journey with the children in their flights of creative play, Conijn is clearly attracted and endears viewers to this alternative way of life, just outside what is acceptable, open-mindedly questioning cultural presumptions in his consideration of the relationship between art and society.

RI-X PAN FILM   KODAK TRI-X PAN

ISEP, The Laycock school and other Experiments

The Islington Schools Environmental Project emerged in the early 1970s as a response to a stark and polarised period of Art History on the tail end of Modernism. Emerging from art school tutors wanting to give their students an education with a focus on collaboration rather than competition and divisiveness, the project became an attempt to draw together elements of art, education and the environment, firmly rooted within the services of a north London education department, providing environmental design services to school communities across the Borough. Similar reactions to the system provoked many individuals and groups at the time to set up alternatives based on ideas of community participation, as discussed in the introduction to this book.

David Cashman and Roger Fagin, both tutors at St Martin's School of Art in London, were frustrated by the expectations and limitations of their roles as artists within a system where values centred on exclusivity and competition. Their concerns were with how art education should overhaul itself, and also with how that overhauling works out when it is applied to outside projects. They started thinking of ways in which they could set up projects and work with a group of students towards a common ideal. In 1973 they started on their first school project at St Joseph's Roman Catholic primary school in Covent Garden, working with a group of students to transform the playground. Roger Fagin, a sculptor who developed large-scale structures with car tyres, explained in the art magazine *Studio International* in 1977: "We are working with a definition of art wider that the one generally promoted in our society. Our art is functional, it relates in a direct way to people and their needs and it is a product of joint endeavour."[1] He acknowledged that there was nothing revolutionary about these ideas: they're common to most cultures at most times. It's only in the west, since the renaissance, that the artist has been elevated to the position of an isolated prophet. Their emphasis on collaboration was a comment on the problems they found in the art school and outside. "People were relating to one another essentially on an individualistic basis, which tends to stress differences both in personal attitudes and in the language one uses. It also encourages a divisiveness among teachers and students which seemed very unproductive." In contrast, the notion of collective activity, the sharing of experience, seemed to provide a basis for a new relationship. Cashman explains: "Because artists are so subtly conditioned by the existing system, I expect they still feel that by entering a collaborative school context they might be sacrificing their liberal notion of personal 'integrity' to the demands of an institutionalised brief: laying aside some of that god-given prerogative to creative 'freedom', and exposing themselves to pressures and compromises."

Their most extensive project is at Laycock School in Islington.[2] Barbara Ryan set the project up as a two and a half year experiment when she was headteacher in 1974.[3] At that time, school grounds often functioned more like a drill yard, a featureless tarmac surface for team games and exercise based on a military model and seen as a way of releasing physical tension built up after hours and hours of sitting at a school desk. While teachers put great care and thought into how they set up their classrooms in a way that would stimulate and support learning, this was not necessarily followed through in the outdoor learning environment. This space might be transformed to offer stimulus to help children develop as effective learners. Fagin felt that an enormous reservoir of creativity was largely untapped and unrecognised: "Education for our society is a cerebral activity to do with educating your head rather than your hands or your heart. Through conditioning we alienate ourselves from our bodies to the point where we don't recognise them as being parts of ourselves at all, but rather as an appendage which we carry around with us and control." This correlates with views expressed by Brian Jackson and others, that in the interests of a capitalist society, a number of children are made to feel unintelligent according to the academic sense, that they are encouraged to think like third-class citizens from a very early stage, being preconditioned, it was thought, for a range of boring, menial jobs. The work at Laycock School included a tyre playstructure, tyre shed, large tractor tyre holes in walls for children to climb through, toilet buildings converted into a play castle and outdoor stage decorated on the exterior with a children's 'snake' mural; a raised garden area built by bricklayer parents; colour-coded jump-grid and maze, large scale murals on the school front facade bordered with children's designs based on tiled designs using the grid of the brickwork and a self-portrait frieze of over 200 figures on the playground perimeter wall. At first the projects did not involve the children.

The Laycock School project was made with students from St Martin's School of Art in their foundation year. Dave Stone joined in 1973 as a painting student with no intention of getting involved at all. He went to St Martin's intending to become a famous artist. His foundation tutor Paul Eachus said, "Well now you've got in you can stop pretending to be an artist and think what you really want to do." This really shook things up. A friend on the Laycock project asked him along to help move some railway sleepers. He ended up spending more time there than any other student (about three days a week). He remembers trying to stimulate the children's imaginations using masks and shadow projections. In his second year St Martin's staff suggested he look at other courses, they had a problem with shared authorship. They accepted the work eventually. He put a lot of effort into the presentation of the Laycock work at college, which seemed to

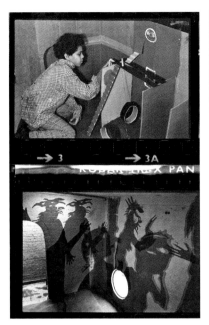

keep them happy. He got a job with the project for one year after graduating, then trained as a teacher before coming back to join the Project with six years' funding from an Inner City Partnership grant. He has been there ever since.

The work was initially always made from free materials. Fagin made large-scale minimal sculptures often using car and tractor tyres. He was inspired by seeing kids play on them and thought this would be a good context for teaching artists. He and Cashman were also blown away by student Clare Calder-Marshall's film *Our Playground*, a short documentary on the St Joseph's project exploring the children's visual responses to playgrounds. Partly as a result of this they decided to get children more involved at Laycock rather than just working with their students. A context very different to the classroom was extremely attractive to particular kids. In some cases it was the kids who were thought of as anti-social and trouble-makers who were most attracted to working in this way. "The art class at a primary school is conventionally based on free expression, which is probably too much for most children to cope with. In working with four- to 11-year-olds we discovered that the more clearly the projects are structured, the more they encourage inventiveness, lateral thinking, spontaneity and genuine creativity.... We make the limitations very, very clear, so that they know what they can and can't do. The important thing is that within those limitations anything is possible."[4] They devised a simple kit to enable children to make small-scale models of their design ideas for playstructures. Fagin said:

> One child was extremely unforthcoming: he didn't say much but started working on his model, and in the process of working went through classic De Bono-style lateral thinking leaps about the material. His model included a trampoline-like grid he made from the frame of the railway sleepers, into which he inserted car tyres as a bed in tension. When we built the large structure with the rope in it, we incorporated this element directly from his model. This child is academically far behind most of the children, and yet in terms of manipulative skills and development of three-dimensional concepts, he was streets ahead of any other children we worked with.

Fagin and Cashman did not see this as the only way for an artist to intervene in society, but were certainly hopeful of wider recognition of this particular role for the artist, because the outcome at Laycock School had been so positive, especially in terms of what the children achieved.

Differences of opinion in the group about the most appropriate ways of working with the children surfaced in a conflict over the designs for the front walls at Laycock School. A very early decision was that these should include designs of the artists' own and that the playground area or other areas would include children's designs. A conflict arose about what they should actually place upon the front walls. They decided that the most appropriate way to resolve it was to take the problem to the children, the staff, and the community of the school. The conflict ran deep enough to polarise a lot of underlying tensions, which already existed in the partnership, to do with the differences in personalities and ways of working. It also had to do with differences in the way they interpreted their role. Cashman talked about their function being primarily catalytic, like technicians executing ideas which had been generated by others; whereas Fagin at that time was arguing very strongly for the place of the artist's image within the overall scheme. After a series of animated talks with the staff and the teachers it was decided that the walls should be painted with children's images alone. Fagin felt "a personal pang of regret that none of my images eventually materialised" but felt retrospectively that the final decisions were the most appropriate. The whole experience helped them to clarify their relationship and the way they worked with other people for the future. The principle established was that it's always important to elicit views from children and the staff in a continuous process informing the basis of further modifications, gaining immediate and unequivocal responses to everything they do. As an indication of the success of their method, 30 years later the murals at Laycock are still intact. Cashman expressed clearly in 1977 that the shape such a project takes will be determined not only by the body of experience and information with which it grew, but also by the incentives, enthusiasm and energy of staff, children and parents in the future. This is entirely the case at Laycock.

The group of artists became known as Islington Schools Environmental Project (ISEP), which continues to run as a practice within the school system designing and building playgrounds collaboratively with school communities across north London.[5] Dave Stone, now Service Centre Manager of ISEP Playgrounds, joined the project as a student in 1973. He likes having a purpose and seeing the benefits of what he is doing, that's what dragged him out of art school in the first place. There is a level of personal satisfaction seeing a job realised. He measures their success by local anecdote: recently as he walked past an anti social family on a local council estate, the guy who was having a domestic with his girlfriend stopped the argument to say, "I know you, you built our playground!"

ISEP act as a catalyst supporting local initiatives. ISEP staff help schools to fund-raise for the material costs of schemes. Schools are encouraged to organise a committee, which will be a consultation and decision-making body, consisting of a child representative from each class in the school, playground assistants, teachers and parents. Although superficially, the transformation of the playground is the object, ISEP believe that the long-term success of the scheme as an 'ongoing' environmental process is dependent upon the continual involvement of the users. In the view of Stone "this changes the hierarchical

structure of the school and promotes equality through representation".[6] It is hoped that through the creation of a stimulating playspace, the children will benefit through improved relationships and behaviour, resulting in a decline in negative behaviour such as racism and other forms of victimisation. The children are involved in a wide range of educational activities through their involvement with ISEP projects. These may include plan drawing, simple surveying and scale model making, photography, mathematics, chart writing, diary writing, discussion and analysis. The work will ideally form an exhibition in the school. The information may lead to class discussions on matters such as territorial conflicts, racial or gender tensions or unconscious inequality of existing facilities and space. The classroom teacher should play a key role in this work. ISEP aim to shift the view of the environment as an impenetrable, unchangeable entity, which is external, alien, with little opportunity to be involved in its planning and design, to a view where people see themselves contributing to the regeneration of the inner city through the provision of safe and stimulating play environments. Through the process of designing and making, the children are involved in transforming their relationship with their immediate surroundings, a potent local symbol of transformation, of having the control and opportunity to express themselves within an environmental context. Over the years, the process has changed somewhat, as restricted funds reduce the time the team can spend working on any project. Nowadays more time is spent planning with teachers and designs are more often devised by ISEP's designer; children rarely get the in-depth involvement which might previously be considered the strength of these projects.

ISEP worked with Patrick Allen on the publication *Playstructures: Participation and Design with Children*, a booklet based on their project at Winton School, Islington. The publication proposes a series of workshops aimed at enabling whole classes, parents and teachers to get involved with environmental work, research and consultation.[7] The first workshop is based on The Kit, which was devised in order for whole classes to be able to build scale models in order to debate and decide on design ideas. Acknowledging that architectural drawings and plans can be difficult to 'read' and understand, this Kit was a useful co-operative design aid, although perhaps restrictive in its choice of elements. The Kit, devised by ISEP, consists of three-dimensional modelling components: miniature poles, tyres, ropes, etc., that can be used by four to six children and carried around in an old tool bag (part of the development plan was to design a case or box which could be efficient in use and easy to store and transport). Children are given a simple idea to work on, for example 'up and over', as a starting point for designing a playstructure. Kits should rotate around the classes of a school, remaining in each class for one week and each child's design recorded in a photograph. Another idea was that the teacher should document the process on video, but unsurprisingly this proved impractical. A second workshop was to investigate where to locate the playstructure in the school's playground, where usually a large central space was dominated by small hierarchies of older boys playing football. Staff hoped the location of a playstructure would provide a forum where children could play across age, gender and race divides.

The project also aimed to identify information from Health and Safety Regulations and British standards on the design of play equipment and collate this in an accessible form. Dave Stone, Director of ISEP later produced "Playground safety: a whole school approach" as part of the BBC Education publication *Playgrounds in the Primary School*.

ISEP in 1990 found itself legitimised in the new National Curriculum when their work was featured in the National Curriculum Council's booklet *Curriculum Guidance 7: Environmental Education*. The Curriculum Council identified environmental education as one of five cross-curricular themes and suggested art education in the school playground as an appropriate project to satisfy a whole range of curriculum objectives in English, science, mathematics, technology and art, illustrating how young children can participate in the planning, design and decision-making processes for creating a more aesthetic and enjoyable environment, demonstrating links with design and technology and how the arts can play a central role in encouraging children to explore and develop a personal relationship with their environment. This threw a life-line to ISEP, giving them a place within formal education which many artists shy away from. Former Minister of State for Education and Science Angela Rumbold states in the opening of the report:

Good environmental education, like any good education, must lead pupils and students out and on from their immediate perceptions and experience to a wider understanding. Education also has a part to play in preparing for a safer, cleaner environment. It must equip you to cope with the complex reality with which we all have to deal. Firstly by becoming knowledgeable and informed; second by being able to reason and consider issues and their consequences in the round.[8]

Learning Through Landscapes, 1990, was another project which promoted initiatives engaging with the outdoor environment as an educational resource, echoing earlier views of education critics such as Colin Ward and Brian Jackson. Its author, Eileen Adams, was responsible for a number of publications where she shows how the playground "can serve as a studio, workshop or gallery for artwork, where pupils can make large-scale, dirty or even dangerous work and display the results, perhaps created from found objects or plant material".[9] Playgrounds, she argued, can offer opportunities for physical education, for theatre in the round, for archaeological digs, opportunities for rich and extensive experience as a basis for learning; children were in danger of missing out on social and environmental experiences that used to be taken for granted as a necessary part of childhood. With carefully designed and stimulating play areas often integrated in school playgrounds today, it is hard to believe that it took some disenchanted artists to change the way schools approached playgrounds. The impact however was felt more in primary schools among four- to 11-year-olds than in the art schools which they were rebelling against, which in many respects have changed little in outlook to this day.

1 Cashman, David and Roger Fagin in conversation with Richard Cork, "Outside the Art System: Collaborative work in schools", *Studio International* 2, 1977, pp. 105-115.

2 The Laycock School project was championed by *Sunday Times* art critic Richard Cork in *Studio International*, 1977, and the exhibition *Art for Whom?* which he organised at the Serpentine Gallery, London, in 1978.

3 Years later, knowing she was dying of cancer, she asked that money not be spent on flowers for her funeral, but on the playground, giving it a new lease of life with the creation of a new Egyptian stage – a design chosen on the strength of children's enthusiastic applause at an image they saw at a school assembly. The current headteacher Chris Miles, a parent when they did the original project, has kept documentation of every phase, aware of its great value for the school community. Laycock was enormously influential, attracting artists from abroad to come and work alongside the original team. John Berger, author of *Ways of Seeing*, was spotted visiting with his mum.

4 Stone, Dave, "The Islington Schools Environmental Project" in *Art for Public Places*, Malcolm Miles ed., WSA, p. 122.

5 Frances Morrell, leader of Greater London Council and previously at Islington council, persuaded the GLC to take on ISEP as a specialist unit of two teachers and a technician. They became part of the local authority, directly linked to Roy Price the education officer for Islington. When ILEA (the Inner London Education Authority) and the GLC were abolished, the Boroughs took over schools; the Boroughs were then privatised with Islington's education services going to Cambridge Education Associates, part of Mott MacDonald, from whom schools could buy in services or opt out. ISEP were advised to set up services like any other business, to charge schools for their services now that schools hold their own budget after 1990-1992. This affects the kind of time they can spend with children; they now find that they spend far more time working with teachers. Dave Cashman, who was good at thinking out systems and process-orientated designs for tile work, went on to set up a small knitting company, giving up his teaching position at the Royal College of Art. Roger Fagin became a Sinyassen.

6 Stone, "The Islington Schools Environmental Project", p. 117.

7 Allen, Patrick, *Playstructures: Participation and Design with Children*, CSV, 1988.

8 National Curriculum Council, *Curriculum Guidance 7: Environmental Education*.

9 See for example Eileen Adams, "School Grounds", in *Kid Size The Material World of Childhood*, Milan: Skira Editore, 1997; Eileen Adams, *Making the Playground: A Key Stage 2 project in Technology, Art and Mathematics*, Trentham Books, 1993; Eileen Adams, *Machi Work: Education for Participation*, Trentham Books, 2001; Eileen Adams, *Changing Places: Children's Participation in Environmental Planning*, The Children's Society, 1998.

Creativity with purpose
Heads Together productions
Adrian sinclair

"Creativity With Purpose" is the tag line of Heads Together. It's easy not to give weight to creativity with a government obsessed with social change, but if we lose sight of the creative basis of our work, it will die and we will lose our incentive. The creative climate has changed enormously from ten years ago. Now people actually want to be creative, it's considered cool. The way we work has not changed, but the climate means that people listen now to what we have to say. Many artists still like the pretence of being poor and repressed, but now that there is real money for artistic work in this field, the key issue is whether artists are prepared to take on the responsibility to set up and run challenging projects. Creative Partnerships reflects this by saying "let's go for it", but we as a sector fail to use the money well, as we don't have adequate capacity. As artists, this is a failing. Our sector is very weak.

Heads Together projects may start with a place or an issue we feel we need to do something about. For example, the Home Zones initiative started because there was no public space for kids to play except the streets, so we started a creative process that resulted in us laying 800 metres of turf on a street. This gesture impacted nationally and led to changes in policy and a £30 million ($53 million) government programme of Creative Home Zones. Home Zones are an attempt to strike a balance between vehicular traffic and everyone else who uses the street, the pedestrians, cyclists, business people and residents. Some see Home Zones as a way of 'reclaiming' local streets from a traditional domination by cars. Others see it more modestly as a way of trying to restore the safety and peace in neighbourhoods that are becoming overwhelmed with speeding traffic. The success of a Home Zone scheme is not just dependant on effective and well thought out plans, but also requires the whole community being encouraged to get involved from the start. We do not consider ourselves strategists but we work closely with organisations such as Transport 2000, the independent national

Artists collaborate with young people in their community

body concerned with sustainable transport. They look for answers to transport problems and aims to reduce the environmental and social impact of transport by encouraging less use of cars and more use of public transport, walking and cycling.

Transport 2000's vision is of a country where traffic no longer dominates our lives, where many of our journeys can be made on foot, by cycle or using public transport and where you don't need a car to enjoy the countryside or city life. We also work with the Children's Play Council, an alliance of national and regional voluntary organisations, local authorities and partnerships researching and promoting children's play since 1988. Our street turfing project is a clear example that work can have an impact if you work in allegiance with other organisations. Impact is also achieved through good documentation. For example, we made a book of *2,000 lines* which means that I can still walk down any street in the area with it and someone will start talking about the project. The book also earned a National Design Award and is a very creative project in itself; the designer loved working on it. We laid all the work out on the school hall floor for a week to see how to bring things together and the page spreads started to emerge. We don't see any difference between the timing involved in sequencing and laying out a book and rhythm in theatre; they are equally time-bound.

Image is our starting point. That's my background. Ian, another member of our team, had worked as a documentary photographer for 30 years and came to us wanting to do written and oral work. We all double up offering different skills. There are generic creative skills, to do with how things fit together, what might work well, what could happen next, it's like creating theatre for other things to happen. What eventually happens can surpass expectation, although at the same time you always imagined it going there; as an artist I never want to repeat the same thing twice.

The idea

Our idea is to give people licence to dream a bit, to work from imagining into reality. Unless we dream we don't explore, so we ask of teachers and communities to dream a bit. We ask ourselves, what can we do for a community and for individuals? We want to push where things feel stuck. Children can lead the way in this: they are more imaginative and less inhibited. "Some communities round here are just coming out of mourning after 20 years", commented an adult in a former mining community. Kids have a different perspective: one said they thought the mines closed down about 100 years ago. They are not weighed down by the past. We often get different people in communities working together. In our radio project we have three generations of the same family working together, we provide these opportunities without thinking about it.

The radio station *ELfm* which we ran in east Leeds followed the success of the previous year's radio project, which had involved over 100 people aged four to 80. Now we have handed the running of the radio station to a steering group that includes kids who have never been invited to an evening meeting before and now find themselves coming to a cafe for steering group meetings. 50 per cent of the radio schedule last year was led by under-16s. People say they don't often hear children's voices on the radio. Some kids are much better at interviewing than adults, they ask some very direct questions. They even had the leader of the council in. Radio encourages participation on many levels. We have shared ownership of the idea of the station (although we authored it); a sign of success to us is when the synergy of people makes something happen.

The idea for *2,000 lines* came from a Leeds Education Authority Literacy Advisor, who approached us saying that kids had forgotten how to write creatively, that writing in schools was now an everyday task but no longer a wonderful thing, so what could we do to give writing status? There are no bookshops in east Leeds, so we decided to make a book and give it a proper launch at Waterstone's bookshop in Leeds as well as the local Fabergé Lever workplace, the main employer in the area. We started by getting the kids to write about things they knew about. Teachers often don't know the places the kids come from, so we get artists in to work with them who know the area. *2,000 lines* started under the CAPE Initiative (Creative Arts Partnerships for Education) which is about establishing long-term partnerships which will have a real impact on the quality of teaching and learning in education, connecting schools with arts organisations, community and business. The timing was right for us to do a project looking at past, present and future. We took the project a lot further than people really thought we would. We will often write a proposal based on the aspirations of people who have approached us, and remain true to the original concept even if we take it further than they ever thought was possible. Delivering on our promises is key.

2,000 lines took about a year. This is short for us, but we had worked for three years previously with one of the schools involved, John Smeaton High School. Our key observation was that the schools did not trust their communities and were not ready to work with them. In *2,000 plus*, an environmental project the following year, the schools really struggled to place artworks off-site out of the schools. In terms of our ambitions for the project we didn't succeed. Sometimes we find we are too far ahead of the game, too ambitious, we are wary of leading too much. My problem is I think it's so obvious, I forget I need to explain and give reasons over and over again, for example, why it's important to site an artwork in your community. People may well ask: "What's it got to do with education?" You have to think in other people's terms, you have to be calm and patient, not arrogant – it's much easier to sit and talk to other artists. But if we don't think in other people's ways why should they think in our way?

The People

Nowadays we select our partners carefully. You are only as good as they are; you have to choose where you are going to be effective. A school needs a committed headteacher for us to work with them, and unless certain management issues are sorted out, we can't change the way a school works. Sometimes we have tough issues to address, such as blocks in teaching (where a particular teacher is preventing learning or development opportunities), and we may have to report back to the head, which could have huge consequences.

Once we pulled out of a project despite the kids at the school raising £10,000 ($17,600). A new headteacher came in who promised to get back in touch with us but never did. We decided to pull out of working with that school as we are not prepared to fail the kids. Schools are sadly so dependent on one person, the head. Under a poor head other good teachers and good energy will quickly disperse.

Artists collaborate with young people in their community

One teacher said, "the trouble is, you get to do all the good bits" (even though they had given us all the worst kids from their class). Now we won't do that. The temptation is to believe that you can solve everything, but actually we can't and feel that putting all the low achievers together is not good, it's better to bring different ages and communities together to make a functional group.

My practice as an artist is collaborative, this is my only practice, it's work that I really believe in. There are vast opportunities to do things that we believe in, we don't do money-making projects to allow other projects to happen. I previously worked for ten years at Shipley College where I really enjoyed working with other professionals in an educational team. They taught young people through dance, theatre, car mechanics, finding the one thing that turned each individual on to learning. Once you find this spark, other things fall into place. These were kids who hadn't done well at school, who disappear into schools and society, no-one knowing what they are interested in; who get through school illiterate with no-one noticing. I wanted to find out, when these kids were in their late 20s, what impact the teaching at Shipley College had had on them. I have incredible respect for the dedication of colleagues there. Keith would go to one child's home who suffered from agoraphobia, and literally fetch him out of his wardrobe. They even took him to Ireland where he saw the sea for the first time and found himself shepherding sheep across a hilltop. No-one today would know he had suffered from such a condition. I have incredible respect for teachers. I like to work in partnership, as an accompanist, although I'm not afraid to take the lead when required. I feel I complement teachers but can't replace them. I love working with other professionals.

The impact

If we can change how a school works with young people we can make an impact for the next few years and provide systemic change. As an organisation we focus less on collecting evidence from young people and more on different professionals to see how we impact on work with young people. We are concerned most of all with those people who deal with them every day. It's all about being honest. We look for a creative response to a situation, that's achievable. As an artist nothing you ever do is new, it has always been done before. But when we hear someone say, "no one's ever done anything like that round here before", that's fantastic! Sharing ownership is key, for example when people say "It's our radio station." Even though my official title is Director, I don't pretend I don't exist; we can do a project like this *and* share the ownership; although ultimately I may know that the concept was originally mine.

I like how the bears are shaped!

Shakeema
Patterson

The mom is taking care of the baby.

FqTi˙mq

The mother bear has very big feet!
The baby bear is much smaller than
the mother bear.

It looks like it is made with tree bark.

Anel

The mother bear looks like the baby
bear. It's very nice and brown. The
mother bear has big ears.

Lady Bugs by: Katherine Bazan

children make sculpture: the work of Elizabeth Leyh

People living somewhere have a much greater understanding
of the place than an architect who is plotting on paper. Nothing
is better for a ten year old that to be involved in planning their
neighbourhood. Kids and neighbours can solve problems in
landscape design, contribute to the place they live, it can take
someone coming in to activate this process, maybe an artist,
maybe a community group. When kids take their artwork into
the public domain and get credit for doing something positive
in the community I can't think of anything better, that's when
they're becoming citizens.
Elizabeth Leyh

American sculptor Elizabeth Leyh has made sculpture collaboratively with
young people since the late 1960s. Her first collaborative project was in a
school playground at Shoreham-by-Sea on the south coast of England. She
has run special units for children with children with severe learning difficulties.
She worked as Milton Keynes Town Artist, 1974-1978, in Ashkelon, Israel,
1980-1986, the USA, and in London from the 1970s to the present. Her two
books *Children Make Sculpture*, 1972, and *Concrete Sculpture in the
Community*, 1978, are classics of their time.

Leyh's book *Children Make Sculpture* is a stunning visual source book
beautifully illustrated with black and white photographs, almost like a coffee
table art book, providing visual inspiration for anyone wishing to make sculpture
with children.[1] Her foreword to the book explains that sculpture is "something
that occurs everyday in everyone's life and should not be looked at as an 'artistic'
concept or pursuit". She emphasises the simple idea that children enjoy making
things, valuing the activity in itself and the knowledge gained by the child
of form and material. The book is organised in five sections: "Putting Things
Together", "Modelling", "Working with Plaster", "Carving" and "Sculpture is

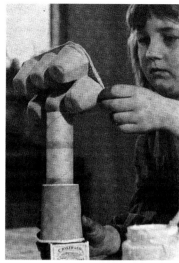

Everywhere." The message is that accessible art materials can be found all around us and that every child has the capacity to make and enjoy sculpture. Photographs show children wearing robot suits made of cardboard boxes, pouring plaster, working with wood and stone, building assemblages with egg boxes and toilet rolls (resonating with a generation brought up on the childrens' UK TV series *Blue Peter*), along with photographs of children climbing on Egyptian statues or a David Smith sculpture. A plate of Swiss Roll cake slices is presented for inspiration along with an ancient Greek temple frieze.

Leyh to this day remains single-minded in her intention to show that anyone can be creative, in groups or as individuals, in their own environment. Her second book *Concrete Sculpture*, published in the Inter-Action Community Arts Series, includes a foreword which describes the remarkably simple method of group creativity she evolved in the practice of making group concrete sculpture: "The process is both social and artistic, it's about groups of people making useful structures (call them 'sculptures') in concrete for their own neighbourhoods, using their own images."[2] Her projects involved not only children, but the entire age range of a community in the creative process, using everyday materials and working in spontaneous response to situations; she introduces her work with the classic community arts belief: "art can be both a group process and socially useful without abandoning aesthetic standards". Berman, founder of Inter-Action Community Arts, reminds us:

> The participation by a group of assistants in an artists' work is by no means new. The Old Masters had ateliers – workshops where apprentices and assistants laboured anonymously. What is new is that no prior training is required to be part of a community arts or social arts atelier. Under the guidance of an artist working in a community local people become a community atelier. They are local adults and children; they don't think of themselves as being artists or apprentices.... The problem is they probably didn't think of themselves as being 'creative' either. The very fact of having helped to make a single worthwhile item in their own environment can ignite the realisation that they too can be creative and constructive. Also some intensely interested but formerly untrained members of a project might carry on from this on-the-job training to lead projects themselves in the future.

Leyh's art practice aims to enable others to feel empowered, so that they too can create and can make a useful contribution to a group effort. Her first collaborative sculpture was made in Shoreham-by-Sea, in the playground of her son's school. She had moved to Shoreham in 1967 after completing the postgraduate sculpture programme at the Pratt Institute, New York. Finding herself in a context where her training appeared to have no relevance, she decided to put her skills to use to brighten up the environment, working collaboratively with other parents at weekends to build a playground sculpture of a crocodile for the kids to play on. The playground felt to her dingy, dreary and prison-like, so they added a mural based on kids' drawings, but this only lasted a few weeks as the Local Education Authority sandblasted the wall as the schools' inspector believed that it was unsuitable to have childrens' work on a playground wall. Such an attitude may seem shocking today from where we can easily fail to appreciate the radical nature of the work that Leyh was initiating.

She was then invited to become head of a school for children with special educational needs in Southampton, her five years at university being sufficient qualification for this. She recalls helping children learn the letters of the alphabet by taking them to the sea shore and writing their names in the sand; baking cookies in the shape of a child's initials or moulding letters in clay. She then moved to West Sussex Psychiatric Services, working with children whose mental disabilities caused severe motor control difficulties, where she involved children in the business of mixing cement and working it to make large outdoor sculptures. She was later asked to a similar project by a school principal in Downey, California, where new law required that special needs children be educated along with non-special needs, which meant they would lose their building. Liz's large collaborative sculpture attracted media and TV interest, which helped their campaign to save the school. Out of their wheelchairs on the ground working directly in cement, this scenario might seem unthinkable today. The optimism embraced in her projects attests to the strength of her belief that everyone has potential for creative engagement, every person can participate in a large-scale, physically ambitious project and gain something meaningful from it.

Concrete Cows at Milton Keynes, which gained her notoriety, was a collaborative project made over two years with adult and children groups, one of many projects which she developed as artist-in-residence in Milton Keynes from 1974-1978, having been appointed as the town's first Arts Council Town Artist. *Concrete Cows* became synonymous with the concrete new town and inadvertently became one of the most well known artworks in Britain, still attracting media interest today and featured on 31 websites, whilst ironically the name Liz Leyh is little known.[3] When offered the Milton Keynes bursary, the Arts Council of Great Britain had said they could not appoint her without seeing a portfolio of her work (the playgrounds work was considered not art but social work, she would need to show portfolio of her own artworks. Going home she begrudgingly took photos, which seemed to her such a fixed idea of what artists do. As the first artist appointed for a new town, she felt very aware that her success, or otherwise, had great implications for arts funding outside of London, which was an important political debate at the time. In terms of creating new ways for artists to work she was part of an important new field, a new area for consideration. There were no national networks or projects available outside of London, the Milton Keynes artists truly felt they were contributing to a whole new way of thinking.

Concrete Cows, made in 1978, was the culmination of a series of concrete community sculptures for this new town designed seemingly for cars, so lacking in distinguishing landmarks that according to writer-in-residence Jack Trevor Storey, it was impossible to recognise one road junction from the next. Leyh allegedly sited *Concrete Cows* on a roundabout to provide Trevor Storey with a marker to find his way home. The grazing cows captured the public imagination attracting a range of responses from civic pride to mockery. The art world of the day appeared to shun their simple pleasure and lack of complexity, which is fascinating in comparison with the latter-day popularity of Antony Gormley's sculpture *Field*, a series of installations made in collaboration with different communities in which thousands of hand-sized clay figures were made by 'participants' and for which Gormley was awarded the Turner Prize in 1994, or *Mother and Child Divided*, 1993, by Damien Hirst, in which four sections of a bisected cow and calf are displayed in tanks of formaldehyde between which the viewer can pass. (Incidentally, both these artists are represented by the gallery White Cube, London.) The *Cows* have been subsumed by a civic desire to conserve one of the few identifiable aspects of Milton Keynes' heritage. Child participation in the making of *Concrete Cows* is now largely forgotten and the imagery is left to work on a purely symbolic level.

Leyh always astutely identifies how her projects engage with larger issues. A project with students of the Sacred Heart Academy New Orleans, 1997, involved a private Catholic girls' school working with a neighbourhood school which the girls drove past but never connected with. The girls made a carved mahogany doorway and a ceramic relief for their neighbouring Catholic school, Our Lady of Lourdes, so close geographically but yet so far away culturally, part of another world. Most importantly the project articulated questions about cross-cultural understanding.

A long-term project in the village of Neve Avivim, Israel, on the Israeli-Lebanon border, aimed at community rebuilding. After discussions the community decided they wanted to build a monument to 12 children killed 20 years previously in a terror attack on their school. The project enabled families to create an identity for themselves. Having gone to do a month, she ended up

Artists collaborate with young people in their community

staying there from 1980 until 1986, charged with physical rehabilitation of a neighbourhood under Project Renewal, an Israeli government scheme to bring in overseas expertise, twinning neighbourhoods with different Jewish communities around the world. The clean-up campaign provided ample supplies of waste rubble to build sculpture with local people.

Miwon Kwon describes what she considers a dominant principle, or operative basis of community-based site-specific work, a "presumption of a unity of identity between the artist and the community, and between the community and the artwork".[4] Kwon is critical of what she sees as a "crucial representative function of labour in community-based art practice" of labour seeming to secure the participants' sense of identification with 'the work' or at least a sense of ownership of it through the recognition of one's own labour in the creation of, or becoming of, 'the work'. Kwon considers that involving large numbers of people in a collective act sets up "a drive toward identificatory unity predicated on an idealistic assumption that artistic labour is a special form of unalienated labour, provisionally outside of capitalism's forces".[5] Leyh argues stridently that children and adults obtain great satisfaction from the chance to make something, to make a difference, to participate in real physical labour towards an enjoyable end result which they can share. She offers a gift to share, not a one-way act of exploitation.

Many who worked with Leyh on the Milton Keynes *Cows* still remember the experience fondly. Lesley Bonner, local artist and one of the original participants in the cow-making project, put her point of view on a web page:

> She enjoyed building the cows and being part of the group of artists at that time as there was a lot of energy and enthusiasm, resulting in many community projects. Amongst these were the bonfire night celebrations where huge models of the Houses of Parliament and large moving political figures were made and burnt! After years of feeling responsible for the maintenance of the cows (which of course had no maintenance budget) Lesley feels that the cows had their day a long time ago and that they should have been allowed to gradually fall into disrepair and be gracefully moved away.[6]

This was the fate of other projects of the time that enjoyed the same notoriety, including numerous underpass murals, a Griffin, Tin Man and Mushrooms on Beanhill. *Concrete Cows* was valuable not only because it generated community pride and participation, but it also established a marketable identity for the town. This is a phenomenon which by the 1990s becomes official policy for many cities and towns across the world and is often the main reason today for towns commissioning public artists.[7]

Concrete Cows attracted many commentaries: "Often the source of amusement, over the years they have been stolen, rearranged and painted. They were once even beheaded", states the Milton Keynes official website. They list under "Cow Crimes" the "many exciting things have happened to the cows":

> A year after they were put in place, the lone calf (nicknamed 'Millie Moo') was stolen by evil-minded rustlers with heavy lifting equipment. Sadly, Millie Moo was never seen again.
> A few years later, in 1988, Millie Moo Two (the original Millie replacement), was also stolen in a daring midnight raid on that hitherto peaceful field. This time the aim was ransom.... Despite their obvious grandeur, indigenous pranksters have often made

Kids + Concrete = ART

MAMA BEAR AND BABY BEAR

A permanent concrete sculpture

Children's Museum

311 Main Street
Utica, N.Y. 13501

State of the Arts

NYSCA

artists collaborate with young people in their community

Lavonda Mathis

the cows targets for practical jokes, usually in the poorest taste. They have been painted as zebras, bedecked in pajama bottoms (by a presumably more prudish sort of vandal) and, memorably, a papier mâché bull was added to the group, causing considerable damage to the hind quarters of the cow it was attached to. Most disturbingly of all, on one occasion, the cows were completely beheaded.... Today, the cows still stand peacefully in their field, and can be visited by the curious or the more criminally-minded members of the young farmers fraternity.

Despite *Cows* being quietly retired, almost 30 years later they are still central to the town's image. A *Guardian* article in 2004 titled "A Little Piece of Heaven Among the Concrete Cows" interviews locals about the prospects of Milton Keynes being the fastest expanding city in the UK. Ken, a retired IT manager, said "People who have never been here always talk about the *Concrete Cows*, but I don't know anywhere else in the country where you can walk more than a mile and a half into the city centre without having to cross a main road... It is a well conceived and well thought out town, but if they expand it the way they are planning it will spoil everything that makes it unique." Steven Heap, the city chaplain thinks:

> If you accept there is a need to build more houses in the south east then Milton Keynes has a track record of building and creating communities, and that is something that is paramount.... It is no good just rolling out houses, but my fear is that despite the rhetoric of [Labour deputy prime minister] John Prescott that the government will not build soulless housing estates, that is what will happen. Yes, we accept that there will be growth, and in some ways that is quite exciting. But does the government have sufficient understanding of what it takes to create a community and, if it does, will it be prepared to make that investment?

In *Kids + Concrete + Art*, 2001, Leyh involved local children in building a park of permanent sculptures in the land next to the Childrens Museum in Utica, New York. In a town lacking middle class parents to take kids to the Museum, the grounds of this museum are pretty much these childrens' back yard. Her main concern was how to integrate Bosnian and black children and get them into the museum. The Mayor stated "isn't this how you build communities and make citizens?" The permanent sculptures were made through after-school programmes with kids from local housing at Washington Courts, Saturday classes, a 70-year-old woman and children with cerebral palsy. "We build it with rocks and cement and little bits of metal armature, and eventually model it into the shape of the bear... They do the modelling, I bite my nails", said Leyh in the local press. She insisted on having city money to create the park, that they bought into the proejct. As with all her projects they are carefully designed and constructed to minimise future maintenance needs. The colouring on the statues of animals comes from minerals, and will not peel or ever need repair.

'Client groups' such as authorities or funders are not Leyh's prime consideration, it is the participants who she is working for. Participation relies on her energy and encouragement, her ability to enthuse and motivate – which is not always the case in 'participatory' art projects which are increasingly mediated by curators, administrators, galleries, funders, facilitators and a range of middle people intent, for many different reasons, on orchestrating 'participatory' scenarios.

1 Leyh, Elizabeth, *Children Make Sculpture*, New York: van Nostrand Reinhold, 1972.

2 Berman, ed., foreword to Elizabeth Leyh, *Concrete Sculpture in the Community*, London: Inter-Action Community Arts Series in association with the Institute for Social Enterprise, 1978. Inter-Action was founded in Camden, London in 1968 and by the time they published this book employed 65 workers – teachers, theatre workers, accountants, architects, video/filmmakers, artists, etc. – all of whom worked as animateurs (otherwise known as "community artists", "motivators" or "enablers"). Inter-Action followed the concept of "Social Enterprise", applying the initiative of creative persons from the arts, community work and business worlds towards the solution of social, educational and financial problems within the community.

3 The notoriety of *Concrete Cows* has led to commercial spin-offs. A computer company has bought up the domain name *concretecows.com*, an American sound engineer trades off the name and a cartoonist promotes his wares with their story.

4 Kwon, Miwon, "Sitings of Public Art: Integration versus Intervention", in *One Place After Another: Site-Specific Art and Locational Identity*, Boston, MA: MIT Press, 2002.

5 Kwon, *One Place After Another: Site-Specific Art and Locational Identity*, pp. 96-97.

6 Website of the Silbury Group of artists.

7 Zukin, Sharon, *The Culture of Cities*, Cambridge, MA: Blackwell, 1995.

Magic Me
intergenerational arts
Jan Stirling

When Magic Me began, it aimed to use arts activities to give older people living solitary, often socially isolated lives in nursing homes, the chance to be enlivened by interaction with young people. Of course, we soon recognised that older people can enliven the lives of children too, making a qualitative difference to a child's experience in their larger community. We've become very interested in the ways that children and older people can partner each other productively, finding ways to consider and meet the needs of their partners through shared creative activity.

Magic Me's core philosophy is that all people are individuals with the capacity for growth and change no matter where they are in the natural process of living, ageing and dying. That an individual's capacity to grow and change can be strengthened and enhanced through relationships with others is an extension of this philosophy.

Magic Me works in the London Borough of Tower Hamlets in the East End of London. This area is one of the most socially deprived areas of London and indeed the UK. Traditionally a working class area, it has historically been home to many newly arrived immigrant populations. In the early part of last century the area was a largely Jewish community with some Irish and white British residents. In recent years it has become home to an increasing population of Bangladeshi and to a lesser extent Somali residents.

Many of the older people with whom we work are white or Jewish, and have lived all or most of their lives in the area. These populations are now diminishing and gradually the older population is becoming ever more diverse. The younger people involved in Magic Me projects tend to be mainly Bangladeshi with some white, Somali and other cultural groups in the minority. Much of our work could be described as development work or community building, as more and more we are designing projects that set out to respond creatively to the complex social needs of a diverse community. Indeed much of the funding we currently receive is through government initiatives aimed at regenerating neighbourhoods and alleviating social exclusion in deprived inner city urban areas.

The arts are a large part of Magic Me's way of building community. By engaging culturally diverse groups of young and older people in shared arts activities we help to enable relationships to develop and flourish between people that might not otherwise meet. 'Meeting is making' is central to my practice. When people are enabled to meet, the product of that meeting (a relationship) is a creative product. Similarly, the reverse is true: 'making is meeting': people naturally begin to discover each other through the creative process and build meaningful relationships. Meeting and making are equally important.

The importance of relationships extends to the organisation itself. We need to build strong working relationships with partner organisations such as schools and residential or day care settings; with funding agencies and with organisations and institutions linked with arts and culture. We also need to work collaboratively with teachers, care workers, managers, funders and the freelance artists we contract to co-deliver our projects.

Projects will often involve two or more art forms, making a relationship between expressive forms part of the work. The art forms are chosen in partnership with the people we will be working with.

Core staff at Magic Me, including Director Susan Langford and myself as Arts Development and Training Manager develop, oversee, and usually co-deliver projects. Magic Me takes responsibility for raising most of the project funds. Magic Me typically also provides project management, project materials and specialist arts staff. Our partners tend to provide the venue, and access to and support for participants.

Over the years *Magic Me* has evolved a variety of project models ranging from short intensive holiday projects of three to five days, to projects lasting for a year or more. Most often a *Magic Me* project will bring a small group of ten to 12 school children accompanied by their teacher, into contact with an equally small group of older adults who are supported by a care worker or activities co-ordinator. Sessions usually happen weekly for an hour or two over a period of one or two school terms (ten to 20 sessions). These usually take place in the adult participants' day-centre or residential home. However, some school-based work may also happen and adults are occasionally invited to visit a school.

Project artists carefully prepare the young people (aged nine or older), and the older people (aged 55 or older) to meet each other. They meet separately with each group in discussions and activities aimed at eliciting thoughts and feelings about the prospect of meeting their older or younger partners. Hopes and fears, assumptions and experiences may be expressed. Younger participants might rehearse greetings and meetings with their prospective older partners before they actually meet, whilst the older adults will be encouraged to consider how they would like to welcome their young visitors.

Young and older participants are supported equally during a project to reflect on their on-going experiences of working together. This happens within the sessions themselves between older and younger partners, but it also happens after the intergenerational part of a session is over, when participants are back with their own peer groups. In this way the project artists, teacher and care-worker can each support the participants both to savour the enjoyable aspects of the project and to work through any experiences that feel problematic or difficult.

Often a project will revolve around a certain theme which is sometimes linked to wider community events or to particular aspects of a school curriculum. Each project will work towards an event of some sort. This might be a performance, an exhibition, a publication or a celebration. Some events might involve an invited audience whilst others are reserved for the participants only.

If a project has as one of its goals a public event, this event is never the final encounter for the group. There will always be at least one follow-up session so that the group can reflect on the experience of showing their work. Participants also need time at the end of a project to remember their journey together, to notice the progress they have made individually and collectively over their shared time, to pass some of their observations on to us so that we can improve our work and they can say a little about what they will be taking away with them. Finally the group members will need the chance to acknowledge that the project has come to an end and to say goodbye to one another.

Recent curriculum developments within primary and secondary education in England have placed a focus on 'citizenship' as a subject in itself. In essence, the citizenship curriculum sets out to encourage young learners to think about themselves in the larger context of their school community as well as their local, national and global communities.

The curriculum also endorses out-of-school learning experiences that put students into contact with people from different backgrounds and age groups in order to attempt to answer these questions. There are very rich links to be made between the citizenship curriculum and Magic Me's work as providers of intergenerational arts activities. The use of arts processes and our emphasis on the development of relationships within intergenerational groups makes us uniquely placed to contribute to curriculum delivery.

One project that is about to begin will link a group of 15-year-olds who are finding it difficult to engage in school and are at risk of being excluded or excluding themselves, with a group of older users of a nearby resource centre. Together they will try to answer some of the questions posed above. A later stage of the project is designed to coincide with the GCSE exam in Citizenship and the older participants will have the opportunity to take the exam alongside their young partners if they choose. Often older participants are very keen to spend time with young people but are anxious when they realise that they are participating in a project that's linked to a young persons 'education'. Comments like, "I wasn't very good at school", and "I'm not expert enough", are indicative of this anxiety. They also worry that they won't be able to learn or do it well.

Unlike the adults, young participants may be compelled to attend a Magic Me project as part of their studies. Whilst the prospect of meeting 'old people' might not at first appeal they may be enticed by the promise of arts-based activities. Like their older partners, young people potentially have their own anxieties in relation to learning. They may be going through the very experiences of education that their older partners remember with such dread. And they may be lacking in sufficient self-confidence to engage fully and fruitfully in more conventional learning opportunities.

It's our role to reassure participants, and to value them as personal historians, with experiences and knowledge that only they can bring to the project. We also need to dispel their belief that they can't learn and present them with something new and different and interesting enough that they can begin to experience themselves as learners again, and to become confident in their capacity to learn.

We do this by providing activities that are fun, creative, expressive and that incite the groups' curiosity about each other. Once engaged, group members are more able to share their personal experiences and to become interested in each other and in the similarities and differences that their stories reveal.

Stranger Than Fiction was conceived as a drama project that would draw participants from three different age groups. 12-year-olds from a local secondary school were set to meet with older people aged between 70 and 92 at a nearby day-centre. The third group of participants, in their early 20s, were students drawn from an applied drama course offered by the theatre department of a university in the neighbourhood (Queen Mary College, University of London).

The project was developed with partners over a 14 week period in the autumn of 2002 and then sessions (some preparatory and others intergenerational) ran over a further 14 weeks between January and April 2003. The project led to a small studio performance based on the life experiences of group members which was shown before an invited audience. The performance also incorporated improvisation and audience interaction.

Two Magic Me artists including myself were primarily responsible for the delivery of the project. We also collaborated creatively with another colleague who was running the applied drama course, who contributed to the conceptualisation and delivery of the project and we simultaneously contributed to the content and delivery of the course. The third group were young aspiring professionals learning to deliver intergenerational arts projects, and their involvement was as participant /animateurs.

Stranger Than Fiction was the final project in a series that ran over three years on a housing estate, funded by a ten year regeneration programme Ocean New Deal for Communities. This body of work by Magic Me and its partners, in a consortium called *Standing On Common Ground*, aimed to provide opportunities for young and older neighbours from diverse cultures to meet and begin to get to know each other. The work did not set out to specifically confront or address problems or controversial issues related to race, religion, gender or age. However, each project implicitly worked with themes that would enable the groups to constructively explore aspects of their diversity.

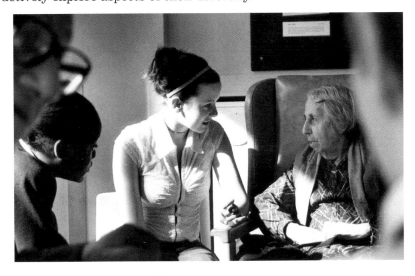

Stranger Than Fiction also coincided with the lead up to, and the early weeks of the Iraq War. The elders participating were all Jewish, and the young participants were a mixture of Muslim, Christian and other religious backgrounds. Some had no religious affiliation. With such media attention on the Iraq and Middle East conflicts the timing of this project was very poignant, providing a backdrop for group members to explore their relationships with each other in the context of both personal and global 'realities'.

In the very early stages of the work we wanted to emphasise a number of things. We wanted to create opportunities for communication, for learning about each others' lives, where we come from and who we are. In the photo on the previous page, 'Jenny', an applied drama student, is helping a younger participant 'Sonia' meet 'Laura', an older participant. Jenny has spent time with Sonia and Laura on their own in previous sessions and is now helping them to come together. It's clear here that the interaction is mainly happening through Jenny. The partners are learning about each other as a result of Jenny encouraging them to talk to her about themselves.

Opposite, we see a similar threesome. However the interaction is markedly different. Each of the three are actively engaged in a conversation that is emerging as a result of their combined contributions. The older man in these photographs looks absorbed in his partners' words and his attention is clearly engaged. This was significant to us at the time because 'Sam' was a man of many words who enjoyed nothing more than singing for an audience. Here he is relaxed enough to enjoy listening to others as well. His youngest partner seems encouraged by his attentiveness and is able to be very open and proactive within her small group. Paradoxically, Sam is getting very positive attention in return for his own attentiveness.

Following an exercise where the older adults were interviewed by the youngest participants the group went on to make visual links that illustrated things people had in common. Several balls of yarn were passed through and around the group resulting in a web of connections. When invited to comment on things people had learned about each other one young person exclaimed: "I never knew older people had aspirations!" The older adults in the room were delighted to have been found out.

In another exercise (not pictured here) older and younger partners described qualities they valued about themselves and created mini dramas that enabled them to invent characters that embodied each other's qualities. 'Ruth' and 'Danny' discovered they shared a love of God. Though Ruth was Jewish and Danny Christian, they enjoyed each other's capacity for devotion and were able to make a scene that celebrated this quality in each other.

Here 12-year-old 'Shaheda' is working collaboratively with her older partner 'Abe'. They are writing down ideas within a larger group of participants who are discussing life experiences and writing together. They have started with a warm up game of 'pass the squeeze' and moved on to work with the idea that they will finish the sentence: "If I ruled the world...." 'Abe' says that if he ruled the world he would "abdicate, give away all his money and sail away on a boat". He wouldn't want the job! 'Victor' says he would make a world where no one would have to feel shame and where everyone would respect each other. Both men have in their own ways made links between corruption, oppression and power. This small group has begun to notice that their interaction and sharing is a contrast to the images of war and conflict in the media. Other participants who hear their statements later in the session remark on how close people feel in the room despite differences of religion and colour.

The group worked together for seven intergenerational sessions before inviting an audience to come and view some selected scenes, songs and poems from their time together. The studio performance also incorporated an interactive element and some improvisation. All of the content was made possible in such a short space of preparation because the group had been enabled to strengthen their capacity to listen and to speak, to watch and be watched, and to use simple interactive structures that supported them to inhabit the moment-to-moment of an encounter with new and different people.

The performance did not explicitly address the conflicts in the larger world. However, what was implicitly present both in the group of performers and in the gathering of friends, colleagues and family who watched them was the sense that this diverse group of people living and working along side each other had found many things in common and many reasons to enjoy one another.

When asked what advice the young people on the project might give future students in relation to participating in intergenerational arts, here is what they wrote:

Dear Future Students,
Don't be shy
Jump in with both feet
Be prepared to have lots of fun
The best is yet to come
Age is not an issue
Listen to each other
Don't be afraid of the older people
They like the same things
Working with older people is quite fun
Its OK to be afraid, you'll be surprised who else is afraid too
Be confident, and always start with a smile
Guts come out of the blue!

Planet VOLCO

a project by Loraine Leeson

VOLCO, which stands for Virtual Online Co-Operative environment, is a planet in cyberspace, which evolves according to information put into it. It has been designed as a learning resource for schools. Children and young people are taking part in the creation of an evolving virtual planet through subjects across the curriculum and linking with schools in different parts of the world. The technical requirements to run this project are very simple and include equipment now common to most schools: online computers, scanner, digital camera, basic visual and word processing software.

The project was devised and realised by Loraine Leeson, an artist who has worked collaboratively and creatively with communities in east London since the mid 1970s. VOLCO emerged from her interest in making a situation in which many children could input into something much larger than themselves, glimpsing that they can be effective and have a role in creating their own futures. She hopes that this virtual experience will give them confidence that they are capable of creating a new society on their own planet. As she says, reality is in your imagination, in any case. Leeson's experience of developing the project has brought to light many discrepancies between the theory and practice of how the new equipment in schools is actually enhancing education. Schools have computer hardware but teachers often have little time or expertise to make productive use of it, despite government efforts at widespread training. Most schools she has worked in have had scanners and digital cameras, but it has not been an unusual experience to find that they have never been used, that few children she has encountered (primary or secondary) have not yet learned to make a web page, or that use of equipment has hitherto not extended beyond word processing and browsing. There have been even sorrier tales of schools that have resorted to remote management of their resources, which disallows anything other than minimal interaction, despite sometimes quite

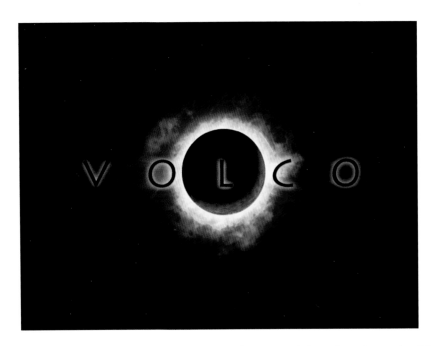

sophisticated equipment. This results partly from provision of equipment without salaries or staff to manage it. Though not its main intention, the VOLCO project has ensured use of all of a school's digital equipment, often for the first time, checking that it is in working order and that some teachers know what to do with it. This hands-on approach to building confidence in technology is completely different from the frustration that busy teachers often experience from 'do it yourself' types of training or trying to develop digital projects themselves.

The project was inspired by a story about the Planet Glub, written by Loraine's younger son at the age of seven for school homework. She was frustrated that children playing commercial computer games had limited freedom to invent their own characters, and could only build characters from a predetermined set of choices. (For example when you create your own pet on *Cbeebies* website, choose your soldier's outfit in the Playstation game *Metal Gear Solid* or select your preferred car in Playstation *Gran Turismo*, you appear to have choices but ultimately the range of options is limited.) She was also intrigued by the fascination young people have in playing with identities online, such as in instant messaging, chat rooms and multi-user domains (MUDs, MOOs, and MUSHes), where they seemed to be far more inventive than with stereotypical figures provided for them. For example in some MUDs participants build their own characters and dwellings, choosing artefacts and environments to complement the character they would like to be. She was interested in marrying the creative potential of these virtual experiences with the real lives, identities and futures of young people.

The whole planet, and indeed its inhabitants, exist in fragments and are never directly depicted. As in life, it becomes a whole through putting it together in your imagination. Her approach was to put clear structures in place. VOLCO has a framework of basic categories through which the children's creative work develops. Basic template formats are used into which they learn to enter their own images and words in order to build up characters plus their ideas about life on the planet. It is through combining these with the ideas of other children via the website and without being prescriptive, that their collective ideas emerge.

On the website, class groups choose a location for their settlement using co-ordinates on the Volcan map. Ideas are developed in a range of ways, aiming to support children with different styles of learning. Both navigation and information are as visual as possible. Individuals in the group create online identities for themselves using scanned, photographed and downloaded imagery as well as text. Avoiding external appearance, incoming Volcans express themselves through their choice of habitat, clothing, accessories, alien pets, etc.. Their next task is to invent all aspects of life on this virtual planet. Ideas for this are discussed online through the Volcan Forum, which links participants from different settlements. In this way, children find themselves talking to others who they do not know, and who may have very different life experience to themselves. The ideas developed in this way are then uploaded as image and text to the archive, where all Volcan knowledge is stored. It's important to her that the website is visually attractive and easy for children to navigate and that the process enables the children's ideas to be represented in a way that does justice to the quality of their imaginations. A simple template format ensures that all images the children produce will look good online, and guidelines are given to help them create and adjust their imagery for best effect. For instance, scanned imagery is set against a coloured or black background, and filling the frame is recommended for photography. Children learn how to adjust their source imagery using the school's imaging software. They are shown how to enhance and crop, change proportions and colours, though the template can also cope with unadjusted imagery as a failsafe. By the end of the project she wants every child to see their own work online and to be able to say "wow! Isn't that brilliant!", while also feeling that the planet is their own.

Leeson developed the project with children from east London living in areas with high levels of unemployment, where most of the population have English as a second language, and educational achievement is low. Experience tells her that children, particularly from disadvantaged backgrounds often have little feeling of self-worth or effectiveness. In this project they have an opportunity to not only do something exciting that may motivate them to learn, but to work towards an output that becomes part of the real world, existing in the public domain as a website, which friends or family in other parts of the world may look at and which the children can feel proud of.

The project offers children a number of things in addition to the computer skills, which they pick up very quickly. It gives them a chance to create something of their own, which is of high quality, and that will also be displayed in the public domain. VOLCO offers its young participants preparation for a world where future generations will need to make creative use of whatever technologies are at their disposal, through teamwork, in a multi-cultural environment. Above all it offers them an early experience of their power to create and change the world around them.

After five years' development and the input of over 600 children, Leeson has set about creating national and international partnerships that are creating a breadth of inter-cultural experience for participants. She no longer delivers the project herself, but now trains teachers to run it themselves. It will be available online as a learning resource for schools and other educational institutions, a lesson in how transferable her method is, and in the potential for digital projects to work in schools without outside experts. She has trained teachers in London and Berlin, artists who work in children's hospitals in Chicago, and has plans to take it to the Shetland Isles, Austria, Luxembourg, Venezuela and Ireland.

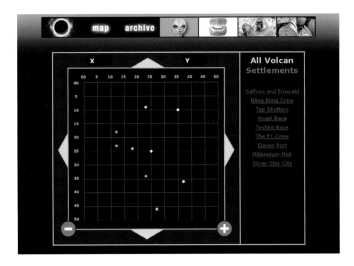

Leeson's working method is informed not only by her fine art training but also being active in co-ops and collaborating as an artist with non-arts organisations in the 1970s and 80s, which provided lessons such as a need for clear structure and learning how to share without creating power struggles and without killing off good initiative. During this time she trained in conflict resolution and for six years worked as a volunteer mediator and neighbourhood conciliator. These experiences gave her an understanding of how creativity may be brought to bear on the possibility of meeting a variety of needs through a single outcome. It crystallised her understanding of difference as a dynamic force and taught her that this energy could be directed in a positive way rather than erupting into conflict, producing innovative and unexpected results. In her work she attempts to minimise the fear that in her view often comes with difference, using fantasy to create safe spaces to facilitate communication, though her real interest is to bring this thinking back into the real world.

East London, where she has spent her working life, offers a multi-cultural context to inform and allow development of this practice. Her conflict management background has become particularly invaluable in dealing with the constraints of schools, and other institutions, with meeting different needs and agendas, including the artistic. It has also enabled her to create ambitious multi-institutional projects such as *Cascade*, 2000-2005, using some of the approaches learned through conflict management to simultaneously involve many participants from different educational levels, while ensuring that each achieves what they specifically need from the experience. In her words, "going into a class can be like going into chaos, not knowing how you will enable coherent expression to emerge... art happens on that fine line between order and chaos". For VOLCO she prefers working with primary schools rather than secondary schools, as there are less management issues involved in working across subject areas.

Leeson sees her projects as encouraging aspiration, fantasy, imagination and projecting identities into the future, which is of high value in the regeneration of depressed communities. Her work aims at offering young participants a glimpse into the possibility that their ideas count, are of interest to others and that they have the power, if open to change and working in collaboration with others, to ultimately change society.

contributors

Anna Harding is Chief Executive of SPACE, London. She was programme director of the MA in Creative Curating at Goldsmiths College, University of London from 1995-2003. She was previously Director of Kettle's Yard Cambridge, exhibitions organiser at Camerawork London and has worked for the Hayward Gallery and Whitechapel Art Gallery in London.

Ruth Maclennan is an artist who was recently artist-in-residence at the BIOS centre at the London School of Economics where she conceived and co-curated the project *State of Mind*. http://www.lse.ac.uk/collections/BIOS/state_of_mind.htm.

Richard Wentworth is an artist and Professor of Visual Arts at the Ruskin School of Art, University of Oxford. Recent solo shows include Tate Liverpool and Lisson Gallery, London.

Faisal Abdu' Allah graduated from the Royal College of Art, London in Printmaking. A Londoner of Jamaican origin, he has shown widely internationally and participated in numerous museum and gallery exhibitions, completed a number of public commissions and has been featured extensively on BBC TV. In 2004 he was a recipient of the Arts Council England decibel visual arts awards.

Shona Illingworth is an artist working with video, film and sound. Her work examines issues of transience and dislocation as central to contemporary experience and explores the role memory plays in the psychological construction of place. She is currently working on projects with Professor Martin A Conway, a specialist in autobiographical memory research. Recent solo exhibitions include *Pianissimo*, Contemporary Art, Milan 2005.
Bare Dust was made with the support of Danny Brade at Trowbridge Youth Club with Aman, Craig, Warren, Scott, Robert, Caspen, Courtney, Junior, David, Michael, Pangy and Christopher. It was curated by Alice Sharp at SPACE Studios and Lucy McNenemy at Hackney Wick Public Art Programme.

Lise Autogena is a Danish artist living in London. Her projects involve long processes of development where the social, political and professional networks, collaborations and communities created around the making of her projects are an important part of the work itself – often resulting in the creation of unexpected connections, diversions and insights. She was recently awarded a three year Fellowship by the National Endowment of Science, Technology and The Arts in the UK.

Juliette Buss, Education Project Co-ordinator for the *Sound Mirrors Project* for Creative Partnerships, is a freelance arts education specialist based in south east England. She was Project Manager (Education) for the inaugural Brighton Photo Biennial, and Education Project Co-ordinator for *Wonderful: Visions of the Near Future*, a Wellcome Trust and NESTA collaborative project. She is an Assessor for Artworks (the Young Artist of the Year Awards) for the Clore Duffield Foundation, course leader for Working With Audiences at the University of Brighton and a council member of ENGAGE.

Ben Sadler was born in Birmingham in 1977. He graduated from the Royal College of Art in 2004. He is currently based between London and Birmingham. In addition to his solo work Ben Sadler is also one half of juneau/projects/ with Phil Duckworth.

Martin Krenn is an artist and activist living and working in Vienna. He has written and published on his work and has been written about by political theorists such as Gerald Raunig, Gunter Jacob and Marina Grzinic. (www.martinkrenn.net).

Walter Riedweg & Mauricio Dias have exhibited extensively and internationally, including major projects in Barcelona, Paris, Zurich, Atlanta, Liverpool and The Hague. Their own text here presents fresh material which has not yet been available to criticism.

O+I is an ongoing practice which has successfully negotiated and carried out a substantial number of placements with major companies such as Esso Petroleum, British Steel, and Help the Aged. The APG archive has recently been acquired by Tate Britain, with a retrospective of Latham's work at the gallery in October 2005.

Gerald Raunig, philosopher and art theoretician, lives in Vienna and is co-director of eipcp (European Institute for Progressive Cultural Policies) and co-ordinator of the transnational research project *republicart*. He is a lecturer on political aesthetics at the Institute for Philosophy, University of Klagenfurt Austria and at the Department of Visual Studies, University of Lüneburg Germany, and editor of the Austrian journal for radical democratic cultural politics, *Kulturrisse*.

David Harding set up the Environmental Art course at Glasgow School of Art, where he tutored many celebrated artists. He has regularly collaborated with the Border Arts Workshop in Tijuana and the Mexico borders and has contributed to many books on community arts since the 1970s, including editing the book *Decadent*.

Kristin Lucas, new media artist, was awarded one of five New York Urban Visionaries Awards 2003 and was winner of the Emerging Talent award for recent works including *Celebrations for Breaking Routine*.

Robert L Sain is Director of LACMALab, Los Angeles County Museum of Art.

Deborah F Schwartz is The Edward John Noble Foundation Deputy Director for Education, Museum of Modern Art, New York.

Carmen Moersch is Associate Professor at the University of Oldenbach, Germany. She is an artist and art educator with a PhD in gallery education.

Lars Bang Larsen is an art critic and a regular contributor to *Springer* (Vienna), *Frieze* (London) and *Nu* (Stockholm).

Steve Herne is Lecturer in Art Education at Goldsmiths College Univerisity of London. Janice McLaren is Head of Education at the Photographers Gallery London. They have written together previously for *JADE* (*Journal of Art and Design Education*).

Heads Together Productions is an artist-run organisation based at The Media Centre in Huddersfield, England. Led by Artistic Director, Adrian Sinclair, they have worked in community settings around east Leeds and beyond since 1992. Their work has informed the development of national policy such as the Home Zones campaign for streets safe for play and Kick it Out, the UK national campaign against racism in football.

credits

Cover Image
© Ben Sadler

Introduction
Nigel Henderson photograph © the Henderson Estate.

Creativity with Purpose
By Anna Harding based on a conversation with Faisal Abdu' Allah,
January 2005.
Faisal Abdu' Allah photographs © Faisal Abdu' Allah, courtesy
the artist and Camden Arts Centre.

Bare Dust
By Shona Illingworth based on a conversation with Anna Harding.

**Sound Mirrors a Proposed Artwork involving Secondary School
Pupils in Kent, England and in Dunkirk, France**
Images © the Sound Mirrors Project.

Room 13: One Artist, 11 Years, One School
Images © Room 13.

**Adaptation for Change: The Southwark Education Research
Project O+I**
Photographs © O+I, courtesy Barbara Steveni.

**De- and Re-territorialising the Classroom and Art:
WochenKlausur in School, Vienna, 1995-1996**
Images © WochenKlausur.

We are 17
Images © Nosh van der Lely, courtesy Galerie Paul Andriesse,
Amsterdam.

**Shape of Ideas: Rolls-Royce Apprenticship Training Scheme with
Tate Liverpool**
Images courtesy Tate Liverpool and Rolls-Royce.

**Celebrations for Breaking Routing with Flamingo 50, Venus and
Exit 3**
By Anna Harding, Kristin Lucas and Marie-Anne McQuay.
Images © the artist and FACT.

Kids of Survival
By Tim Rollins, adapted from a talk at the ENGAGE conference at
Tramway, Glasgow, 4-5 October 2001. Courtesy of ENGAGE.

**Student Reinstallation of a permanent Collection Gallery, Los
Angeles County Museum of Art, June 2003-March 2004**
Installation photography from The Michael Asher Project ©
2005 Museum Associates/LACMA, courtesy Los Angeles County
Museum of Art.
Gallery view p. 183: Rene Magritte, *The Liberator* © ADAGP,
Paris and DACS, London 2005; Isamu Noguchi, *Cronos*, 1947,
cast 1986 bronze © The Isamu Noguchi Foundation and Garden
Museum/Artists Rights Society (ARS), New York.

Art Inside Out at the Children's Museum of Manhattan
Photographs by Frank Oudeman, courtesy Children's Museum of
Manhattan.

**Application: Proposal for a Youth Project dealing with Forms of
Youth Visibility in Galleries**
Photographs by Carmen Moersch © Carmen Moersch.
Thanks to artist Lottie Child and Whitechapel Art Gallery for
support, collaboration and openness in discussion.

**Play and Nothingness The Model for a Qualitative Society, an
Activist Project at the Moderna Museet, Stockholm 1968**
Photographs courtesy Palle Nielsen *The Model for a Qualitative
Society*, Moderna Museet Stockholm, 1968.

**A Toe in the Water: Giving Young People a Voice at the
Whitechapel Art Gallery**
Earlier versions of this case study/evaluation appeared on the
Whitechapel Art Gallery Website: www.whitechapel.org, and in
JADE, 20.3, NSEAD, 2001.
Images courtesy Whitechapel Art Gallery.

**Siddiequa, Firdaus, Abdallah, Soeleyman, Moestafa, Hawwa,
Dzoel-kifi**
Stills from *Siddiequa, Firdaus, Abdallah, Soeleyman, Moestafa,
Hawwa, Dzoel-kifi*, 2004: DVD (42 minutes) by Joost Conijn
© Joost Conijn.

ISEP, The Laycock School and Other Experiments
Images from exhibition display panels © ISEP.

Creativity with Purpose Heads Together Productions
By Anna Harding based on an interview with Adrian Sinclair,
March 2004.

Magic Me Intergenerational Arts
Images © Lisa Woollett, courtesy Magic Me.
Text © Jan Stirling.
Pseudonyms have been used for the participants and all
photographs reproduced with their permission.

Planet VOLCO
Images © SPACE.

Translation of texts by Martin Krenn, Carmen Moersch and
Gerald Raunig from German to English by Lisa Rosenblatt at
Dream Coordination.

All images and texts are © and courtesy the artists and authors
unless otherwise stated.

acknowledgements

Of the many people who have given generously of their advice
at different stages in the development of this project I owe
particular thanks to Peter Jenkinson, Deepa Patel, Vivienne
Reiss, Steve Herne, Rebecca Sinker, Jenni Lomax, Christopher
Naylor, Eileen Adams, Alicia Miller, John Slyce, Jane Sillis and
Phillip van den Bossche. For their research assistance in the
early days Sophie Hope and Bridget Crone, and for editorial and
design Tahani Nadim and Marit Münzberg. Above all thanks to
all the contributors of images and texts, whose work inspired
this project, for their patience and optimism.

© 2005 Black Dog Publishing Limited, the artists and authors
All rights reserved

Edited by Anna Harding

Designed by marit@graphic-shapes.co.uk

Black Dog Publishing Limited
Unit 4.4 Tea Building
56 Shoreditch High Street
London E1 6JJ
Tel: +44 (0)20 7613 1922
Fax: +44 (0)20 7613 1944
Email: info@bdp.demon.co.uk
www.bdpworld.com

All opinions expressed within this publication are those of the authors and artists and
not necessarily of the publisher.

British Library Cataloguing-in-Publication Data.

A CIP record for this book is available from the British Library.

ISBN 1 904772 28 5

All rights reserved. No part of this publication may be reproduced, stored in a
retrieval system, or transmitted, in any form or by any means, electronic, mechanical, photocopying,
recording, or otherwise, without prior permission of the publisher.

Every effort has been made to trace the copyright holders, but if any have been inadvertently overlooked
the publishers will be pleased to make the necessary
arrangements at the first opportunity.

This publication was made possible by the financial support of Creative Partnerships
and Arts Council England

Creative Partnerships